The Technopolitics of Communication in Modern India

The Technopolitics of Communication in Modern India

Paper Chains and Viral Phenomena

Pragya Dhital

BLOOMSBURY
NEW DELHI • LONDON • OXFORD • NEW YORK • SYDNEY

BLOOMSBURY INDIA
Bloomsbury Publishing India Pvt. Ltd
Second Floor, LSC Building No. 4, DDA Complex, Pocket C–6&7,
Vasant Kunj, New Delhi 110070

BLOOMSBURY, BLOOMSBURY ACADEMIC INDIA and the Diana logo are trademarks of Bloomsbury Publishing Plc

First published in India 2025
First published in Great Britain 2025

Series design by Charlotte James
Cover image: Wall-art graffiti at Shaheen Bagh Protests © DTM, CC0, via Wikimedia Commons

This edition published with permission from Bloomsbury Publishing Plc, 50 Bedford Square, London, WC1B3DP, UK

A catalogue record for this book is available from the British Library.

ISBN: 978-93-61315-96-1

Typeset by Newgen Knowledge Works Pvt. Ltd., Chennai, India
Printed and bound in India by Replika Press Pvt. Ltd.

Contents

Acknowledgements

Many people, places and institutions have gone into the making of this book, which started life as a doctoral thesis. Firstly, I would like to thank Jan-Peter Hartung, Andrea Janku and Cosimo Zene, who made it possible for me to complete my PhD at the School of Oriental and African Studies in 2016. Saul Newman was a generous PhD examiner and has continued to provide effective support. The Berlin Graduate School for the Study of Muslim Cultures and Societies and British Association of South Asian Studies funded preliminary research and language training. A British Academy Postdoctoral Fellowship supported me financially whilst I was working on the manuscript from 2018 to 2022.

Roy Foster was an excellent postdoctoral mentor. Despite severe difficulties, he provided sharp and timely feedback on every chapter of the book. Jörg Haustein and Javed Majeed also took the time to read and discuss many of the chapters. The publication of this book owes much to Aditya Nigam's encouragement and advice. Rochana Bajpai, Julie Cyzewski, Santanu Das, J. Daniel Elam, Syed Mohammed Faisal, Laurent Gayer, David Gilmartin, Mark Hobart, Robin Jeffrey, George Kunnath, Jagjeet Lally, Daniel Ryan Morse, Caroline Osella, Rahul Rao, Nils Riecken, Mayur Suresh and Keren Weitzberg offered very useful responses to individual chapters.

Early versions of Chapters 2 and 3 were published as 'From "Imam ul-Hind" to *Azizul Hind*: The "One Man Media House" in Modern India', *South Asia: Journal of South Asian Studies*, *42*(3) (2019): 452–68 and 'Media Satyagraha in the Broadcast Age: Underground Literature and Populist Politics during the Indian Internal Emergency of 1975–1977', *Interventions*, 21(7) (2019): 942–58. I was motivated to write those articles and this book whilst a Visiting Research Fellow in the Institute of Advanced Studies at University College London from 2017 to 2018. I finally laid the book to rest in 2023–4, whilst working at the Sarah Parker Remond Centre, UCL, and the School of Advanced Study, University of London. I am grateful to Tamar Garb,

Paul Gilroy, Tariq Jazeel and Claire Langhamer for providing thinking and breathing space within those institutions.

This book was also fostered by the vibrant intellectual and cultural life in and around various Indian universities, colleges and research centres. In Delhi these included Jawaharlal Nehru University, the Delhi School of Economics and the Centre for the Study of Developing Societies. Librarians and archivists at CSDS, the Central Secretariat, Jamia Millia Islamia, the National Archives of India, the Nehru Memorial Museum & Library and the P. C. Joshi Archives on Contemporary History were efficient and helpful. The officers of the Directorate of Advertising and Visual Publicity, Registrar of Newspapers in India, National Council for the Promotion of Urdu Language, and Anjuman Taraqqi Urdu were also generous with information and time. In Uttar Pradesh, I was assisted by staff in various newspaper archives (*Aag*, *Amar Ujala*, *Dainik Jagran*, *Inquilab*, *Rashtriya Sahara*, *Roznama Rashtriya Sahara*, *Sahafat* and *Shah Times*), the Urdu Academy, the American Institute of Indian Studies, and the late, great Ram Advani's bookshop in Lucknow. I also thank the staff and volunteers I met across UP in untold party headquarters and election war rooms, District Magistrate offices and counting centres, press agencies and newspaper offices.

Ali Abbas, Arjumand Ara, Azhar Masud, Timsal Masud, Ishrat Zaheer and Mohammad Yusuf patiently taught me Urdu. Arjumand was especially long-suffering, and I was lucky to have her as a teacher and a friend. I was hosted in Delhi and Lucknow by Arjumand, Hoda Bandeh-Ahmadi, Karolina Hedström and Kiran Kothari, Sofia Nasir, Francesco Obino, Najma Seth and Anita Sharma. Finally, I'd like to thank Angela Becher, who accompanied me for much of the writing and saw me across the finish line.

Introduction

Over the past decade, forms of popular politics once seen as confined to the geographical south or the historical past have come to threaten liberal tenets and institutions everywhere. From the Brexit referendum in 2016 to the phenomena of 'Trumpism' and 'Putinism', there has been much speculation about the role played by new media technology in this apparent return of illiberal politics and primordial identities. *The Technopolitics of Communication in Modern India* addresses these concerns with reference to India, a country seen as both exception and exemplar in political studies. Post-independence, India had been cited as a successful example of democratic transition in a newly independent state, despite not meeting standard criteria for democratic stability (ethnic homogeneity, high income and literacy levels). More recently it has been seen as exemplifying both the progressive potential and regressive risks of new media.

In India and elsewhere, an earlier optimism about decentralised forms of collective mobilisation enabled by social media has by now curdled into anxieties about more insidious types of manipulation and control of information. The surprise 2007 election victory in the state of Uttar Pradesh by the Bahujan Samaj Party (BSP), a party representing the interests of the Scheduled Castes (formerly known as 'Untouchables'), had been attributed to agile campaigning at the grassroots level through the medium of cheap mobile phones (Jeffrey and Doron 2013). Whereas the 2014 general election victory by the Bharatiya Janata Party (BJP), one of the first in a series of victories by right-wing nationalist parties across the globe, has sown doubts about the efficacy of electoral democracy as a mechanism for capturing popular will in an era of mediatised populism.

Within India both election results also seemed to reflect sociopolitical changes that confound identity-based explanations of social and political behaviour: greater electoral volatility and alliances amongst disadvantaged groups, which cut across lines of caste, religion and ethnicity. Vote bank politics, voting on the basis of identity, was apparently superseded by the BSP's overtures to upper-caste voters in 2007 and the BJP's inclusive development agenda of '*sabka sath, sabka vikas*' (together with all, development for all) in 2014. Both parties addressed constituencies that did not meet classic criteria for either ascriptive identity (language, culture, religion) or class location (role in the division of labour). These included the *bahujan* (loosely, 'majority' or 'mass') and a group identified in the 2014 BJP election manifesto as 'the neo middle class' (BJP 2014: 15), said to consist of those who had 'risen from the category of the poor' but were 'yet to stabilize in the middle class' (ibid.: 17). Appeals to this amorphous class seemed to be part of the BJP's attempt to shake off its upper-caste Hindu image and counterpoise the newly founded Aam Aadmi Party's appeals to the *aam aadmi* (ordinary man).

The penultimate chapter of this book will discuss the 2014 general election, and the final chapter will look at the BJP's subsequent recourse to an even more openly Hindu nationalist politics. But across the book I argue that these convolutions could best be understood by not taking identity for granted as a static and exclusive form of affiliation. I focus instead on the processes through which various groups are ventriloquised – the nation, the people, this or that community or class – whilst remaining mindful that these labels neither seamlessly map onto those they describe nor remain external to their formation.

The subjects I deal with might be easily identified as political: state language and media policy in post-independence India, seditious writing in the colonial and postcolonial period, and attempts to control public communication through emergency ordinances and election law. But I deal with political communication – attempts to articulate constituencies through communicative practices – whilst eschewing the cybernetic (Deutsch 1963 and 1966) and mass communications (Shannon 1998) models often used to understand this process by political scientists. The book covers similar ground to earlier studies of communalism and separatism in modern India, which build on and nuance these theories.[1] But I diverge from this literature in not

1 See in particular Brass (1974), Robinson (1974) and Minault (1982) and also more recent work on the rise of Hindu nationalism and 'Islamism': Jaffrelot (1998); Hansen (1999); Hansen and Jaffrelot (2000); Ahmad (2009); Chatterji, Hansen and Jaffrelot (2019).

looking at ethnic groups singly and separately, and by proceeding from a non-instrumentalist understanding of political communication.

Scepticism about the coherence and efficacy of state and 'elite' intentions informs my heuristic of technopolitics, which understands the technical and material as interwoven into human thought and action rather than acting upon them externally. This is a variant of a communicative understanding of power as corresponding to the human ability to act in concert rather than being the property of an individual (Arendt 1969: 44). But in this translational model, power is a consequence rather than a cause of collective action and commands are transformed as they are disseminated (Latour 1986). Proceeding from Bruno Latour's interesting suggestion that power does not exist and political science should therefore become a branch of disability studies (2005a: 30), I focus on the means and ends that make a grouping '*reach* a bit further and *stand* a bit longer' (Latour 2005b: 35, italics in the original): the paper chains along which messages are sent by various agencies, and through which groups are mediated.

This means I pay attention to newspapers and journals, party manifestos, policy documents, laws and codes. But I also deal with non-textual aspects of their production and dissemination – from how they are financed to how they are printed and interact with other media. By considering the technopolitics of communication, I modify standard models of the transparency of speech without replacing the intentionality of human actors with material or ideological constraints. I instead propose an expanded conception of both technology and speech, which would render the concept of material or ideological determinants redundant and allow more possibilities *for* speech – encompass non-verbal communication and non-human agency.

I accordingly draw upon understandings of representation from science and technology studies and aesthetic theory, which are aware that it involves a great deal more than the 'simple transmission' of a message or force (Disch 2008: 91). The models for this type of mediation might be the microprocesses of negotiation involved in the construction of facts in a laboratory (Latour and Woolgar 1986) or film and photographic reproduction, in which an image is not a duplication of a thing but 'an alteration that occurs in a chain of images which alter it in turn' (Rancière 2009b: 93–4). This is distinct from a model of communicative action that assumes its elements are pre-constituted. Its understanding of representation as work – an act of construction and translation – is more attuned to the contingent and uncertain process of political representation in mass democracies than the ideal of an 'enchanted individual' voter, who stands outside the world as an observer, and is the 'bearer of an almost mystical autonomy' (Gilmartin 2012: 411).

In addition to being unrealistic, the myth of authentic democracy that underlies this ideal has often favoured the interests of representatives over and above those of the people they claim to represent. In his history of the rise of popular sovereignty in England and America, Edmund Morgan highlights how by claiming power in the name of '*the* people' they were able to shed 'the local, subject character that made them representatives of a particular set of people' (1989: 50). This distance was even presented as an advantage in colonial India, as the state set itself apart from a society it configured as communally divided and backward, and as therefore the best representative of the collective interests of the people of India. In an essay on continuities between the 1935 Government of India Act and the post-independence Indian Constitution, Sandipto Dasgupta describes how into the postcolonial period the authorial subject position of India's constitution has remained that of an anxious administrator, called upon to govern a potentially dangerous alien population (2014: 231–2). I explore how that conjoined sense of mission and threat has informed state attempts to regulate communication from the colonial period through to the Covid-19 pandemic.

This book outlines an alternative basis for popular representation, one that does not sacralise the people and assume power in their name. Based on the substitutability of persons rather than in a metaphysics of co-presence, the alienability of the word rather than faith in transparent communication, this would be better placed to obstruct oligarchic rule and encourage inclusive forms of collective mobilisation. These ideas are worked out through examples in Indian political history ranging from the independence struggle through to resistance to the emergency of 1975–7 and the Citizenship Amendment Act protests of 2019–20. Across these cases, I describe non-exclusionary forms of the people momentarily coalesced by a common experience of subjection on the one hand, and acts of both collective and individual dissent on the other.

Kaleidoscopic communities

Early on in my research, Abid Suhail, a senior Urdu journalist whom I interviewed in Lucknow, spoke to me of 'the complete newspaper':

> No newspaper can become a complete newspaper, but no newspaper has a right to call itself a respectable daily without trying to become a complete newspaper. A complete newspaper must provide all important news from the region, then the country, then of the world. There is a perpetual conflict in the daily newspaper between the regional, national and international. Suppose a government is overthrown in UP and on the same day the USA attacks Baghdad. There will be a conflict. On that day Baghdad will be close to Lucknow because of our Muslim heritage and foreign policy. The defeat of the state government is also of great importance. One of these stories will be first lead. But there is a method to make the first page in such a way that both stories draw almost equal attention without disturbing the make-up of the page.[2]

Suhail acknowledged that this was an 'ideal which is never achieved', but still regretted that contemporary Urdu newspapers continued to make up their pages in a 'random' manner. He spoke of a time when the front page of a newspaper was made by the chief sub-editor himself, who would decide the lead story and its layout. Now it is the compositor who decides, he complained, and greater emphasis was laid on filling space than careful composition of a newspaper. One finds two related stories at a distance from one another on the same page; continuity errors in run-on stories; inconsistent localisation of the various editions of a newspaper; information that should be in the introduction crammed into a subheading; lack of immediate relevance in the selection of editorials; and so on.

He partly attributed this to the impact of television upon the production, contents and layout of Indian newspapers. Previously dailies used to be produced in three shifts: morning, midday and night. Now there was only one shift from 5.00 pm to midnight, and newspapers tended to follow the lead of television in selecting major news items. Even though journalism is 'a craft of direct expression', an 'element of ornamentation' had been introduced to

2 Interview with Abid Suhail, Lucknow, 7 December 2010.

counter the effects of TV. But in describing how the impossibility of these ideals of 'direct expression' and 'completion' paradoxically set the process in motion, he went beyond a normative understanding of the necessity of 'transparency' and 'balance'. Speaking from decades of journalistic experience, he had also arrived at the insight that groups are 'the provisional product of a constant uproar made by the millions of contradictory voices about what is a group and who pertains to what' (Latour 2005b: 31).

This turbulent, multilocal and multilingual media scene differed markedly from Benedict Anderson's description of how large anonymous communities such as nations are created through the practice of reading a newspaper written in a single language dealing with events occurring all over the world (1991). These everyday practices are the bedrock of his ironic faith in 'the goodness of nations', whose 'unbound serialities' he perceives to be the most inclusive forms of community, encompassing, as they do, various ethnicities and races, The Unborn, The Living and The Dead (1998b). But his claim that 'newspapers everywhere' have a universal scope, because it would be unnatural for them to confine their reports to the political realm in which they are published (ibid.: 33), seemed to be disproved by increased localisation of the content of Hindi papers alongside the increasingly international focus of Urdu press. Papers in both languages focused on events within their own differently defined realms rather than the 'world of mankind' generally.

Seeing how state, market and political party pressure affected newspaper content also sensitised me to the quirks of the Indian newspaper market, its lack of adherence to Anderson's allied notion of print-capitalism in terms of both content and business model. According to Anderson, capitalism and print technology created the conditions for 'a new form of imagined community, which in its basic morphology set the stage for the modern nation' (1991: 46). Mass consumption of newspapers established the basic morphological elements of these imagined communities: a conception of empty homogeneous time and universal space, as events occurring all over the world were connected by 'calendrical coincidence' (ibid.: 33).

However, pressures from various directions, as an Urdu newspaper editor pointed out, meant that it was not possible for a daily paper to function as a 'machine', a vehicle for a single ideology, agent or party.[3] This was said to contrast with weeklies such as the Jamaat-e-Islami's *Dawat*, which were cheaper and easier to produce and more didactic in tone. Conversations with journalists who had experienced both colonial repression and the Indian internal emergency of 1975–7 also made it clear that technological improvements and absence of strict censorship laws did not inevitably lead to a freer press. The previously slow and cumbersome nature of Urdu press production seems to have actually restricted state oversight and control of newspaper content.

A different understanding of the mechanics at work is also encouraged by the history of the Urdu language itself. Hindustani, Hindi and Urdu emerged as discrete languages in response to colonial taxonomies and governmental practices. Notably, the decision to declare Urdu (Hindustani in Nastaliq script) court language in the North-Western Provinces in 1837, enhancing the status of that language at the same time as catalysing into existence a Hindi (Hindustani in Nagari script) language movement with Hindu and Indian nationalist undercurrents. But more fine-grained studies of north Indian language politics do not support the view of religio-cultural identities as determined by state intervention or 'elite' machinations. They recount how over the course of the nineteenth century Indian writers and publishers advanced the cause of Hindi and Urdu for both personal gain and altruistic ends, whilst participating in the process of dichotomisation that would lead to the decline of the latter (Dalmia 1999 and Stark 2007).

Urdu's history also does not accord with anthropologist James Scott's account of the autonomy conferred by 'unique languages', which he views as treasuries of local knowledge and formidable obstacles to external control (1998: 72). Illegibility of neighbourhoods and vernacular languages, in particular, are said to be a resource for local political autonomy (ibid.). Histories of Urdu, however, speak of the role played by cultural sensibility, literature, myth, a musical past *and* state knowledge, colonisation, control, manipulation, instruction and propaganda. In present-day north India, one finds both strong state influence on language and media and a range of dialects and languages that baffle attempts to control communication, even at the basic level of linguistic standardisation. Neither aspect of Urdu's history supports

[3] Interview with Aman Abbas, editor of *Sahafat*, Lucknow, 13 September 2011.

a view of the state as an apparatus that is external to the social world, or the opposed but complementary notion of the autonomous subject who refuses state demands from an exterior social space. [4]

The dispositif of state

When thinking of the operations of power, and of state power in particular, in place of this image of the apparatus or instrument I posit the dispositif, heterogeneous assemblies that between them establish a shifting network of relations. These arise at a given historical moment in response to a strategic imperative but are expressed within and influenced by this same network. The concept is central to the first volume of Foucault's *Histoire de la sexualité: La volonté de savoir* (1976), and in an interview he gave in 1977 on publication of that work, he usefully sums up the term: 'Le dispositif lui-même, c'est le réseau qu'on peut établir entre ces elements' (1994: 299). ('The dispositif itself is the network which can be established between these elements.')[5] This describes a much more ambiguous and open-ended relation than the model of interactions contained in Althusser's theory of the ideological state apparatus (Althusser 1977a) or Bourdieu's field theory in which objective structures form the basis for the ' "typical" behaviour of participants' (Bourdieu et al. 2013: 116).

This model of power relations seems particularly relevant to modern India, where, as Ranajit Guha observes, a colonial state exercised 'dominance without hegemony' (1997). Guha attributes this to a structural split between a metropolitan political culture and pre-colonial political traditions. This engendered certain 'paradoxes of power' as two distinct political traditions coalesced and diverged. He emphasises that this involved a process of 'braiding,

[4] For a detailed account of the theoretical assumptions underlying this perspective, see Timothy Mitchell's critical overview of the literature on the state-society boundary (1991). My sense of the state as the sum of its discursive practices aligns with his understanding of the state as a 'structural effect', created by 'detailed processes of spatial organization, temporal arrangement, functional specification, and supervision and surveillance' (ibid.: 95).

[5] The English translation of both the *Histoire* and this interview renders dispositif as 'apparatus' and réseau as 'system', which overstates the coherence of the process. Foucault speaks of a 'jeu' of these elements: 'Bref, entre ces éléments, discursifs ou non, il y a comme un jeu, des changements de position, des modifications de fonctions, qui peuvent, eux aussi, être très différents' (1994: 299). ('In sum, between these elements, discursive or not, it is like a game, [with] changes of position, modifications of function, which can, between them also, be very different.')

collapsing, echoing, and blending of these idioms' rather than a 'mechanical stapling' of a Western liberalism onto an unchanging feudal culture (ibid.: 60–1).

These admixtures of concepts could result in more pervasive exercises of power, such as when the British idiom of 'Improvement' was translated into the concept of *Dharma* (loosely signifying virtue or moral duty), providing a non-antagonistic means for both the state and indigenous elites to legitimise their claims. But he also describes how a British tradition of Rightful Dissent found a non-identical equivalent in the concept of Dharmic Protest, providing an array of spaces and tactics for the non-elite to contest the hegemony of dominant groups. In the process of translation, these concepts could also exceed the intentions of those who coined them. For example, as Gandhi's fusion of the utilitarian idiom of 'Obedience' with a feudal concept of *Bhakti*, in his offer to volunteer Indians for service in the Anglo-Boer War (1899–1902), became a means to assert their rights as British subjects (ibid.: 43–6).

This book is located amongst ethnographies of the state in postcolonial South Asia which extend these insights into the current day. These works are attuned to the state's multilayered and pluricentric nature (Gupta 1995), and to how it is both produced and undone through everyday practices and public representations (Sharma and Gupta 2006). To give an example which resonates with the recent Covid-19 pandemic, in his work on bureaucracy and structural violence, Akhil Gupta proceeds from a Foucauldian, post-structuralist view of the state to describe extreme poverty in India as 'a direct and culpable form of killing' made possible by state policies and practices (2012: 5). Rather than diffusing the operations of power so widely that it makes it impossible to attribute responsibility for such outcomes, sensitivity to its capillary flow allows him to calculate the number of excess deaths in India, the number of people missing from the population due to malnutrition and morbidity, to be 'approximately 140 million' (ibid.).

His reckoning is in direct contradiction to Amartya Sen's claim that no major famine has ever occurred in an independent and democratic country with a relatively free press (1999: 6–7). Sen's argument is lent force by childhood memories of the 1943–4 Great Bengal Famine, which reverberate through his writings on development. Gupta, however, not taking official pronouncements at their word or locating power in a single place, perceives how 'thanatopolitics' works despite proclaimed state policy and regardless of the intentions of bureaucrats. Ethnographic observation of development programmes, in which officials are revealed to make decisions on the basis of 'guesswork and contingency', attunes him to how they are shot through with 'barely controlled chaos' (2012: 14). The resulting scepticism about bureaucracies as representing 'the rationalization of power in a disciplinary society' sensitises him to the irrational faith in qualifications and documents held by officials and those who appeal to them (ibid.). This leads him to argue that 'bureaucratic action repeatedly and systematically produces arbitrary outcomes in its provision of care' (ibid.: 6).

With reference to state attempts to regulate public communication, I expand on these insights to describe how concatenations of ignorance and inaction produce outcomes that are arbitrary *and* prejudicial in the areas of language and media policy and electoral law. By looking at the unintended effects of state interventions, I highlight the slippages between the state's central and local levels, the incoherence of its policies, and the unfaithful nature of their implementation by state functionaries. Through close reading of 'elite' communications (the words of politicians, journalists, and bureaucrats), I deal with the gap between speech and utterance, and the techno-material means through which both are shaped. By paying attention to how these messages are disseminated and received, I suggest the presence of a subject that exceeds any pre-formatted outline of the people.

The orphan word

Towards this end, I outline an alternative, technopolitical model of communication: an alchemical combination of speaker, audience, and context, which both shapes the content of a message and alters the constituent elements in the communication network. Some aspects of this approach draw upon Judith Butler's work on censorship, in which she emphasises that 'speech is always in some ways out of our control' (1997: 15) and that censorship precedes the text and is in some sense responsible for its production (ibid.: 128). Both assumptions are premised in a post-sovereign view of agency, in which it is 'an effect of power' rather than the property of the subject, and therefore constrained but not determined in advance (ibid.: 139). Butler locates the space of discursive agency in the break that occurs when speech is taken out of context in utterance (ibid.: 129). This encompasses 'impossible speech', the ramblings and rantings of the asocial and the psychotic, which haunt the rules that govern speech (ibid.: 133). But it also includes 'the political promise of the performative' (ibid.: 161), 'the insurrectionary 'force' of censored speech as it emerges into 'official discourse' and opens the performative to an unpredictable future' (ibid.: 142).

The political potential of the open temporality of the performative is an important aspect of this book. But whereas Butler counterpoises bodily 'excess' to the force of habitus (1997: 155), and in subsequent work expands on the 'chiasmic' relation between linguistic and bodily performativity (2015: 9), I am concerned with the dissonance between doing, being and saying that is an affordance of alienable media technology such as writing. For Butler vocalisation requires some sort of prosthetic (a larynx or a technological prosthetic) but acting in concert always involves an equivocal relation. As she puts it, 'this movement, or stillness, this parking of my body in the middle of another's action, is neither my act nor yours, but something that happens by virtue of the relation between us' (ibid.: 9). Proceeding from a different understanding of technology and communication, I view the relation between humans and prostheses as no less equivocal.

I also draw upon the keener sense of the power of the written word expressed in Rancière's concept of literarity. Instead of viewing writing as secondary to and dependent on spoken language, he emphasises its insurrectionary possibilities. The 'community of readers' is 'a community without legitimacy, a community formed only by the random circulation of the written word' (2011c: 14). Literary intransitivity is set apart from all transmitter-message-receiver models of communication in which a message leaves 'the proper transmitter and goes to the proper receiver by the proper channel' (ibid.: 55). The groupings that emerge from literary circulation differ from Anderson's imagined communities not just in their illegitimacy, but also in the indifference to market logics (print capitalism) demonstrated by the randomness of their organisation and the openness to appropriation of the texts around which they momentarily coalesce. These communities are produced by the alienability of the word rather than its exchange value. The play of languages without hierarchy is different from 'the simple fact that a euro is worth a euro and that two commodities that are worth a euro are equivalent to one another' (ibid.). Rather, it is a matter of knowing that 'absolutely anyone can take over and redirect the power invested in language' (ibid.).

This disruptive potential is the property of various forms of media, and in recent times the audiovisual properties of social media induce the same alienation effect without requiring literacy on the part of either their authors or readers. This potential is also evident in certain types of politically resonant acts, which derive expressive power from their transgression of codified norms of social conduct. In earlier work, both Butler and Rancière refer to an action when illustrating how the insurrectionary possibilities of speech and writing might work in practice: Rosa Parks' violation of racial segregation laws in the United States (Butler 1997: 147; Rancière 2006b: 61). Butler emphasises that Rosa Parks had no prior right to sit at the front of the bus in Montgomery, Alabama. It was only through the act of doing so that 'she endowed a certain authority to the act, and began the insurrectionary process of overthrowing those established codes of legitimacy' (1997: 147). Likewise, Rancière describes Parks' actions as reclamation of the rights of which she had been deprived, and as therefore exemplary of the double manoeuvre of the democratic process: 'the action of subjects who, by working the interval between identities, reconfigure the distinction between the public and the private, the universal and the particular' (2006b: 61–2).

Rosa Parks' protest was both an act of self-assertion and part of a wider struggle for civil rights, which drew upon a global history of non-violent resistance. The sit-in had been adopted by the Indian independence movement from the practice of *dharna* – sitting in attendance on the house of a local notable or divinity to claim a debt or seek a boon. *Dharna* features in Guha's inventory of forms of Dharmic Protest, which are said to have been an incalculable factor in colonial politics because of their grounding in pre-colonial political idioms devoid of any notion of citizenship and rights (1997: 57–60). Indian nationalists, picking up on its subversive effects in rural politics, transformed this act of obeisance into a means to directly oppose British rule. Something similar happened to the religio-cultural practice of the fast when adopted as a political tool by those with limited agency – the disenfranchised, the colonised, the incarcerated. *Dharna* continues to be used as a protest tactic, notably by those whose time and labour are counted cheap or not counted at all. The final chapter will discuss how both *dharna* and digital media featured in protests against the 2019 Indian Citizenship Amendment Act by Dalits and women. Across the book I will also describe individuals and groups who performed this broader rhetorical manoeuvre, who overstepped the boundaries of their allotted identity, laid claim to a right to intervene in the affairs of the community and thereby remade it.

Qaum, millat, ummat

An important example of this manoeuvre for the book is the attempt by certain Muslim thinkers to secure a nationality within India on the basis of an ideology of pan-Islamism, through what Javed Majeed has described as a process of 'simultaneous identification and rejection' (2007: 154). In the colonial period this dialectic was famously expressed in an exchange of words, conducted in the Urdu press, between Maulana Hussain Ahmad Madani (1879–1957) and the poet-philosopher Muhammad Iqbal (1877–1938) regarding the meaning of the terms *qaum*, *millat* and *ummat*. This involved an immanent critique of the nation form, made with recourse to prior and other ways of imagining community.

In the modern era the Arabic word *qaum* has often been translated as 'nation' despite long predating the nation state. The word features in the Qur'an and in English translations is usually rendered as 'people'. For example, in the Qur'an 2.54 (translated by M. A. S. Abdel Haleem) Moses addresses *liqawmihi*, 'his people'. The term became associated with regional nationalism over the course of the nineteenth and twentieth centuries, with the rise of colonial philology and anti-colonial independence movements. In John Thompson Platts' nineteenth century Hindi and Urdu dictionary, *qaum* is variously defined as 'A people, nation; a tribe, race, family; sect, caste' (2006: 796). Platts claimed to have considered both scholarly precedents and everyday usage in compiling his dictionary – poetry and prose, newspapers, and the 'living colloquial language', which he had encountered over a long period of residence in India (ibid.: iv). But his use of terms such as race and caste also reflected orientalist constructions of Indian difference. Platts defined *millat* as nation or, more generally, a society or a company, whilst also acknowledging it could describe a religious community and faith (2006: 1064). *Ummat* (more commonly *ummah*) is now widely associated with the international community of Muslims, but Platts described it as encompassing 'religious sect, people of the same religion; followers; race, nation; caste; creed, religion' without naming any particular group (ibid.: 81).

The unfixity of these terms has led them to be used interchangeably, allowing disputes over their meaning to become a means to define sociopolitical community.[6] During a public meeting held in Delhi in December 1937, Madani is said to have asserted that in the current age 'nations (*qaumeen*) are based on homelands (*autaan*, pl. of *watn*), not religion (*mazhab*)' (Metcalf 2005: 37). Urdu newspapers reported Madani as claiming that *millat* was based on territory, provoking Iqbal to write a Persian verse mocking Madani's knowledge of Arabic. When Madani responded with a clarification of the terms he had used, Iqbal dismissed this as philological quibbling. The main point for Iqbal was that territorial nationalism and Islam were incompatible. Thoughts of nationalism would only lead Muslims astray, onto the paths of 'irreligiousness and scepticism' (Iqbal 1995b: 303). He had been opposed to nationalism since before the concept had become known 'in India and the Muslim world', he wrote, from early on identifying it as the most effective weapon of European imperialism, a means to shatter 'the religious unity of Islam to pieces' (ibid.: 301). This attitude he shared with contemporary Muslim thinkers such as Syed Abul A'la Maududi (1903–1979), who regarded nationalism as a modern form of kingship, and both as contrary to the Islamic principle of 'equality of all men regardless of their birth' (Hartung 2013a: 117).

But Iqbal's scepticism about the nation-form involved more than 'Islamism'. He was also working within what Barbara Metcalf has described as a 'minor strand' of international intellectual denunciation of 'the 'black' side of modernity: competitive nationalism and its resultant militarism, imperialism and consumerism' (2005: 40–1). This strand, and the influence of Bergson in particular, is expressed in his assertion, in a lecture printed in the Report

[6] For an interesting recent example, see Mohamed Abdou's work on Islam and anarchism, which attempts to wrest the Arabic term 'Qawmiyyah' from the modern meaning of regional nationalism or peoplehood (2022). He enlists the concept in the service of a decolonial, non-racialised and non-territorial conception of an *ummah*, which could apply to both Muslims and non-Muslims (ibid.: 112–46).

of the 1911 census, that Islam is in its essence 'non-temporal, non-spatial' (1995a: 121). Through Walter Benjamin's concept of 'empty homogeneous time', Anderson would later go on to claim this as the ideal space-time of the nation, in his description of how everyday practices 'rooted in industrial material civilization … displaced the cosmos to make way for the world' (1998b: 29), that is, displaced cosmological notions of time and the centripetal and porous spatialisations of dynastic states.

Conversely, Madani's counterarguments in favour of territorial nationalism were based in particular circumstances of discrimination and oppression rather than faith in the 'open-to-the-world plurals' of capitalist modernity (Anderson 1998: 117). Indians who travelled abroad were regarded as members of the same *qaum* regardless of religion and despised accordingly – hence it was a real category (Madani 2005: 55). If nationalism was such an effective weapon, why should Muslims themselves not use it to undermine the power of the British? Madani proposed an 'Action plan for India', a 'composite nationalism on the basis of national unity' as a means to throw off the yoke of colonial rule (ibid.: 106). Far from being irreligious, this would be on the lines of the Constitution of Medina, which the Prophet Mohammad had formed between Muslims and Jews in that city. In this view, the nation form itself was a historically contingent dispositif rather than an instrument of oppression and one that was compatible with Islamic and pre-modern types of political organisation.

These approaches inform my understanding of the modern, used to describe a period that spans India's experience of both colonisation and independence. Each chapter deals with the colonial and postcolonial period, not just to see how the former influences the latter, but also to trace the outlines of a shared intellectual environment, spanning ideologies as well as epochs, whose progressive ideals are based in what Timothy Mitchell describes as the spatiotemporal 'staging' of capitalist modernity (2000). I am particularly interested in the possibility of 'shift, displacement, or contamination' inherent in each 'staging' of the 'historical immediacy and spatial extension' of the social world and 'the unified global history of modernity' (ibid.: 23–4). In both periods, I focus upon such moments of slippage, look for vestiges of other ways of imagining community and conceptualising the movement of time.

Background and outline of the study

When dealing with media the impediments and instruments that enable communication are particularly obvious, and this was one of the reasons why I chose this focus. I was also drawn to the opportunity it affords to work with people whose task is similar to that of a researcher and writer. By studying media, I attempted to elide the emic/etic distinction, based in the notion of bounded cultural units, which typically informs ethnographic research that focuses on one such group.

This choice of focus was the result of an orientation and a disposition. In India, I was always and variously identifiable as an outsider: a woman, a Hindu, a foreigner, a foreign-language speaker of Hindi–Urdu and a first-language speaker of English. But these different identifiers could counterbalance and inflect one another. Whatever privileges I was afforded as a foreign researcher were offset by how I was placed and would position myself across various axes. Combined with how I was racialised, this meant I was able to access a wide range of environments and to be fairly anonymous within them. My gender allowed me entry to all-female domestic spaces, and as a researcher I could also access predominantly malc offices. My Sanskrit first name marked me out as Hindu, but this was modified by my status as a non-Indian Hindu, and my Nepali surname made it hard for most Indians to identify my caste.

Additionally, many of the people I interviewed had experience of doing interviews or being interviewed. Several suggested books and articles to read, offered advice on topics I should study. Some of the most enjoyable exchanges were with retired journalists who were writing their own books and who welcomed the opportunity to reflect on their experiences. But I also learned a great deal from the offhand comments of more reluctant interlocutors. Both the focus and theoretical outlook of this study changed as a result of clashes and convergences of perspective during these conversations, interviews and meetings.

When I did my first period of research in Delhi and Lucknow between August 2010 and September 2011, my focus was the relationship between Urdu language policy and print media. Over the course of a decade of observing radical changes in Indian media and politics, I started to adopt a broader and more historical perspective on the relationship between state policy and media and linguistic practices. My research involved work in Indian libraries, archives and research centres, government departments and newspaper offices.[7] I also conducted interviews in Hindi–Urdu and English with people involved in public communication: newspaper editors, journalists, advertising agents, government officials, politicians and party workers, religious professionals and social workers.

Interviewees were often hard to get hold of and short of time. Our conversations had to be fitted in around the course of a busy working day – the production schedule of a newspaper, an election campaign. My pre-prepared questions would therefore initially focus on a particular event or the workings of an organisation. As well as clarifying important details, this would establish how familiar I was with a context, and respondents would pitch their responses accordingly. I would then ask more open-ended questions and leave space for interviewees to discuss points beyond those I had raised and those they had prepared to discuss. I complemented interviews in official settings with informal interactions and observations from more than a decade of periodically living in north India. I spent time in newspaper, NGO and government offices, political party headquarters, places of worship, in schools, colleges, shops, private homes and on the street.

This research was not done with the intention to get a holistic picture of a pre-existent field, to judge official representations against actual practices in order to arrive at the truth of a situation, but to capture the mutually constitutive relations between different elements. This process continued when I wrote up my research. This book's five chapters proceed in roughly chronological order, but they are not intended to provide an overview of a period of modern Indian political history. I have selected these cases because they illuminate a different aspect of mediation at a particular time. The first four chapters deal with state and elite attempts at discursive construction of the

[7] In Delhi, I consulted the Central Secretariat Library, Jamia Millia University Library, Jawaharlal Nehru Memorial Library, the National Archives and the P. C. Joshi archive in Jawaharlal Nehru University, looking through material on central and UP state language and media policy, emergency-era censorship and its precedents and electoral regulation. I also consulted the archives of Hindi and Urdu newspaper offices in Delhi, Lucknow, Meerut and Muzaffarnagar: *Aag*, *Inquilab*, *Roznama Rashtriya Sahara* and *Sahafat* (Urdu); *Amar Ujala*, *Dainik Jagran*, *Rashtriya Sahara* and *Shah Times* (Hindi).

people during special periods such as wartime, emergencies and elections, and also through mundane regulation of a language that flouts most of the criteria for official language status. The last outlines a model of communication, which exceeds the diktats of states and 'elites'.

The first chapter looks at the workings of language policy with reference to Urdu in post-independence India and the state of Uttar Pradesh. I take on board the significance of ideologically motivated non-recognition of Urdu but describe how policy can be undercut by the way it is interpreted, implemented and received. In a survey of BJP election manifestos, I look at how the party's post-Partition hostility to the language has been tempered by electoral calculations and an enduring attachment to Urdu across India. I also look in detail at the incongruence of an apparent boom in Urdu newspapers accompanying a perceived decline in Urdu readerships. This chapter attempts to go beyond pointing out obvious inconsistencies to understand how various factors worked together to produce these apparently arbitrary outcomes. Instead of offering a standard ideology critique, I pay attention to the role of ignorance in both the marginalisation of Urdu and its continued relevance.

The second chapter picks up on the preceding discussion of Urdu's ambiguous status to deal with the attempts of two Urdu-language newspaper editor-journalists to address a *qaum* conceived in their own image, Abul Kalam Azad (1888–1958) and Aziz Burney (1952–). I deal with these attempts through their response to a series of international and domestic crises and to political organisations that attempted to unite Hindus and Muslims. In particular, the nascent Khilafat movement for the defence of the Ottoman caliph, which was key to their coming together in the independence struggle and Congress Party following the First World War, and Congress's ambiguous relationship with Muslims in the post-independence period. By comparing speech conditions for Azad and Burney, I describe how new combinations of audience, speaker and context have changed the boundaries of the *qaum*. I return to this theme and the figure of Azad in the fifth chapter. The chapter's discussion of possibilities for successful mediation of sociopolitical community beyond the agency of the state is further developed in all the subsequent chapters.

The third chapter, 'Emergency pedagogy', deals with another national and cross-denominational political movement, resistance to the internal emergency of 1975–7. I extend the previous discussion of state censorship by describing how repressive mechanisms once again worked to coalesce sociopolitical groups across ideological and identity lines, and the role played by media in this process. The focus here is on audiences rather than the state or spokesmen. I look at how news of an event in Bangladesh, the assassination of President Sheikh Mujibur Rahman (1920–1975), was written about in the prison diaries of two political leaders arrested in connection with the emergency in India – Jayaprakash Narayan (1902–1979), leader of the anti-Congress movement for Total Revolution, and L. K. Advani (1927–), Jana Sangh and later BJP politician. But I also consider the role of a wider reader response resulting in Congress's defeat in the 1977 general election.

The fourth chapter extends the preceding discussion of the technical mediation of the people by looking at attempts to regulate public speech during Indian elections, through imposition of a special electoral time when many kinds of political activity are restricted. I describe how during the Uttar Pradesh phase of the 2014 general election, the local election office's preoccupation with print, public space and the official election period left it unable to span the informal spaces, unofficial periods and new media fora in which the BJP's election campaign was conducted. I conclude by outlining an alternative basis for electoral regulation and democratic representation guided by the anarchic principle of democratic equality.

The fifth chapter extends the discussion of the interplay between formal and unofficial politics and returns to Abul Kalam Azad and the figure of the *qaum*. It looks at the 2019–20 protests against nationwide extension of the National Register of Citizens and the passing of the Citizenship Amendment Act. These protests are discussed in historical perspective, with focus on three different invocations of the *qaum*: Abul Kalam Azad's famous post-Partition speech, delivered from the Jama Masjid in Delhi in 1947, Dalit and anti-CAA activist, Chandra Shekhar Azad Ravan's intervention on the same site in December 2019, and a *dharna* by the women of Shaheen Bagh, New Delhi, in 2019–20. This chapter brings together the preceding discussions of the possibilities for a post-sovereign articulation of the people.

Texts produced by voluble actors are the main focus of these chapters: acts, codes and constitutions, reports and manifestos, newspapers, and magazines. But I do not view them as discrete documents or deal solely with their content. I read them against the findings of archival research and fieldwork, with a view to understanding something of their context, how they were disseminated and the ways in which they were received. I also pay attention to how they were produced and relate to other media: the printed image, spoken and broadcast word, and video message. By reading along the grain, I discern the outlines of the groups that were sought to be constructed by the authors of these messages. By reading against it, I try to avoid making assumptions about the success of their attempts.

Across these cases, whether through media, institutions or policy, there is little in the way of unidirectional transmission of univocal symbols to homogeneous audiences. The circuitry is more twisted and knotted than the developmental state's model of knowledge diffusion and nation-state formation allows. The groups articulated by these means are also more volatile. Unlike the mass reading publics described by Benedict Anderson, which are characterised by repetition and synchronicity, the collectivities that emerge from these processes are constantly being made and remade. In its more reflexive moments, this technopolitics of communication provides the shifting ground for a non-exclusionary form of the people, a people articulated by messages that are alienable from their immediate context (not exclusively involving face-to-face communication) but responsive and responsible to the communities they coalesce.

1

The immense writing-machine

Writing in 1853 on the occasion of a debate on renewal of the East India Company's rule over India's territories, Marx noted the absurdity of a senate ruling more than 156 million people putting its heads together to ask, who is the governing power in India? On looking deeply into 'the framework of this anomalous government', he identified 'a third power', supreme but hidden from public view, the two thousand stockholders who had no interest in India other than securing dividends on their revenue (2011: 34). The men elected from this pool being unfit for their duties, the real government was said to consist of 'the permanent and irresponsible *bureaucracy*' who had transformed it into 'one immense writing-machine' (ibid.: 34–5). The combination of automation and inscription suggested by this image looks forward to the fragment on machines in *The Grundrisse*, in which the automaton, 'a moving power that moves itself', is said to supplant the worker (1973: 693). Unlike the instrument, which the worker 'animates and makes into his organ with his own skill and strength', the machine 'is itself the virtuoso':

> The science which compels the inanimate limbs of the machinery, by their construction, to act purposefully, as an automaton, does not exist in the worker's consciousness, but rather acts upon him through the machine as an alien power, as the power of the machine itself.
>
> (Ibid.)

Both the article on India and the text on automation contain the suggestion of a blurring of boundaries between humans and non-humans, which renders labour and the act of inscription mindless. Decentring the subject of these operations makes it hard to ascribe authorship for actions and to assign responsibility for their consequences. Although in India there was 'a financial deficit', an 'over-supply of wars', 'no supply at all of public works' and abominable systems of tax, justice and law, no party was held responsible for any of this (Marx 2011: 31). Early on in the history of the Government of India, Marx was describing how extraterritorial rule exacerbates the subversive potential of paper and signature,[1] and his insights anticipate much work on bureaucracy in contemporary South Asia.[2]

In this chapter, I pick up on the post-sovereign understanding of agency contained in Marx's image of the writing machine to oppose a model of state–society relations in which the former is portrayed as imposing its rigid order on society through repressive and ideological means. In political theory, a well-known version of this is Althusser's account of the state apparatus (Althusser 1977a), which extends Marx's theory of subjectification to describe how individuals are interpellated as subjects through ideology. In social theory, a particularly influential version is found in the close and critical reading of Marx, which informs Weber's multidimensional model of class and descriptions of the bureaucratic state and capitalist market (Weber 2013). I instead look at the state's writing practices to question the coherence of its policies and argue against understandings of social group formation that view language as a fixed marker of identity, with reference to the fluctuating fortunes of Urdu in India.

Associated with the camp and the court, the soldier and the courtesan, Urdu has long existed in ambiguous relation to the categories of mother tongue and national language. Urdu emerged out of congeries of languages known by many names and written in a number of scripts, which coalesced into Hindi and Urdu over the course of the nineteenth century and came to be conflated with Hindus and Muslims respectively by the twentieth.[3] These associations were reinforced by Urdu's post-Partition status as the national language of Pakistan, where it serves as a lingua franca for communication

[1] The articles on India that Marx wrote between 1853 and 1862 as London correspondent for the *New York Daily Tribune* were written just prior to *Capital* and *The Grundrisse*. For a discussion of the publication history of these articles and the likely effect they had on his later writings, see Iqbal Hussain's preface and Irfan Habib's introduction to *Karl Marx on India: From the New York Daily Tribune (including Articles by Frederick Engels) and Extracts from Marx-Engels Correspondence 1853–1862*. 2011. New Delhi: Tulika Books.

[2] See Fuller and Bénéï (2000), Gupta (2012), Hull (2012), Mathur (2016), Piliavsky (2014), Poole and Das (2004) and Tarlo (2003).

[3] See the accounts of this history in Brass (1974), Robinson (1974), Rai (1984), Lelyveld (1993), King (1994), Bayly (1999), Dalmia (1999) and Rai (2001).

between groups speaking various 'mother tongues'.[4] Because of the recency of its association with Muslims and mutual intelligibility with spoken Hindi, Urdu offers a good case study of how sociopolitical labels come to be attached to cultural phenomena and the extent to which they can be made to stick.

Through the case of Urdu, I specifically respond to the assumptions that inform Bourdieu's work on symbolic power (1994, 1987a, 1987b, 1984) and Paul Brass's multi-symbol congruence theory (2004, 1991, 1989 and 1974), both of which describe the role played by language in political legitimation and social cohesion and, in the latter instance, deal with language politics and nation-state formation in north India. Both theorists seek to denaturalise the categories of class, ethnicity and nationality by paying attention to how they are made through communicative practices. But I argue that their continued reliance upon these categories, and instrumentalist understanding of how they are achieved, ultimately favours a view of society in which actors are fitted within a network whose coordinates are determined in advance.

Both Brass and Bourdieu oppose the idea of social cohesion as determined by coercive control and instead emphasise the role of symbolic mediation. Bourdieu seeks to transcend 'energetic models, which describe social relations as relations of force, and cybernetic models, which turn them into relations of communication' through the concept of symbolic power, which by 'dissimulation and transfiguration' efficiently transubstantiates power relations by rendering 'recognizable and misrecognizable' the violence they contain (1994: 170). For Bourdieu, misrecognition (méconnaissance) is both a question of embodied durable dispositions as well as consciousness, and language is of special interest to him because it partakes of the two.

Brass also opposes cybernetic theories of national 'integration', according to which the gap between the modernising elite and the masses is 'reduced or overcome by the communication to the mass of the goals of the elite and the transformation of mass values to make them compatible with the aspirations of the elite' (1974: 5–6). He emphasises that shared differences do not in themselves produce a subjective sense of identity. Some kind of political

[4] The 2017 Pakistani census records only 14,706,159 mother-tongue speakers of Urdu amongst a survey of 207,684,626 census participants: https://www.pbs.gov.pk/sites/default/files/population/2017/tables/pakistan/Table11n.pdf (accessed 7 February 2024).

agency is required to effect the transition from ethnic group to community to nationality, in particular, state policy and elite politicking. Symbols play an important part in this process too. Nationalist elites are said to 'emphasize one symbol above others' in order to foster a national identity coextensive with the modern state, whilst indigenous elites, who place more value on caste, religion and region, 'seek to induce multi-symbol congruence in their groups to achieve separateness and political rights' (Brass 1974: 45). Such an approach does not begin with the nation and process of modernisation and ask how each territorial group of people reaches these goals. It instead begins with the ethnic group and asks 'under what conditions do ethnic groups develop into nations' (ibid.: 7).

Brass is aware even this is problematic given that 'objective' differences are themselves 'highly variable' (ibid.: 405). Nevertheless, his definition of ethnic groups is orthodox in its reference to 'language, culture, territory, diet, and dress [rather] than to a role in the division of labor' (ibid.: 8). He persists in thinking of ethnicities and nations as discrete and quantifiable units. Similarly, Bourdieu continues to use the term class even as he rejects the usual economist understandings of it. Their attachment to these labels ultimately favours an objective view of social reality, which verges on being deterministic if not essentialist, and a corollary of this view is a kind of instrumentalism. Brass speaks of 'the ways in which a people creates its own history through a conscious process of symbol selection' (1974: 121) and Bourdieu of 'deeply buried corporeal dispositions, outside the channels of consciousness and calculation' (Bourdieu, Wacquant and Farage 1994: 14). But both describe how symbols are instrumentalised by states and elites to construct social groups (ethnicities, classes) on their own terms. Elites are the main agents in these operations and the state is the motive power – owner of 'meta-capital' in the work of Bourdieu (ibid.: 4), and therefore capable of spanning the various fields, the catalyst for subjective consciousness of identity in Brass.

Brass was to modify his opinions in response to criticism of this early work and reject an 'extreme instrumentalist perspective' that would deny history and agency to the groups it describes by representing their pre-existing cultural and religious practices as 'infinitely malleable by elites' (1991: 77). But he reiterates his basic thesis on language politics and applies it to a wider pan-Indian context in an article published decades later (2004). Bourdieu's understanding of the state is also more nuanced than Althusser's theory of the state apparatus, but he speaks of it in familiar totalising terms as 'the *culmination of a process of concentration of different species of capital*' (Bourdieu, Wacquant and Farage 1994: 4, italics in the original). From this process, the state emerges as 'a sort of meta-capital granting power over other species of capital and over their holders' (ibid.). Those such as Marx who question the seamlessness of its monopoly are said to ignore the effects of its 'obligatory reference to the values of neutrality and disinterested loyalty to the public good', including upon bureaucrats themselves (ibid.: 17). Through these unfold 'the long work of symbolic construction', whereby 'official representation of the state as the site of universality and of service of the general interest is invented and imposed' (ibid.).

To this notion of top-down symbolic construction, I oppose the productive effects of the slippage between a communicative act and its reception and underline the role played by ignorance rather than knowledge in state–society relations. Accordingly, I look at the practices and associations as well as ideologies and instrumental rationalities that influence language policy. This perspective does not downplay the significance of power dynamics and the ideas and intentions of actors. I instead pay close attention to how they become effective in particular contexts and reflect more broadly on the relationship between post-independence linguistic, education and media policy, and the multiple readerships for Indian media incompletely distinguished by language, region and religion.

I work through these ideas across three case studies spanning the areas of state policy, party politics and market forces in post-independence India. In the first, I look at language policy and politics nationally and in the north Indian state of Uttar Pradesh, where post-Partition Urdu has been marginalised in education and bureaucracy despite constitutional and central government safeguards for minority languages. In the second, I consider the paradox of the Jana Sangh's and its successor the Bharatiya Janata Party's at times avowedly pro-Urdu platform. Finally, I consider the Urdu newspaper market, which has continued to expand into the 2020s despite the apparently declining significance of Urdu.

Instead of singling out a single factor to account for these apparent anomalies (ideologies *or* interests *rather than* the market) and relegating others to context (historical *background*), I describe how various factors have worked together to produce these outcomes. Through these examples I demonstrate how on the ground, history and policy combined to inform practices that did not adhere to the writ of various 'laws': of the state, of ascriptive attachments and ideological allegiances, of supply and demand. I conclude by outlining a non-instrumentalist aesthetics of politics, sensitive to the liberatory potential of a reflexive form of ignorance, which helps account for the continued relevance of Urdu in post-independence India.

Ignorance and power

In his influential essay, 'The Census, Social Structure and Objectification in India', Bernard Cohn proceeds from the notion that 'culture equals symbol systems', to describe how the colonial census played a key role in making objective to Indians themselves their own culture and society (1987: 225). By paying attention to how colonised peoples responded to these governmental processes, Cohn moves beyond the traditional focus on 'westernised' elites and provides a nuanced account of the impact of the census on caste politics. However, he limits its effects to the enumerators who then as now were responsible for filling in census forms. According to Cohn, the 'act of a census enumerator asking a question of a peasant' did not contribute much to the process, especially as many enumerators may have filled out the forms on the basis of their own knowledge of their neighbours (ibid.: 248).

In this section, I advance a different understanding of mediation by looking at how census language statistics are collected and deployed in order to question their efficacy in producing an objective account of Indian culture and society. State-sanctioned censuses may be political rather than purely philological documents, but they are also part of a bureaucratic process, subject to bureaucratic inertia and opacity, with repercussions for any biopolitical project of knowing the population in order to manage it. I specifically look at how census questions left unasked and answers misrepresented make the bias and arbitrariness of state classifications legible to those whom they marginalise. I then go on to consider how this marginalisation is reinforced by those who interpret census data and implement state language policy.

Any census would struggle to capture the complexity of linguistic practices in India, but the three questions relating to them in the 2011 census form offered a particularly stark assessment of language and literacy.[5] Question ten asked for 'Mother Tongue'; question eleven for 'Other languages known' (a maximum of two could be listed); and question twelve for 'Literacy status' – giving two options 'Literate' or 'Illiterate'. Categories such as Mother Tongue and Literate/Illiterate did not consider how multiple languages/dialects could be spoken within a family, how and to what extent literacy had been acquired, and which language respondents were literate in. Only sixteen languages are listed on the census schedule, encompassing hundreds of 'mother tongues', a term which covers both dialects and languages.[6]

Because the distinction between dialect and language is not self-evident, and mother tongue no less contentious a term, schedule listing is fiercely contested and often quite arbitrary. Linguists have described the terms as existing on a continuum rather than in opposition. The decisive shift from dialect to language is said to result from selection, codification and community acceptance of a norm, rather than cut-and-dried linguistic differences, and to be closely related to the rise of nationalism (Haugen 1972: 237). Mother tongue has also been described as an alien concept in South Asia, where multilingualism is pervasive. Modern instances of 'linguism', manifested in the creation of linguistic states, are said to be of recent stamp and exogenous origin (Pollock 2006: 507).

This multilingualism is attested to by the profusion of terms deployed in colonial censuses to record spoken, as opposed to written, languages. These included 'mother tongue', 'parent tongue', 'language ordinarily used', and 'language ordinarily spoken in the household' (Brass 1974: 193). In the 2011 census handbook, enumerators were instructed to take its meaning literally as 'the language spoken in childhood by the person's mother to the person'.[7] The

5 http://censusindia.gov.in/2011-Schedule/Shedules/English_Household_schedule.pdf (accessed 15 March 2015).

6 The examples of 'Mother tongue' given in figures 6.55–6.58 of the enumerators handbook (Sadri, Hindi, Malayalam and Bhojpuri) encompass two dialects or 'bolis' – Sadri and Bhojpuri, which are both classified as languages and mother tongues grouped under Hindi: http://www.censusindia.gov.in/Census_Data_2001/Census_Data_Online/Language/Statement1.aspx (accessed 16 March 2015).

7 http://censusindia.gov.in/2011-Documents/Updating%20of%20Abridged%20Houselist-English.pdf, p. 54 (accessed 16 March 2015).

only exception was someone whose mother had died when they were a child. In such instances, the language used in the person's childhood home was said to qualify. Both the category and its exception overlooked multilingualism within the Indian family, where the language you speak with your mother could be different from that used to address your father, which could differ yet again from that spoken amongst siblings.[8]

In the eyes of its critics, simplifications were compounded by distortions as it was left to census workers to complete the form. In the handbook for the 2011 census, enumerators were instructed not to attribute religion on the basis of 'caste names' and also not to establish any relationship between religion and mother tongue.[9] Those who suspected that 'due to any organised movement', religion was not being accurately recorded were to make a report to their supervisory officer for verification.[10] This instruction, and the attempt to monitor its implementation, suggest that these practices may have been quite common, as has historically been the case. According to Brass, no census of Hindi and Urdu speakers in the north Indian states of UP and Bihar has ever accurately reflected the number and relative proportion of Hindi or Urdu speakers (1974: 190). Before 1951 the goal was subverted because enumerators were told to record as mother tongue 'something different from what they were told by the people' (ibid.) (e.g. with various languages/dialects grouped under the label 'Hindustani'). Following Partition, when Urdu became the national language of Pakistan, Hindi an official national language of India, and Hindustani, which encompassed them both, gradually disappeared from the Indian census, they have been viewed with no less scepticism.[11]

8 The 2020 New Education Policy acknowledges multilingualism *within* the family, as well as between families, with its category of 'home language', a language spoken between some family members that might differ from both mother tongue and local language. It recommends that 'the medium of instruction until at least Grade 5, but preferably till Grade 8 and beyond, will be the home language/mother tongue/local language/regional language' – the profusion of terms reflecting the complexity of India's linguistic situation. See 'Multilingualism and the power of language', in *The National Education Policy* (GI [Government of India]) 2020: 13).

9 http://censusindia.gov.in/2011-Documents/Updating%20of%20Abridged%20Houselist-English.pdf, p. 45. (accessed 16 March 2015).

10 Ibid.

11 Although Hindustani lost official language status following independence, it continued to be a census category until a sharp decline in recorded speakers led to its disappearance from the 1971 census schedule. The *Report of the Committee for the Promotion of Urdu* records that 6,742,937 Hindustani speakers were recorded in Uttar Pradesh in 1951; 100,530 in 1961 (although 'Nil' were recorded in urban areas); and a statistically negligible number in 1971, which meant there are no figures given for Hindustani in this year (GI 1975: 19).

Over the same period, the numbers of Hindi and Urdu speakers increased as these languages became equated with Hindus and Muslims respectively. In a post-Partition context, declaring yourself a mother tongue Urdu speaker would become a means to assert a religio-cultural identity. A census enumerator's decision to ignore your claim and record the language you 'actually' speak would also be read politically. Brass describes Urdu movement leaders dismissing the 1961 census as bogus on the basis that it recorded two million fewer Urdu speakers than Muslims in UP (1974: 189). In recent times, during fieldwork in Uttar Pradesh, I was repeatedly told by Muslims that they had been misidentified as mother-tongue Hindi speakers, in what they perceived to be a deliberate attempt to underestimate the number of Urdu speakers in India.

There is also nothing straightforward about how census statistics have in turn been read by the state. The census matters to language activists because it forms the basis for provision of facilities, but in practice the census's recording of a certain number of Urdu speakers has been insufficient to secure its position in India. Article 347 of the Indian Constitution declares that the President may authorise recognition of a language, if he believes a 'substantial proportion' of the population 'desire the use of any language spoken by them to be recognised throughout that State or any part thereof'. However, the vagueness of Article 347's wording has hampered its implementation. When the central state-appointed Gujral Committee called on legal experts to clarify the term 'substantial proportion', they expressed the view that it suggests a percentage of no less than 15 to 20 per cent in a state as a whole (GI 1975: 28). According to the census, Urdu did not have that many speakers in any Indian state. Urdu may have officially been the sixth most widely spoken language in the country, but, unlike most of the languages in the census schedule, it was not spoken by the majority of people in any state.

The report produced by the Gujral Committee sidestepped the question of how Article 347 should be interpreted but commended use of Urdu for official purposes where there were 10 per cent or more speakers of Urdu (ibid.: 147). Despite these recommendations, no such recognition was accorded to Urdu in UP until The Uttar Pradesh Official Language (Amendment) Act was passed in 1989. This was only ratified after a decades-long and bitterly fought struggle in the courts, which concluded in 2014 when the Supreme Court upheld

Urdu's status as second official language for seven administrative purposes. But even these concessions were limited in scope, as was observed when they were first proposed by the 1990 report on the implementation of the Gujral Committee's recommendations.[12]

Alongside its marginalisation in bureaucracy, Urdu gradually disappeared from state school education despite constitutional safeguards and central state policy guidelines for education in minority languages. Article 350a of the Constitution requires state governments to provide facilities for primary-level instruction in the mother-tongue language of children belonging to linguistic minority groups, but this requirement has been unevenly applied across regions and languages. In implementing Article 350a, the state of UP was guided by the '10–40' formula issued by the Department of Education in 1952, which stipulated that in a primary school class of forty students, ten would have to request instruction in their mother tongue for such an arrangement to be made.[13] The *Gujral Committee Report* pointed out that this formula had proved unworkable because of its unwieldiness (GI 1975: 44). A follow-up report recorded that there were only 1375 Urdu medium primary schools in UP, despite the presence of 10,767,175 Urdu speakers, and that most of these were religious schools run by the 'linguistic minority' itself (GI 1990: 69). The situation was said to be even worse at the secondary level, where there is no constitutional obligation for representation of minority languages. The same report claimed that in Uttar Pradesh 'there is not a single Government Urdu medium secondary school' (ibid.: 12).[14]

In addition to the virtual disappearance of Urdu-medium state schools, Urdu as a subject was affected by a particular understanding of the Education Ministry's three-language formula of language learning, which was introduced in The National Policy on Education (1968).[15] According to the formula,

[12] SC upholds Urdu as second official language in Uttar Pradesh', *India Today*, 4 September 2014

[13] This was later officially sanctioned by the state government. See *Report of the Uttar Pradesh Language Committee* (GUP [Government of UP] 1962: 32–3).

[14] The situation appears to have deteriorated over the subsequent period, despite intermittent pro-Urdu policies by the state government. According to the National University of Educational Planning and Administration's report for the academic year 2017–18, there were only ninety-nine Urdu-medium primary schools in Uttar Pradesh, which were either government managed or aided, and no government managed or aided Urdu-medium secondary schools. http://schoolreportcards.in/SRC-New/AdvanceSearch/AdvanceSearch.aspx (accessed 17 July 2019).

[15] http://mhrd.gov.in/sites/upload_files/mhrd/files/document-reports/NPE-1968.pdf (accessed 7 April 2015).

secondary school children in the Hindi-speaking states would study Hindi, English and a modern Indian language apart from Hindi, and those in the non-Hindi-speaking states, the regional language, Hindi and English. The National Policy on Education recommended that Hindi-speaking states choose a modern Indian language from the southern states, but the decision was left to their discretion. In the Hindi-speaking states, where the choice of third language was dependent on the wish of the majority of the students, there was little incentive to study another regional language whilst English and Hindi continued to be official languages of the Union. Urdu might seem to be the natural choice of third language, given that prior to independence both Hindi and Urdu had been used in state education, but this was discouraged by the decision to recognise Sanskrit as a modern Indian language.

Sanskrit was available as a choice of 'Modern Indian Language' because it had been listed as such in the Eighth Schedule of the Constitution. Rather than being the result of an ideologically motivated Hindu nationalist attempt to promote Sanskrit, this was the outcome of three years of fraught deliberation on the future of India's languages. The cause of Sanskrit as a national language had coalesced a wide range of people during the Constituent Assembly debates, including non-Hindu politicians such as Ambedkar and Naziruddin Ahmad of the Muslim League in Bengal. They had supported Sanskrit's designation as a Modern Indian Language because it was perceived to belong to 'no one single region, caste, or religion, even while belonging to all of them' (Ramaswamy 2009: 122). Sanskrit resembled Urdu in its detachment from any particular region, and was therefore able to supplant it as third language in the Hindi-speaking states. Faced with a choice between Urdu and Sanskrit, the former for many students requiring acquisition of a new script, students had little incentive to opt for Urdu in Uttar Pradesh.

A combination of census politics, bureaucratic processes and constitutional provisions led to the decline of Urdu in a state where it was formerly the predominant language. But rather than arising from a concern with control on the basis of knowledge, the drafting, interpretation and implementation of policy was characterised by willful blindness and ignorance. Marginalisation was also achieved through collateral effects rather than direct means, and by the unfaithful implementation of incoherent state directives.

Split publics, forked tongues

Over the years, pro-Urdu measures by political parties and governments have been a standard way of dealing with Muslim voters, although the way this has worked has been paradoxical. On the one hand Hindu nationalist organisations have continued to play a role in the marginalisation of Urdu. At the same time, the BJP's origins in north India (both 'Cow-belt' and Hindi–Urdu heartland), and a section of its leadership's appreciation for Urdu and its associated culture, mean that a sentimental attachment to the language exists within its ranks. Even more significant has been the impact of electoral calculations: the presence of concentrations of Muslim voters across the country, the need to form coalitions with other political parties and to avoid alienating voters of all denominations who might not share the party's Hindutva ideology.

In this section, I look at how Urdu's historical status as a link language worked out in the post-independence period through an analysis of the Jana Sangh's and its successor the BJP's Urdu policy, as expressed in their election manifestos. Apparent Hindu nationalist support for a language associated with Muslims is un-anticipated by theories of multi-symbol congruence and symbolic power, premised on objectively verifiable and fixed ethnic and social locations. The twists and turns of Jana Sangh and BJP policy highlights how the multivalence of symbols can work to bring groups together as well as be manipulated to separate them.

The 1954 Jana Sangh manifesto, the first to mention language policy, promised to introduce Hindi as a national language, whilst encouraging the development of 'regional languages', with the proviso that they accept Nagari script and a common scientific and technical vocabulary based on Sanskrit to further 'the growth of national solidarity and goodwill' (BJS 2005: 280). It pointedly refused to recognise Urdu as both a regional and national language and promised to remove Urdu from the list of languages recognised in the Constitution. It also declared that 'Hindi will be secured its rightful place in Jammu and Kashmir' (ibid.: 281). Hindu nationalist claims over this disputed territory would be affirmed through imposition of Hindi on the only state where Urdu was the official state language.[16]

[16] This policy was implemented by the BJP government after Kashmir's special status was revoked in 2019, when Hindi joined Kashmiri and Dogri as official languages in the 2020 Jammu and Kashmir

This attitude towards Urdu was to remain largely unchanged in the 1950s and 1960s, but a mellowing in attitude was discernible in the 1971 manifesto. A section titled 'Developing Indian Languages' proclaimed that '*Swarajya* is incomplete without *Swabhasha*' ('self-rule' and an 'autonomous language') and promised to 'expedite the replacement of English by Indian languages at the State level' and develop Hindi as a link language (ibid.: 171). But it also promised to 'pay attention to the promotion of the Urdu language, and ensure that facilities due to it under the law are accorded to it', whilst being opposed to making it the second official language of UP, Bihar and Madhya Pradesh (ibid.: 172). The last comment responded to pro-Urdu agitations that took place around the time of the 1967 elections, during which second language status for Urdu was the plank of several political parties. This movement gained impetus from non-Hindi states' success in pushing for amendment of The Official Languages Act in 1967, affirming the use of English as an associate official language. Although the Jana Sangh had expressed vocal resistance to the amendment, the party ultimately agreed to it out of a concern to extend its national support base into areas such as the Punjab, where it had a relationship with the Akali Dal, and Kerala, where it had been making some headway.

Congress fragmentation was also an important factor in these developments. Congress had won a slender majority in the 1967 general election but failed to secure an outright majority in several states, leading to the formation of Samyukta Vidhayak Dal governments in north India. These consisted of broad-based coalitions between Jana Sangh and other parties, including, in Bihar, the Communist Party of India. These volatile combinations showed early signs of strain, and Congress would return to something approaching its former stature in the 1971 election. But these forces would reunite during the emergency period, go on to form the Janata Party, and contest and win the 1977 election.

The 1977 Janata Party manifesto stated that it would implement the three-language formula and protect the rights of linguistic minorities, and accord

Official Languages Bill. This was justified on the basis that Urdu, the official vernacular, was only spoken as a mother tongue by 0.16 per cent of the population in Jammu and Kashmir. However, the same census also recorded that a mere 2.3 per cent spoke Hindi. See 'Parliament passes Jammu and Kashmir Official Languages Bill, 2020', *The Hindu*, 23 September 2020: https://www.thehindu.com/news/national/other-states/parliament-passes-jammu-and-kashmir-official-languages-bill-2020/article32677107.ece (accessed 31 July 2022).

'due importance and encouragement' to Urdu and Sindhi (BJS 2005: 139). Urdu and Sindhi are non-regional languages mostly spoken by Muslims and displaced Hindus from Sindh, so this was a carefully balanced combination. This was toughened up in the 1980 manifesto, in response to doubts about the secularism of the Janata Party given its incorporation of the Jana Sangh party and members of the Hindu nationalist paramilitary organisation, the Rashtriya Swayamsevak Sangh (RSS). This document mentioned its commitment to implementation of the recommendations of the *Gujral Committee Report*, and to the Urdu language generally, 'which originated in India, and whose contribution to the country's literature and culture has been immense', with special provisions for Urdu as a medium of instruction for Urdu-speaking children 'wherever there is adequate demand' (BJS 2005: 95–6).

The coalition was soon to come unstuck, leading to the formation of the Bharatiya Janata Party in 1980. The BJP's stance towards Urdu hardened during this decade, a period of increased communalisation of Indian politics, and the BJP strongly opposed moves to make Urdu the second state language of UP in 1989. BJP state President Kalyan Singh threatened a 'violent and gigantic' agitation in response, sentiments reportedly 'echoed' by party leader Atal Bihari Vajpayee and manifested in a gathering of more than 250 Shiv Sena men 'brandishing spears and trishuls' outside the Vidhan Sabha (legislative assembly) building in Lucknow.[17]

The BJP manifesto for that year also mentioned the Act in a list of examples of Congress appeasement of Muslims:

> By negativing [sic] the Supreme Court judgment in the Shah Bano case, the government has put a premium on communalism and obscurantism. And by recognizing Urdu as second official language in Uttar Pradesh on election eve, it has shown more interest in Muslim votes than in Urdu language. In the process it has only given the country so many corpses. By not allowing the rebuilding of the Ram Janma Mandir in Ayodhya, on the lines of the Somnath Mandir built by the Government of India in 1948, it has allowed tensions to rise, and gravely strained social harmony.
>
> (BJP 2005: 358)

[17] Dilip Awasthi, 'Urdu uproar: Fracas over second official language status to Urdu in Uttar Pradesh', *India Today*, 15 October 1989 http://indiatoday.intoday.in/story/fracas-over-second-official-language-status-to-urdu-in-uttar-pradesh/1/324017.html (accessed 31 August 2015).

The abrupt transition from Urdu to Ayodhya indicates how language and religion were connected in Hindu nationalist thinking. However, even in this year, in the section on language, there was a promise to assist in the development of Indian languages 'which are neither State languages nor regional languages, but have contributed to the enrichment of Indian culture' (ibid.: 384). This could mean Sindhi and Sanskrit, but both these languages were explicitly mentioned elsewhere (ibid.: 378 and 384) and the wording was left vague enough to encompass Urdu.

There was no direct reference to Urdu in the 1991 and 1996 manifestos, but there was a striking use of Urdu in the latter's description of Congress rule:

> never since the scourge of the Pindaries [mercenaries, often Muslim, who were active in the Maratha region] has the writ of our state been as enfeebled as by this Congress misrule. The primary task, therefore, is to restore to the state, and to governance, its honour and prestige – *izzat* and *iqbal*.
>
> (BJP 2005: 250)

On the one hand, there was a reference to Muslim treachery and, on the other, a use of Urdu words to express noble sentiments. Both were the legacy of centuries of Muslim rule in India, which had left a corpus of political heroes/villains and Arabic, Persian and Turkic words, many of which relate to politics. *Izzat* and *iqbal* may have been chosen for their association with the glamour of an 'exotic' court culture, which voters across India would have been familiar with. The BJP's recourse to Urdu, even when making communally tinged public statements, indicates how hard it was to eliminate the language in favour of *shudh* ('pure', Sanskritised) Hindi or English.

Nineteen ninety-six was also the year that saw the formation of an abortive BJP government. When the BJP returned to power in 1998, with a coalition of smaller and regional parties in the National Democratic Alliance, its official policy towards Urdu had cooled to carefully balanced and vague statements about encouraging 'the enrichment, preservation and development of all Indian languages, including Sanskrit and Urdu' (BJP 2005: 182). This document also mentioned the diversity that is 'an inseparable part of India's past and present national tradition', which comprised not only the Hindu holy books but 'also the Indian traditions of the Muslims, Christians and Parsis' (ibid.: 142). This existed alongside sections on 'the cultural nationalism of

India which is the core of Hindutva', and the 'integrative' ideas which led it to support the Ram Janambhoomi movement (ibid.: 146). But the tone of these statements was very different from that of earlier manifestos. When elections were called the following year after the Tamil All India Anna Dravida Munnetra Kazhagam's exit from the coalition, there was no mention of Hindutva in the 1998 National Democratic Alliance (NDA) manifesto. There was also little mention of the BJP. All emphasis was on the new coalition, as the NDA mission statement proclaimed: 'The NDA is new, the NDA is the future and the NDA is a broad-based movement for progress and justice' (ibid.: 122).

By the time of the next polls in 2004, the BJP had been holding power across India and at the centre in a coalition government for five years and needed to consider other parties, Muslim voters and a general distaste for blatant communalism after more than a decade of riots and violence. The sitting BJP Prime Minister, Atal Bihari Vajpayee, was himself seen as an embodiment of composite Indian culture. Vajpayee was socially comfortable around Muslims, a product and proponent of *ganga-yamuni tehzeeb*, and even a Hindustani poet of sorts. It was during his term in office and just prior to the Lok Sabha elections that a series of pro-Urdu measures were announced. Notably, Vajpayee's 2004 promise to recruit 200,000 Urdu teachers and spend Rs. 740 million on madrassa education. This, again, reinforced the conflation between Urdu, Muslims and a certain type of religious education and was opposed on this account by some prominent Muslims and Urdu language advocates.[18]

The move was condemned by the Vishwa Hindu Parishad as 'an insulting slap to all Hindus, Christians and others', but both the proposal and the VHP's reference to 'Christians and others' in its critique of it mark a shift from the communal rhetoric of earlier periods, including that expressed by Vajpayee himself.[19] Just two years earlier, in 2002, on the eve of the burning of the Sabarmati Express, ostensible trigger for the Gujarat pogrom, he had

18 Ather Farouqui, General Secretary of Anjuman Taraqqi Urdu, dismissed it as 'unconstitutional' (from personal communication with Ather Farouqui).

19 'VHP flays Vajpayee on support to Urdu, madrasas', *The Times of India*, 23 April 2004: http://articles.timesofindia.indiatimes.com/2004-04-23/india/28324162_1_madrasas-urdu-general-secretary-praveen-togadia (accessed 21 June 2012).

proclaimed that the BJP could win the upcoming UP assembly elections without Muslim support.[20] The menace in this statement was underlined by events that were to unfold a few days later. The proportion of Muslim voters being unlikely to have changed significantly during this time, a roughly similar number was being addressed quite differently over a two-year period.

How to understand these sudden shifts and apparent incongruities? You could argue that they result from deficiencies in Indian democracy that have created 'an incompletely modern polity' with a 'split public' sphere, in which there is a divide between the political society desired by modernising elites and 'its actual historical forms', a central fault line being the 'the unfulfilled mission of secularism' in a country where a compromise between Hindu orthodoxy and progressive nationalism launched an anti-colonial independence movement, culminating in the creation of a secular state (Rajagopal 2001: 152). The emergence and success of the Hindu nationalist BJP in an officially secular country might be proof of such a split, as would the BJP's double discourse on Muslims.

Setting aside for a moment the sincerity or otherwise of the party's intentions, for whatever reason, it is notable that the BJP was seeking to demonstrate its secularism through this policy rather than gesture to the historical form of, say, a Hindu kingdom. The VHP's critique was also ostensibly secular. Both the BJP and VHP alluded to a view of secularism as a state of equilibrium between the faiths, only differing on how this balance should be maintained. The BJP here seeming to think that it entailed support for religious minorities, the VHP that it meant not favouring one group above others. These understandings are commonplace and even said to be distinctively Indian, although something like it can be seen in other countries where the predominant religion does not support the separation of church and state because, like Hinduism, it has no church.

Moving beyond the idea of both primordial attachments and instrumental rationality makes it possible to think in terms of kaleidoscopic configurations, and to look at the ways such measures worked across various levels. Without dismissing their divisive local effect, the fact that they were introduced prior to a general election encourages reflection on how they might have been received

20 'BJP can win even without Muslim votes: PM', *The Hindu*, 20 February 2002: http://hindu.com/thehindu/2002/02/20/stories/2002022003000100.htm (accessed 21 June 2012).

nationally, where distinct elements come into play. Muslims who do not read Urdu or even speak Urdu, and who might prefer their children to be educated in English (or Hindi or Tamil), could still interpret pro-Urdu measures as signalling that a party is attuned to their presence. These measures may also have been aimed at non-Muslims, an attachment to secular values, however defined, not being exclusive to religious minorities.

A decade later, during the 2014 general election, a non-Muslim audience seemed to be implicit for measures listed in the section on equal opportunities for minorities, which included a commitment to 'preservation and promotion of Urdu' (BJP 2014: 17). A pro-Urdu stance allowed the BJP to gesture towards secular ideals despite its controversial choice of Narendra Modi as leader. At the same time, adoption of Hindi allowed Modi, the first Chief Minister other than, briefly, Charan Singh, to assume the position of Prime Minister, to counter charges of parochialism. Standing from Varanasi and speaking in Hindi allowed this Gujarati politician to lay claim to a regional identity now viewed as national: Hindu, Hindi-speaking, Hindustani, Banarasi. He even attempted to parlay this into the international arena, delivering his first speech to the United Nations General Assembly in Hindi.[21]

All of these ideological convolutions seemed to be less indicative of elites rallying pre-constituted groups through an appeal to shared, 'given' characteristics, than parties semaphoring their intentions, voters reading and sometimes reading between the lines of these signals, and meanings being created through these circuits. Through such impure processes of semiosis, popularly known as dirty politics or opportunism (*gandi siyasat*, *mauqaparasti*), sociopolitical constituencies are continually being mediated.

The file paper

In this section, I consider the idiosyncratic workings of the Indian newspaper market, focusing on Urdu dailies in the state of Uttar Pradesh in the 2010-20s.

[21] 'PM Modi's US visit: Modi follows footsteps of AB Vajpayee, speaks in Hindi at UN' in *The Economic Times*, 27 September 2014: http://articles.economictimes.indiatimes.com/2014-09-27/news/54377095_1_hindi-divas-prime-minister-narendra-modi-pm-modi (accessed 31 August 2015).

In continuity with earlier work on the East India Company, I also look at a 'power-laden world of documentary transactions' (Raman 2012: 18) and at how contradictions between rules and their bureaucratic implementation are the central problematic of the modern state. But in dealing with the post-Partition and post-Second World War era, I consider further contradictions resulting from an international consensus on the importance of free speech as a pillar of democracy and a postcolonial state's concern for communal harmony and national unity.

Into the twenty-first century, repressive colonial-era legislation continues to frame Indian newspaper production (1860 Penal Code, 1867 Press and Registration of Books Act, 1885 Telegraph Act, 1898 Indian Post Office Act, 1923 Official Secrets Act), and the Constitution lacks a provision on freedom of the press. Until the introduction of The Freedom of Information Bill (2000) and The Right to Information Act (2005), regulation seemed to have been weighted towards control rather than freedom of expression. Even then it departed from 'the American folk ideology of free speech, which fosters the sense that speakers control language', contextualised by Western, vernacular belief systems that naturalise language standards through 'metaphors such as that of the free market' (Woolard 1998: 26 and 21).

This belief is more commonly described as universal, and a conflation of free speech with free markets can be discerned in one of its most famous proclamations, The Universal Declaration of Human Rights (1948). Article 19 of the UDHR defines freedom of expression as the right 'to hold opinions without interference and to seek, receive and impart information and ideas through any media and regardless of frontiers'. Reference is made to the imparter, seeker and receiver of information and ideas, to the opinion holder, but there is no mention of any wider context except for references to the media through which ideas, information and opinions flow, and the interference and frontiers that are said to potentially restrict their circulation.

The Indian Constituent Assembly adopted the UDHR in 1949, but the turmoil of Partition and socialist sympathies of Congress Party leadership encouraged a cautious attitude towards both freedom of speech and free markets. The first restrictions on the Indian Constitution's provisions on

'Protection of certain rights regarding freedom of speech etc.' were introduced in 1951, as part of The Constitution (First Amendment) Act.[22] This subjected Article 19(1)(a), concerning freedom of speech, to 'reasonable restrictions' in order to safeguard India's sovereignty and integrity, 'friendly relations with foreign States', and public order, decency and morality. When justifying the amendment in parliament, Nehru emphasised his appreciation for the press as 'one of the vital organs of modern life' but maintained that the 'concept of individual freedom has to be balanced with social freedom and the relations of the individual with the social group' (Austin 1999: 46). Nehru also questioned the idea of the press as guardians of free speech, given the existence of newspaper monopolies: 'When gigantic newspaper chains spring up and undermine the freedom of the independent newspapers, when the press in India is controlled by three or four groups of individuals, what kind of a press is that?' (ibid.).

The Indian state initially attempted to harness the double-edged power of print capitalism to both create new forms of sociality and threaten the integrity of social groups by rationing newsprint and attempting to control the price of newspapers through The Newspaper (Price & Page) Act (1956) and The Daily Newspapers (Price & Page) Order (1960). This legislation was intended to protect small newspapers from unfair competition by preventing big newspapers from cutting prices whilst increasing volume. Rationing and restrictions on the import of newsprint were eased in 1992 and have been inoperative since 1997.[23] More recently, continuity with pre-censorship through indirect pressure can be seen most clearly in the significance of state advertising revenue. Advertising has traditionally been a major support for newspapers around the world. Although this business model no longer works so well in countries with high levels of internet penetration such as

[22] http://indiacode.nic.in/coiweb/amend/amend1.htm (accessed 17 April 2015).

[23] The Supreme Court vetoed price controls on the basis that stipulating a minimum price for a newspaper would 'deter a class or section of its readers from purchasing such a newspaper' and would, therefore, be an infringement on freedom of expression as guaranteed by the Indian Constitution (Basu 2010: 287). Both the legislation and the Supreme Court judgement overturning it referred to social harmony, but viewed the role of state and markets quite differently. In justifying state intervention, *The Daily Newspapers (Price & Page) Order* cited the risk of creating monopolies that would drive smaller newspapers to the wall and in this way skew the whole newspaper market, whereas the Supreme Court judgement expressed faith that self-regulating markets could meet consumer demand.

the United States,[24] it still seemed to in India, into the 2020s, where papers continued to proliferate despite fast growing rates of internet usage. Up until the period 2016–17, the RNI annual report, *Press in India* was recording increases in the number of registered daily newspapers. Numbers fell following the introduction of a more stringent verification system in 2016 but then largely continued to increase.[25]

The First and Second Press reports claimed that almost half the revenue of Indian newspapers came from advertising,[26] and, according to some accounts, following the economic liberalisation policies of the early nineties the proportion increased significantly. Vanita Kohli Khandekar, in her survey of the Indian media business, estimated that 80 per cent of a print publication's revenue came from advertising, the exact amount varying according to 'language, frequency, price, the market it addresses' (2010: 29). More modest figures were recorded in the Government of India's own *Press in India*, but in

[24] See the Pew Research Center's Project for Excellence in Journalism's 2012 report *The Search for a New Business Model*, which describes how American newspapers struggle to build up digital revenue to make up for print losses (accessed 12 May 2020): https://www.pewresearch.org/wp-content/uploads/sites/8/legacy/SEARCHFORNEWREVENUEMODEL.pdf. The Pew Research Center's 2019 fact sheet reports that increased digital readership has still not made up for losses in print revenue. Additionally, in recent years, a steady decline in readership for print newspapers has been accompanied by a levelling off of online readership from 2016 onwards. *Newspapers Fact Sheet*, 9 July 2019, https://www.journalism.org/fact-sheet/newspapers/ (accessed 12 May 2020).

[25] Registration and submission of annual statements went online in 2014, and an enhanced verification process was introduced in 2016. *Press in India 2017–18* states that in 2017–18 there was a 1.45 per cent decrease in the number of daily newspapers who submitted annual statements to the RNI; 8,930 as against 9,061 for 2016–17 (GI 2018: 313). But except for the period 2019–21, recent years appear to have seen an increase in the number of daily newspapers. The most recent report for 2021–2 records 10038 daily newspapers, an increase of 2.95 per cent over the previous year (GI 2022: 336). Additionally, during the period in which the RNI registered a decline in newspaper numbers, certain dailies appear to have increased their circulation, as per the Audit Bureau of Circulation statistics for January–June 2018. See *Exchange4media* report, 'Indian dailies have grown in the past one year, shows ABC Jan-June circulation data' https://www.exchange4media.com/media-print-news/indian-dailies-have-grown-in-the-past-one-year-shows-abc-jan-june-circulation-data-93546.html (accessed 22 September 2019). Audit Bureau of Circulation figures are self-reported by newspapers, verified by accountants hired by the ABC, and then used to attract advertising revenue, meaning that its figures are viewed with scepticism. But they are subject to more external verification than the largely self-reported data presented by the RNI, and the ABC membership fee is thought to disincentivise false reporting – the phenomenon of 'file' (spurious) newspapers that I go on to discuss. I am grateful to Robin Jeffrey for discussing the merits of both surveys. For a comparison of the RNI and ABC see Jeffrey (1994).

[26] The *Report of the First Press Commission* estimates that net circulation revenue for the daily press is Rs. 60,000,000 and advertising revenue, Rs. 50,000,000 (six and five crores respectively) (GI 1954, Vol. 1: 44). The second report claims that advertisements bring in roughly as much revenue to a newspaper as sales and that the 'financial viability of a newspaper depends, to a large extent, on its pull with the advertisers' (GI 1982, Vol.1: 112).

the report for 2020–1 income from advertising was said to still be the main source of revenue for print publications.[27]

Private advertising revenue is greater for newspapers with large circulation and written in English because of what is perceived to be their more affluent readership, meaning that Urdu papers tend to be reliant on state advertising revenue but also relatively independent of consumer demand. Hence the increase in the number of registered Urdu newspapers, in part facilitated by new technology, despite the apparent decline of Urdu in India generally and Uttar Pradesh in particular. The editor of *Sahafat*, an Urdu paper headquartered in the UP state capital, Lucknow, and catering to a Shia readership, claimed that advertising made up more than 90 per cent of the income of his paper and that almost all of this came from the central- and local-level governments.[28]

The Directorate of Advertising and Visual Publicity (DAVP) is the main body for coordinating conferral of central state advertising to newspapers and journals, and regional information departments often follow the lead of its policy in selecting newspapers in which to advertise and fixing rates. According to this policy, 'the DAVP does not take into account the political affiliation or editorial policies of newspapers/journals' when releasing adverts.[29] However, these claims to impartiality have been contradicted by preferential treatment of certain papers because of their political affiliations, most notoriously during the internal emergency of 1975–7. The report of the Shah Commission enquiry into emergency-era abuses described how the DAVP categorised newspapers as 'friendly, neutral and hostile', and government advertising was awarded or withdrawn on this basis (GI 1978, Vol. I: 40). Then as now, vernacular language newspapers seem to have been particularly vulnerable to this kind of pressure.[30]

[27] Of the 10,038 registered daily publications, 2364 dailies reported that they derived more than 75 per cent of their income from government advertisements; 1757 claimed to derive 50 per cent to 74 per cent of their income from this source; and 1757 dailies, 25 per cent to 49 per cent (GI 2022: 354). A separate table provides figures for income derived from 'advertising' (presumably private advertising): 887 dailies derived more than 75 per cent of their income from advertisements, and 1,586 got 50–74 per cent of their income from advertisements (ibid.).

[28] Interview with Aman Abbas, Editor of *Sahafat*, Lucknow, 13 September 2011.

[29] http://www.davp.nic.in/Newspaper_Advertisement_Policy.html (accessed 15 November 2011).

[30] The *Shah Commission Report* cites the example of *Dastan-e-Watan*, an Urdu paper published from Delhi, which had its advertising resumed after the journal ceased to follow a pro-Jana Sangh

In 2007, the DAVP attempted to introduce greater transparency into its workings through a written advertising policy and online empanelment process. But there were still anomalies in its distribution of adverts, notably overrepresentation of Hindi and Urdu papers proportionate to their readerships and of the north Indian state of Uttar Pradesh relative to its population. Almost half the daily newspapers registered in India for the period 2017–18 were written in Hindi (3,838 out of 8,930), and the second most significant language for a daily paper was Urdu (1,145 papers – GI 2018: 313). The Indian census does not indicate which languages respondents are literate in, merely records spoken language and literacy per se, and its definition of Hindi is very broad. In the 2011 census the scheduled 'language' Hindi encompassed more than 56 'mother tongues'.[31] Even if the recorded 43.63 per cent Hindi speakers and 4.19 per cent Urdu speakers were also able to read these languages, this would still not account for their prominent position amongst registered newspapers.

With regard to regional concentration of registered newspapers, according to the 2011 census, UP had an overall literacy rate of 69.72 per cent as opposed to the national average of 74.04 per cent, putting it in twenty-eighth place out of a total of thirty-five states and union territories in the literacy table. Nevertheless, Uttar Pradesh had the largest number of registered daily newspapers in India: 1,963 according to the RNI annual report covering the period 2017–18 (GI 2018: 314). That was more than twice as much as the next territory, Madhya Pradesh, which had 962 registered daily newspapers (ibid.), and out of proportion to its population. According to the 2011 census, UP was home to 199 million of India's 1.21 billion people.

The first explanation for these apparent anomalies that comes to hand is DAVP advertising policy, which in many ways seems to provide greater incentive for Hindi and Urdu papers to register with the RNI than those written in other Indian languages and to therefore disproportionately favour

policy and started to support Congress. The report concludes that the government during this period had 'utilised its advertising policy as a source of financial assistance or denial of financial assistance to newspapers' (GI 1978: 41) and had even put pressure on private advertising agencies to do the same (ibid.: 42).

31 http://www.censusindia.gov.in/2011Census/C-16_25062018_NEW.pdf (accessed 17 July 2019).

north Indian newspapers.[32] (Registrar of Newspapers of India membership was one of the requirements for empanelment with the DAVP.)

Clause 3 of the DAVP's advertising policy

Language

30 per cent (approx.) of its advertising budget is devoted to English publications.
35 per cent (approx.) to Hindi
35 per cent (approx.) to papers written in 'Regional and other languages', in keeping with its concern to encourage unity and communal harmony. ('Other' languages include Bodo, Dogri, Garhwali, Kashmiri, Khasi, Konkani, Maithili, Manipuri, Mizo, Nepali, Rajasthani, Sanskrit, Santhali, Sindhi, Urdu and state government certified Tribal languages.)

Size

15 per cent minimum to small papers (with a circulation of 25,000 copies per publishing day)
35 per cent minimum to medium sized newspapers (with a circulation of between 25,001 and 75,000 copies per publishing day).
50 per cent maximum to big papers (with a circulation of more than 75,000)

Hindi and English, the two official languages of the Union as per The Official Languages Act (1963), received the bulk of central state advertising, as did big newspapers. But this was balanced against a concern for smaller and medium-sized papers, which are less well placed to attract lucrative private advertising, and newspapers written in 'Regional and other languages'. The requirement to be 'uninterruptedly and regularly under publication' for thirty-six months was relaxed for the latter. Proof of only six months continuous publication was required from papers written in these languages.

Because of the history of Hindi, Urdu and English in India, of all the 'Regional and other languages', Urdu is the most widespread print language in the post-independence period. Additionally, according to Audit Bureau

[32] http://www.davp.nic.in/Newspaper_Advertisement_Policy.html (accessed 5 July 2012).

of Circulation figures for 2022, there was no Urdu newspaper with 'big' circulation, meaning that they have also benefited from concessions for small and medium papers.[33] The government rationale for this policy was expressed in the *Report of the Second Press Commission*:

> Among the Indian language newspapers, small and medium newspapers serving a district or a group of districts can play a more direct role in the process of democratizing communication than newspapers aiming at State-level or multi-State circulation.
>
> (GI 1982, Vol. I: 21)

By these means the state would be able to control and channel socially disruptive market forces. In state hands, newspapers would become an instrument to increase participation in public life.

However, in practice this goal has been subverted by the phenomenon of what are informally known as 'file papers'. Concessions for small, medium and vernacular papers have led to a proliferation of newspapers that exist to cream-off state advertising, only publishing a nominal number of copies which are then distributed to and filed in government offices, as all registered newspapers are required to be. This practice is in contravention of Clause 2 of the DAVP policy, which stipulates that government advertisements should not be offered as financial assistance for newspapers/journals. The existence of these 'file papers' was recorded in the *Report of the Second Press Commission*, in an appendix titled 'Spurious Newspapers: The U.P. Experience', which described the 'mixed consequences and unforeseen bad results' of help given to small newspapers (GI 1982, Vol. II: 75). It cited a report commissioned by the UP government which discovered the prevalence of newspapers practicing the art of 'Sam-Dam-Dand-Bhed' (by hook or by crook), whose periodicity was determined by their need 'to harass or oblige some individuals', and whose circulation bore no relation to reality 'although they are certified by their chartered accountants' (ibid.). In more recent times, I was surprised to learn

[33] As per the ABC's table of Highest Circulated Daily Newspaper (language wise) the highest circulating Urdu paper is said to be *Munsif* with a circulation of 51,030 for the period January–June 2022 and 50,419 for July–December 2022: http://www.auditbureau.org/files/JD%202022%20Highest%20Circulated%20(language%20wise).pdf (accessed 20 February 2024).

that 2521 Hindi papers were published from Lucknow in 2018 (GI 2018: 10), given that only a dozen or so regularly appeared on the market.

When I spoke to officials at the RNI and the DAVP about 'file papers', they wearily acknowledged the phenomenon and said that they were unable to control it because of lack of resources and, in the case of Urdu papers ('minority media'), minded to overlook it.[34] Frank Noronha, Director General of the DAVP, was moved to exasperation when I brought up a campaign by the Urdu Newspaper Editors' Union to increase Urdu newspaper's share of advertising revenue to 15 per cent, as in his view they were hardly ill-served by the existing policy.[35] Fifteen per cent is commonly thought to be the percentage of Muslims living in India, although Hasan Shuja, the President of the union and main instigator of the campaign, denied that this was how he had arrived at the figure.[36] According to him, 15 per cent was an accurate reflection of the number of people who read Urdu newspapers in India if one took into account readerships rather than sales or circulation, the idea being that many people read a newspaper over the course of a day.

Shuja's words recalled the romantic image of a teashop *adda* in which men huddle around a single paper and discuss the day's events. This scene recurred in my conversations with senior journalists, when they imagined their readerships. However, then as now most Indian newspapers were delivered to private homes. Urdu literacy in north India being increasingly limited to certain demographic groups (the elderly, the madrassa educated), it was also unlikely that all members of a household that received an Urdu paper would have been able to read it. This was reflected in the growth of Hindi supplements in Urdu newspapers, sections of Urdu newspapers that were written in Hindi, and papers that published dual Nastaliq and Nagari editions or were written in Nagari script entirely.

Set against this context, the mass Urdu readership imagined by some Urdu journalists seemed to be illusory. But the spurious papers that attempted to maintain this illusion did not just evade the state, they used its rules and regulations to their own advantage. Conversely, the state turned

[34] Interview with Frank Noronha, Director General of the DAVP, New Delhi, 26 August 2011. Interview with Manoj Roorkiwal, Registration Supervisor at RNI, New Delhi, 4 August 2011.

[35] Ibid.

[36] Interview with Hasan Shuja, New Delhi, 21 August 2011.

a blind eye to minor infringements in order to keep the peace, to avoid overstretching itself and preserve communal harmony. Instead of limiting discretion and fostering continuity by maintaining 'papereality' (Dery 1998), the bureaucratic operations of the documentary state continued to generate slippages between rules and their implementation, public office and private gain, captured by Marx in his image of the 'immense writing-machine'.

An ignorance which liberates

Local government–level subversion of constitutional injunctions and central state policy directives, based on a restricted understanding of what constitutes a substantial proportion and a flexible understanding of the modern, seem to have led to the decline of Urdu in a region where it was formerly the predominant language. The attitude that led to this situation is conveyed by J. B. Kripalani, the Chairman of the UP Language Committee, in his introduction to the Committee's 1962 report on the status of Urdu following the creation of linguistic states:

> I would like to remind you that though Urdu is the language of a minority of people living in this State, it is not the language of a particular minority community or religious group. Only a minority of the whole population of Uttar Pradesh speak and write in the Urdu style of language. This minority consists of members of both the majority and minority communities, as also of some Christians and Sikhs. When, therefore, we say that Urdu is a minority language, it does not mean that the minority belongs to a particular religion or religious community.
>
> (GUP 1962: 7)

These equivocating statements about the 'Urdu style of language' are justified in the report's emphasis on how Indian culture being a harmonious fusion of various influences, it was unfeasible 'to demarcate different cultural groups in India or term any of them as "cultural minorities"' (ibid.: 19). Kripalani dismissed calls for Urdu to be made second language of UP with reference to the States Reorganisation Commission's recommendation that second language status only be accorded to those spoken by 30 per cent or more of the population, and he emphasised that linguistic facilities should 'be in tune with the larger interests of national integration' (ibid.: 25).

In his analysis of this document, Brass underlines the 'remarkable sophistry' at the heart of the assertion that although a certain number of people speak Urdu as their mother tongue and it is the language of a minority of people living in the state, Urdu speakers do not constitute 'a particular minority community or religious group' (1974: 204). But Brass himself similarly struggles to describe Indian Muslims as an objective community given the multiplicity of Muslim ethnic groups and communities across the country, which, as he acknowledges in a later work, are 'nowhere defined by descent' (1991: 102). In both instances, talk of objectively verifiable social positions provokes the obvious question: who is to judge? Specifically, who is to say what language someone is speaking or should learn?

This is the crux of Rancière's critique of Bourdieu, and more generally of a sociological method which would presuppose the result that it is supposed to establish (2006c: 7). To this knowledge, he opposes 'an ignorance which liberates', the deregulatory effect of aesthetic experiences which elude the distribution of roles and competences in a hierarchical order (ibid.: 3–6). This liberatory potential is exemplified by artisans who act 'as if they were at home in the house that they otherwise know is not theirs' (ibid.: 6). Far from being an example of false consciousness, this 'as if' supplements their identity as a worker at home in a defined regime with 'a *proletarian* identity', which for Rancière means 'the identity of a subject capable of escaping the assignment to a private condition and of intervening in the affairs of the community' (ibid). For both Bourdieu and Rancière, class is a conceptual category rather than an exclusively socioeconomic one, but in the latter's work proletarian identity opens up the possibility of escaping structural determinants rather than establishes its coordinates.

As well as allowing more room for 'proletarians' to manoeuvre, this aesthetic perspective also better accords with the pre- and post-independence history of Urdu. The idea of the universal imposition of a national culture and language does not account for the survival of Urdu and failure of attempts to legitimise the imposition of Hindi, from creation of linguistic states in 1956, amendment of The Official Languages Act (1963) to allow for the continued use of English in 1967, successful opposition to the Draft Education Policy of 2019 and Urdu's continued relevance in the state where it has suffered the worst decline in official status.[37] Linguistic states, the amendment of The Official Languages Act and the New Education Policy were brought about because of protests and pressure from the non-Hindi speaking states.[38] Urdu remains significant in UP largely because of the support of religious establishments who run Urdu-medium schools in the informal education sector, in rural and remote areas, often stepping into a state-created vacuum,[39] and also its continued presence in media. Informal educational institutions and private media organisations might sometimes be supported by the state, but neither can be seen as pure and anticipated outcomes of its policies.

A striking recent example of this is the popular Urdu poetry and literature site *Rekhta.org*, which presents Nastaliq, Nagari and Roman versions of Urdu poems, with crowd-sourced translations and links to YouTube videos and audio recordings. In an interview with the *Hindu* newspaper, Sanjiv Saraf, the entrepreneur who founded the site, declared 'Urdu is not my mother-tongue but the language of my heart because Urdu poetry embeds every emotion in it'.[40] As discussed earlier, attachment to Urdu as a literary language does not preclude support for policies that reduce its role in education and

37 Coming soon after the BJP's victory in the 2019 elections, the Draft New Educational Policy, which stipulated the study of Hindi as part of the three-language formula, seemed to confirm anxieties about Hindi–Hindu majoritarianism and was robustly and successfully resisted on these grounds. See Partha Chatterjee's article 'Populism Plus', *The India Forum*, 3 June 2019: https://www.theindiaforum.in/article/populism-plus (accessed 21 November 2019). In this article, Chatterjee attributes BJP incursions into eastern India to the circulation of the mass culture of the Hindi region. His analysis overlooks the wealth of languages and dialects spoken in north India, including Hindustani/Hindi-Urdu.

38 For details of the controversy of the New Education Policy, see 'Post backlash from Tamil Nadu, mandatory Hindi goes out of draft education policy', *The Hindu*, 3 June 2019: https://www.thehindu.com/news/national/centre-removes-mandatory-hindi-from-draft-education-policy-after-tn-protests/article27412373.ece (accessed 18 July 2019).

39 In 2019, the website of the Uttar Pradesh Madrassa Board, now in Hindi and prominently featuring the image of BJP Chief Minister Yogi Adityanath, claimed that there were 14677 registered madrassas providing primary and junior high-level education in UP and 4536 providing advanced-level religious education: http://madarsaboard.upsdc.gov.in/About.aspx (accessed 25 July 2019). The National Institute of Educational Planning and Administration's 2018 report on *Evaluation of the Implementation of the Scheme for Providing Quality Education in Madrasas* however recorded that there were 16,000 madrasas in the State of Uttar Pradesh (consistent with earlier Madrassa Board figures and the largest number of any state), and of these, only 560 were fully government aided (NIEPA 2018). See 'Official figures out: Uttar Pradesh has over 16,000 madrassas', *Times of India*, 17 October 2017, https://timesofindia.indiatimes.com/city/lucknow/official-figures-out-uttar-pradesh-has-over-16000-madrassas/articleshow/61110843.cms (accessed 25 July 2019).

40 'Urdu poetry made accessible', *The Hindu*, 17 January 2013: http://www.thehindu.com/todays-paper/tp-features/tp-metroplus/urdu-poetry-made-accessible/article4314372.ece (accessed 16 March 2015).

government. But Saraf here pointedly refused 'the infantile and narcissistic metaphors of mother tongue and mother's milk', a linguistic activism based in 'self-glorification and other disparagement' and a politics of 'mobilization and separation' (Brass 2004: 366). These attitudes also inform state-sanctioned categories such as mother tongue, which Saraf simultaneously recognised and ignored. As a non-Muslim, his statement had clear political resonance in a post-Partition context, in which Urdu was the national language of the Islamic Republic of Pakistan. Wider appreciation of Urdu through *Rekhta.org* was also possible because of a combination of factors rather than a single actor or singular market logic: a wealthy benefactor, new technology, the close concordance between spoken Hindi and Urdu, increased literacy in Hindi and English, and the persistence of poetry as a popular form in India.

Instead of being solely motivated by a biopolitical project of knowing the population in order to control it, the formulation and implementation of state policy in all three cases also seems to have been characterised by ignorance and inaction. In the first, we saw constitutional and central state language policy subject to local level and bureaucratic implementation, which was in turn offset by extra-state forces (media, the confluence between spoken forms of Hindi and Urdu). Then, Hindu nationalist ideological opposition to Urdu was checked at an early stage by national electoral ambitions leading to the incongruence of an apparently pro-Urdu BJP policy. Finally, limited state and bureaucratic oversight of the press combined with Urdu's status as a language of Muslims encouraged the growth of 'file papers', with the result that, contrary to the prognostics of social scientists, the effects (intended or not) of state policy, and both working through and beyond attempts to instrumentalise linguistic and religious identities, Urdu remains a living language in India.

2

The one-man media house

The Indian Urdu-language press has long been subject to close state scrutiny, and not just within India. Wikileaks cable 06 NEW DELHI 5470, dated 4 August 2006 and titled 'Indian Muslim Resentment Smoldering over Lebanon and Gaza', observed that Urdu newspapers had devoted much more space to these issues than English and Hindi papers, speculated that anti-US editorial opinion had been planted by Iranian agents and concluded with a discussion of the 'Muslim Factor' in Congress electoral calculations, in language familiar from colonial-era police reports on the 'Muhammadan' press.[1] During both periods, Muslims and their media were described as an internal fifth column with the potential to ballast or destabilise national politics. Links to co-religionists in other countries made Muslims' loyalties suspect. At the same time, Islam was a major Indian religion, Islamicate culture suffused India's cultural and political life, and long-established Muslim communities continued to live across the entire country. Muslims had to be reckoned with by both states and those who opposed them.

Underlying these concerns about divided loyalties was a more general anxiety about modern political forms such as electoral democracy and territorial nationalism. The presence of a widely dispersed but sizeable minority – in total numbers the largest population of Muslims in any non-Muslim majority country – exposed the limitations of these majoritarian institutions. Muslims were both too politically significant to ignore and too numerically insignificant to count. As previously discussed, this paradox had resulted in the incoherence of India's post-independence Urdu language policy

[1] 'Indian Muslim resentment smoldering over Lebanon and Gaza', 4 August 2006, https://wikileaks.org/cable/2006/08/06NEWDELHI5470.html (accessed 1 September 2015).

and had also played out in an intra-Islamic dispute, conducted in the pages of the Urdu press, between Maulana Hussain Ahmad Madani (1879–1957) and the poet-philosopher Muhammad Iqbal (1877–1938) over whether *qaum* referred to a community of Muslims or could also be applied to a nation. Although holding opposed views on the compatibility of Islam and nationalism, both Iqbal and Madani were concerned with defining a community to which they themselves belonged in terms that went beyond technologies of representation that minoritised Indian Muslims.

This chapter follows this ambition across the colonial and postcolonial period, through a comparison of two renowned Urdu journalist-editors: Abul Kalam Azad (1888–1958), during his editorship of the first version of the weekly *al-Hilal* (1912–14), and Aziz Burney (1952–), editor of the most widely distributed Indian Urdu-language newspaper, *Roznama Rashtriya Sahara*, who in 2013 started to self-publish his own paper, *Azizul Hind*. Although the chapter proceeds chronologically, it is not a historical survey in which two men connected by a direct line of affiliation are compared. I have selected these particular figures because they exist in genealogical relationship to reformist and revolutionary traditions of Indian Muslim leadership – namely, the loyalist tradition of the educator, jurist and writer, Sir Syed Ahmad Khan (1817–1898), and the more radical politics that emerged from engagement with anti-colonial struggles in India and internationally.

Both men had ambitions to be a 'one-man media house', as Burney expressed it in an interview, to combine the power of print and the authority of speech in order to address a *qaum* conceived in their own image.[2] But in practice their messages were subject to numerous pressures, which shaped the content and directed its movement, and in both periods the most significant of these emanated from the state. From publication of the first Urdu-language daily in North India in 1858 to the 'newspaper revolution' encouraged by increased literacy and economic liberalisation, government advertising revenue has been the main support for the Urdu press.[3] State discourses of loyalty have set the boundaries by which its contents are judged, and state language policy has delimited readerships.

[2] Burney's ambition was expressed in an interview on 14 July 2011 and repeated on 4 September 2014.
[3] See Stark (2003) and Jeffrey (1997 and 2000).

In this chapter, I compare how Azad and Burney attempted to exceed these limits in order to invoke an expanded vision of the *qaum*, one that could counterpoise the no less ambiguous category of the people. Towards this end, they played with the range of languages available to them in their editorials and were early adopters of new communications technology: type printing and telecommunications. But I describe how Burney seemed to be stuck within narrower parameters despite the greater speed and ease of Urdu newspaper production and absence of strict censorship laws. As with the previous chapter ('The immense writing-machine'), instead of identifying a single cause for this apparent anomaly, I describe how various factors worked together to produce this outcome. I accordingly look at their writing and the surrounding circumstances for its production and reception: the media through which their words were transmitted, their uneven translation within and across languages, and at the role of technology.

Abul Kalam Azad: Imam ul-Hind

Bearing the title 'The Indian People and the War', a letter written by S. P. Sanyal to the editor of the Indian English-language newspaper, *The Pioneer*, and published on 11 October 1914, described how the Great War had 'taken hold of the Indian mind'. Even in villages people spoke about it, and scores of newspapers were now being bought and sold in small towns. He wrote that he was surprised to hear from a newspaper vendor that illiterate men, 'even sweepers', had been known to buy penny newspapers ('paisa akhbar') and 'have the war news read'. These were said to be sure signs that 'the unchangeable East is moving and moving rapidly'. Sanyal drew particular attention to a 'certain paper' published in northern India and commanding a large circle of readers, which is 'well known to Government' and whose writings needed 'careful watching rather than censoring', lest the 'masses' started to see things from the German point of view.

The paper was not named, but on 2 November 1914 *The Pioneer* published an editorial titled 'Pro-Germanism at Calcutta' to describe the stance of *al-Hilal*, a widely circulating Urdu 'weekly illustrated newspaper' edited by Abul Kalam Azad. It claimed that the paper had so far managed to avoid censorship because the style of its 'most mischievous articles' was 'very allusive and full of veiled sneers and sarcasms and innuendoes', which lost their effect when translated into English. A government that at such a time allowed a British subject to publish such 'malicious insinuations' must 'lay claim to the possession of a most un-Germanic spirit of toleration', the writer concluded.

However, a spirit of toleration had not informed the colonial state's attitude towards the Indian press since the viceroyalty of Lord Curzon (1889–1905). A combination of domestic and international crises brought to an end the policy of informal influence that had characterised regulation of the press in much of the nineteenth century.[4] Internationally, there had been the 1904–5 Russo-Japanese war, the first major military victory in the modern era of an Asian power over a European nation. Within India, there had been a violent response to the partition of Bengal in 1905, which had catalysed a new, more militant phase of the *swadeshi* (home rule) movement.

In response to increasing public criticism of British rule, the easily evaded requirement that books and newspapers bear the names of authors, printers and publishers had been made more stringent with the passing of the 1910 Press Act. The Act rendered all registered publications liable to payment of a security deposit that would be forfeit if a document was found to contain seditious content. In practice the 1910 Act was hard to implement because demarcating where 'seditious' began and the merely 'religious' or 'mythic' ended involved difficult encounters with Indian media – in the case of *al-Hilal*, the 'veiled sneers and sarcasms and innuendoes' referred to in *The Pioneer* editorial.

This difficulty was not confined to the vernacular language press. Questions could also be asked about the motivations behind the letter and editorial. *The Pioneer* had been founded in 1865 by an Englishman, George Allen, for an English readership, but by 1914 the paper had acquired Indian readers and staff. Sanyal is a common Bengali Hindu surname, and Bengal was a centre of both colonial administration and *swadeshi* violence. Sanyal's detailed warning and suggestion that the authorities closely watch – but not censor – seditious writing could be an example of 'sly civility', the double discourse of the

[4] More stringent regulation had briefly been introduced in response to negative coverage of the Second Anglo-Afghan War (1878–80). The 1878 Vernacular Press Act empowered the government to enter any Press suspected of producing seditious writing, but this was repealed in 1881 after Britain's successful conclusion of the war.

colonised, which plays up to the paranoid projections of the coloniser (Bhabha 1985). These ambiguities also shadowed the decorous speech and writing of the Indian Muslims who set themselves up as loyal subjects in response to the activities of the Bengali militants.

Writers and publishers also benefited from techno-material limits to implementation of the Press Act. They were able to evade regulations by disseminating their messages through more mobile and less easily tracked means, such as lithography and word of mouth. As a result, the Act mainly affected letterpress printing technology such as that used by Azad to produce his magazine. Hence both the delay in acting against *al-Hilal*, which combined political polemic and religious fervour in its coverage of the Balkan Wars and the First World War, and the effectiveness of levying an additional deposit in forcing it to shut down. In 1913, alarmed by the pro-German tone of *al-Hilal*'s editorials, the Government of India demanded a security deposit of Rs. 2,000. In response to the edition of 1914 described in *The Pioneer*, the deposit was forfeited and the government claimed a further sum of Rs. 10,000, causing *al-Hilal* to cease production. The last edition of its first version was published on 18 November 1914.[5]

The daily report of the Calcutta commissioner of police for 11 September 1914 described how apparent Muslim support for Germany could only be understood by reference to events preceding the First World War, in particular communal representation in the new local legislative councils in India and efforts to remedy the perceived educational 'backwardness' of Muslims.[6] This awakening had produced a new generation of political leaders and primed them for a more radical politics. Provoked by 'the troubles which have befallen the Muslim world', Indian Muslims were described as imitating 'Hindu methods' in pressing 'what they consider to be claims of the community by active agitation'. They had acquired 'a ready means of inflaming the masses' through the 'new Muhammadan press', and of these newspapers, the tone of *al-Hilal* was 'particularly bad'. There was now 'a definitely acknowledged young party which seeks to thrust the older more cautious men into the background'.

5 Azad published another magazine a year later named *al-Balagh*. It ceased publication within a year after Azad was expelled from Bengal and moved to the state of Bihar. *Al-Hilal* resumed publication in Delhi in 1927, but this version of the magazine only lasted for six months.

6 Home, Political A, November 1914, Nos. 33–38, National Archives of India, New Delhi.

The report's reference to the older, more moderate generation was an allusion to the reformist tradition of Sir Syed Ahmad Khan, who had been hostile to pro-Khilafat sentiment in the late nineteenth century. He had responded to these early stirrings of the Khilafat movement with a series of articles written in 1897 at the conclusion of the Greco-Turkish War. These were collected together and republished in 1916 and 1920 to refute the messages of those who were seeking to 'misguide the ignorant Mussalman masses of the country' (Ahmed 1920: ii). (The editor's preface makes particular mention of a booklet by 'Maulvi Abulkalam Azad of Calcutta' (ibid).) During this earlier period, Sir Syed had dealt with the problem of defining the boundaries of the *qaum* by upholding the colonial distinction between religion and politics, thereby delimiting the authority of the Ottoman caliphate and emphasising the subject position of India's Muslims. In this way, he staked his claim to be an intercessor for the Indian Muslim community he was in the process of ventriloquising for the colonial state.

Building upon Sir Syed's legacy, Azad went on to both use and overstep these boundaries in his pursuit of a broader constituency as a Muslim leader *and* a nationalist statesman through his involvement in the Khilafat movement. In the struggle for restoration of the Ottoman caliphate, Hindus and Muslims came together to oppose British rule and support the Congress movement. Born soon after the founding of the Indian National Congress in 1885, Azad was a prominent leader in both the Khilafat movement and Congress Party. Autobiographical works in Urdu and English have fixed Azad's reputation as 'India's Maulana', a hero of the freedom struggle and apostle of Hindu–Muslim unity.[7]

However, the Khilafat leadership was not a homogenous group, and Azad was something of an outlier within it. He was not affiliated with any of the religious schools with which most of its leaders were associated – namely, Aligarh Muslim University, the Dar al-Ulum Deoband and the Farangi Mahal madrassas – and did not fit the pattern of those who entered politics because of 'institutional rivalries and the quest for followers in that framework' (Minault

[7] In addition to Azad's own *India Wins Freedom*, which he went to the effort of writing in English in collaboration with Humayun Kabir, Abdur Malihabadi produced the 'as-told-to' Urdu biography, *Azad Ki Kahani Khud Azad Ki Zabani* (2008).

1982: 45). The ambivalent nature of Azad's relationship with the *ulama* and his own leadership ambitions can be discerned in both the style and content of his editorials in *al-Hilal*. These were full of criticism of the conservatism of these schools but written in erudite prose laden with Persian and Arabic words, and sometimes, in his *fatiha* (opening) editorials, entirely in Arabic.

In his biography of Azad, Ian Henderson Douglas describes how from 1910 until 1921, Azad thought of himself as 'some kind of *mujaddid* or *imam*, whom God would vindicate in the way He vindicated the prophets' (1988: 97). But far from being unalloyed mixtures of human consciousness and God's word, with no political content or design, Azad's speech and writing often verged upon intercession and even more. The title of 'Imam ul-Hind' was later given to him by the mysterious figure of the Sheikh ul-Islam, but its legitimacy was disputable. Azad was more securely located in the emerging type of 'the professional politician in India, part journalist, part orator, part holy man' (Minault 1982: 3).

Precisely because of his extramural status as a journalist–statesman rather than a full-fledged member of the *ulama*, Azad was open to diverse influences: reformist, revolutionary, English, non-Western and non-Indian. He was therefore well placed to invoke both pan-Islamic and cross-denominational notions of the *qaum*. This allowed him to assume a pivotal role in the dawn of the non-cooperation movement when the independence struggle became a mass movement. Through his use of print and prophetic speech, he participated in the shift from a reformist to a revolutionary Indian Muslim politics and sought to position himself at the apex of this movement.

Print, as has often been noted, came relatively 'late' to the 'Muslim world' and India.[8] Before the 1800s, most Urdu-language books published in India were printed in Nastaliq, the cursive script in which Urdu is most commonly written. But even after moveable type printing in the more adaptable Naskh script was introduced by the missionary presses, lithographic printing and Nastaliq continued to predominate. Cheap, portable and easy to use, lithography played a significant role in 'democratizing print in South Asia' (Shaw 1998: 89). Lithography became the preferred printing medium for South Asian Muslims because of its ability to make possible the 'mass-produced manuscript', which

[8] See Carter (1925), Graham (1987), and Robinson (1993 and 1996).

met the criteria of cultural authority in a way that the typeset text could not (ibid.) – that is, the authority of the person-to-person mode of transmission, which preserved the authentic meaning of a text in the absence of the original author.

There were also technical reasons for this preference. Nastaliq is hard to typeset accurately, meaning that most Urdu newspapers continued to be lithographed until Urdu InPage software was developed in 1994. The first Urdu computer font was invented by Ahmed Mirza Jamil in 1981, who was inspired by a Chinese character keyboard he had seen at an exhibition in Singapore.[9] However, a complicated user interface and incompatibility with standard word processing packages meant that it was not much used in India.[10] Even the Congress Party paper *Qaumi Awaz* (voice of the *qaum*), the most widely distributed and best-resourced Indian Urdu paper of its time, continued to be lithographed into the 1990s.

Azad was therefore making a statement in choosing to print his newspaper using Naskh type in 1912. He was both signalling a modern outlook and grounding in Islamic scripture, as Naskh is the script in which the Qur'an has most commonly been written.[11] The early editions of *al-Hilal* repeatedly drew attention to the magazine's use of type. The first edition (13 July 1912) discussed at length the difficulties that beset its production and apologised for its poor quality. Due to production difficulties the entire magazine could not be printed in specially imported Turkish type as had been promised. The editor assured readers these faults would be fixed in the coming weeks. The second edition (20 July 1912) provided a brief history of printing in eastern countries. The editor regretted that because of a lingering attachment to stone lithography, there was no Nastaliq equivalent to the beautiful Naskh type produced in Turkey and Egypt, in which Arabic and Persian newspapers were printed. These discussions contextualised his choice to publish a weekly magazine rather than a daily newspaper and to print it using technology imported from Turkey.

9 See the account in Kashfi's book on the history of Noori Nastaliq compositing (2008: 12).

10 Kashfi writes that computer font was used to produce the Lahore edition of the Pakistani newspaper *Jang* (2008: 12.).

11 See Safadi's account of the history of Naskh in his book on Islamic calligraphy (1978: 62-67).

In an addendum to this edition, the magazine's production values were said to justify its relatively expensive price, which the editor claimed would be unexceptional for a similar quality English-language magazine. If *al-Hilal* were in English, an annual subscription would cost one guinea and be cheap at the price. Unfortunately, Urdu readers had got into the habit of paying no more than three or four rupees for an annual subscription to a magazine, but most of these papers were printed using litho press and cheap paper and were often devoid of illustrations. Although *al-Hilal*'s annual subscription was Rs. 8, this was not excessive given the expense and effort that went into its production. If the magazine had a cover price of Rs. 15 there would be some hope of covering expenses. But because the real purpose of *al-Hilal* was to raise a countrywide movement, and without producing numerous editions this would be impossible, the expense had been discounted.

Through the direct address of these editorials, Azad made his presence felt and appealed to an audience, whom he addressed as *nazrin* (viewer) and *pablik* (public). The discussion of letters he had received and editorials he had written in response further underlined his presence, notably in an editorial that appeared on 8 September 1912, written in response to a friend's enquiries about the magazine's political purposes: '*al-Hilal ki politikal ta'lim ki nisbat ek khat aur us ka jawab*' ('With regard to *al-Hilal*'s political education: a letter and its reply'). The letter was reproduced, accompanied by a lengthy reply in which Azad both asserted and downplayed his knowledge of Arabic, his religious learning and his extensive library, and emphasised that the authority for his magazine's political policy was based solely on the Qur'an. According to its teachings there was no need to pay obeisance to the colonial state or submit to the Hindus. In these editorials, he appeared to be attempting to conjure an ideal reader: one who would be both attuned to his political message and aware of the practicalities of magazine production, attentive to details of tone and type.

The potential for solipsism was allayed by Azad's awareness of various existing audiences. His authority may have been located in an Arabic language ecumene, but a great deal of space in *al-Hilal* was devoted to coverage of events in the Ottoman empire, and these reports were written with the concerns of Indian Muslim readers in mind. These connections are strongly evident in Azad's coverage of local authority encroachment on and demolition of a mosque in the north Indian city of Kanpur. Similarities with what the Calcutta police commissioner had described as Hindu methods of protest can be seen in both the demonstrations and the coverage of them in 'the new Mohammadan press', in the allusive use of words and images as colonial censorship increasingly began to take its toll. Pushed into the same socio-religious space, and into using the same tropes, those critical of British rule were driven to be both more militant *and* more indirect.

The story ran in *al-Hilal* for many months from 11 June 1913 onwards. When police fired upon demonstrators on 3 August 1913, killing several, Azad responded on 13 August with an article titled, 'A Painful Glimpse of Edirne in Kanpur', a reference to the Turkish town of Adrianople which had been occupied during the Balkan Wars, weaving a local story which had gained national significance into the international:

> The earth is thirsty. It needs blood. But whose? That of Muslims. West Asia is adorned (*rangin*) with whose blood? Muslims. On the soil (*khak*) of Iran, whose bodies are writhing? Muslims. In the Balkan region whose blood is flowing? Muslims. The soil of Hindustan is also thirsty. She needs blood. Whose? Muslims. At last, in the environs of Kanpur blood flows and the earth of Hindustan is intoxicated.

Passages like this seem to validate the criticism of Azad and *al-Hilal*'s 'thick streak of Muslim separatism' (Ashraf 2001: 108). Communal tensions do seem to have been an important part of his response to the mosque's demolition, but the rhetorical devices in the passage also resemble the 'cosmo-politics' of Hindu nationalist discourses of the independence movement (Pinney 2009). Specifically, there are parallels with revolutionaries' use of allegorical devices, according to which historical and present-day events became 'parallel systems with a converging significance' (ibid.: 32). Azad made these connections across space as well as time and not just with reference to what is broadly understood as the 'Muslim world'. In a series of articles on Gandhi's activities in South Africa in the November and December 1913 editions of *al-Hilal*, the events in Kanpur were linked to police brutality against Indians in South Africa. As Muzaffar Alam notes, in these and other early writings, Azad extended an Islamic vocabulary of '*jihād*' and '*azīmat*' (determination) to refer to the actions of non-Muslim martyrs to truth such as Gandhi (2023).

There is also the significance of *al-Hilal*'s non-Muslim readership in a period when Urdu had yet to be exclusively associated with Muslims. Because of Azad's subsequent involvement in the Indian independence movement, *al-Hilal* has acquired the status of a nationalist periodical. Following independence, Azad claimed that through publication of *al-Hilal* he had intended to build up a national public opinion among its multidenominational readership (1989: 8). This does not accord with the difficult language in which the magazine was written, unlikely to have had mass appeal in this period of wide illiteracy. Even if the magazine had been read aloud, it is questionable how much of its language would have been understood by most Hindi and Urdu speakers. Nor does Azad's claim reflect the Muslim readership addressed in *al-Hilal*'s editorials on the status of Muslims in India and around the world. In the 8 September 1912 editorial in which Azad had outlined the political purpose of the magazine, Muslims were urged to abjure the paths taken by both moderate and extremist Hindus. They were not to forget that a true Muslim holds the Qur'an in his hand, and a hand that holds the Qur'an cannot hold a bomb.

But appearing soon after implementation of the 1910 Press Act, these public disavowals of violence arguably reflected Azad's awareness of another particular audience – the colonial censor. Even in the first version of *al-Hilal*, Hindu revolutionary activities were the context for Azad's discussion of the necessity to adopt jihad, when he criticised Muslim leaders, such as Sir Syed, who counseled loyalty to the British, leaving Hindus to take the lead in the struggle for independence.[12] The disavowal of violence in Azad's September 1912 editorial is also contradicted by his later autobiographical writing. In *India Wins Freedom*, he recalled how he had been politicised by the partition of Bengal in 1905, which he described as an attempt by the British to 'create permanent division between the Hindus and Muslims of Bengal' (1989: 4). He even claimed to have joined a Hindu revolutionary group in Calcutta and convinced them to overcome their anti-Muslim prejudice:

> I began to argue with them that they were wrong in thinking that Muslims as a community were their enemies. I told them that they should not generalise from their experiences of a few Muslim officers in Bengal. In Egypt, Iran

[12] See the article he wrote just a few months later, 'Al-jihad! Al-jihad!!', *al-Hilal* (18 December 1912).

> and Turkey the Muslims were engaged in revolutionary activities for the achievement of democracy and freedom. The Muslims of India would also join in the political struggle if we worked among them and tried to win them as our friends.
>
> (Ibid.: 5)

Regardless of the accuracy of these retrospective accounts, they mark a shift from Syed Ahmad Khan's hostility to both Hindu and Muslim Bengalis. In a defensive review of Hunter's *Indian Musalmans: Are they bound in conscience to rebel against the Queen?*, Ahmad Khan had insisted that Hunter's argument was invalidated by a narrow focus upon 'Bengal Mahomedans' (1872: 7). 'As a cosmopolitan Mahomedan of India', he wrote, 'I must raise my voice in opposition to Dr. Hunter in defence of my fellow-countrymen' (ibid.). Writing in English, he used the word 'countrymen' to refer to co-religionists across India and staked his authority to do so in his 'cosmopolitan' origins as a member of the *ashraf*, an elite class of Muslims who boasted of foreign ancestry.[13]

Ahmad Khan's hostility was even clearer in his later contemptuous references to the prospect of Bengali Hindu rule, in the event of the introduction of competitive examinations for government posts, as demanded by Congress:

> Over all races, not only over Mahomedans but over Rajas of high position and the brave Rajputs who have not forgotten the swords of their ancestors, would be placed as ruler a Bengali who at sight of a table knife would crawl under his chair.
>
> (1888: 11)

In this speech, he dismissed the Congress agitation as a Bengali phenomenon, which in that province safely confined itself to 'writing with the pen' and 'mere talking', to '*giz, giz, giz, giz, giz*' and '*buk, buk, buk, buk*', as he expressed it for the amusement of his Lucknow audience (ibid.: 18). Were it to spread to 'Mahomedans and other brave races', he warned, the Government would need 'to pass a new law and to fill the jails' (ibid.: 109). It is notable that the word

13 *Ashraf* first entered the colonial census in the nineteenth century, see David Lelyveld's entry on 'ashraf', in *Keywords in South Asian Studies*, ed. Rachel Dwyer (London: School of Oriental and African Studies, 2005), https://www.soas.ac.uk/south-asia-institute/keywords/file24799.pdf (accessed 7 February 2020).

Ahmad Khan used to refer to Hindu Bengalis in the Urdu original is *qaum*, which is much more capacious than 'race'.[14] His use of the term opened up the possibility of encompassing non-Muslims within this category, a manoeuvre whose potential would be realised in the Khilafat movement. By fusing pan-Islamism and anti-British sentiment in his support for that movement, Azad effected a further innovation. By moving around various socio-technical constraints, between a spiritual register and demotic concerns, a local and international politics, he ventriloquised both a pan-Islamic *and* national community as an Imam ul Hind.

Aziz Burney: *Azizul Hind*

One hundred years after the first edition of *al-Hilal*, a newspaper with the curious title of *Azizul Hind* was published in 2013. This was an Urdu-language paper for the most part, but with certain sections translated into Hindi. The title of the paper drew upon the meanings of the first name of its editor, Aziz Burney. *Aziz* is evocative of various kinds of love and esteem, and also indicates 'a great man; a worthy or pious personage, a saint' (Platts 2006: 761), while *ul-Hind* recalls Azad's honorary title. Through the title of his newspaper, Burney positioned himself in a line of Indian Muslim leaders and in relation to Azad in particular. The title of his 2005 collection of editorials on the Gujarat riots, *India Lose Freedom* (sic), alludes to Azad's book on the independence struggle, *India Wins Freedom*, and a complete set of *al-Hilal* was also prominently displayed in his office.

More than Azad's literary style or ideas, his example seems to have shaped the trajectory of Burney's career. Like Azad, he combined entrepreneurial zeal with political ambition and was prolific in a range of genres and languages. Prior to 2013, Aziz Burney had been head of operations at Sahara Group Urdu Media. After joining its Hindi-language newspaper in 1991, he went on to launch monthly, weekly and daily Urdu-language periodicals in 1991, 1994

[14] See the Urdu text on Frances Pritchett's website: http://www.columbia.edu/itc/mealac/pritchett/00islamlinks/txt_sir_sayyid_lucknow_1887_urdu.pdf (accessed 14 February 2020). In this speech, he addresses his audience as *bhaiyon* (brothers) and *sahiban* (gentlemen), but when speaking of both Muslims and Indians in general, the word he uses is *qaum*.

and 1999 respectively. *Roznama Rashtriya Sahara* grew to become the most widely circulating Urdu daily in India, published in ten editions, including one as far south as Bangalore.

Burney had also published novels, screenplays and books of non-fiction in Urdu, Hindi and English, and used to maintain a multilingual blog.[15] But he was most famous for his full-page Hindi and Urdu editorials on the second page of *Roznama Rashtriya Sahara*: the right hand columns in Urdu and the left in Hindi, with the contents and language of the two varying slightly (i.e. the Nastaliq original was not transliterated straight into Nagari). These texts were dictated to a subeditor in an adjoining office or, when he was travelling, delivered via telephone. The free-form structure and personal voice of the editorials meant that they conveyed a strong sense of the spoken word. These speeches/texts attracted attention beyond the domain of Urdu newspapers after being collected, translated and published in book form.

Even when printed in the newspaper, these editorials carried a certain weight because of their prominent position within the paper and grand title of '*Azad Bharat ka Itihas*' ('The History of Free India'), superimposed upon a photograph of the Red Fort in Delhi. Formerly a seat of Mughal power, the Red Fort is a now a centre of post-independence state nationalism. The Indian Prime Minister delivers a speech from its ramparts on Independence Day, in continuity with Mughal tradition. The tricolour flag that is hoist from the fort on this occasion was visible in the photograph accompanying the *Azad Bharat ka itihas* editorials. In using the Sanskrit terms *Bharat* and *itihas* in this Urdu text, rather than the Urdu terms *Hindustan* and *tarikh*, Burney also situated his editorials within mythopoeic traditions of Indian history writing, which have strong Hindu associations. *Itihas* is synonymous with the royal epics the *Ramayana* and the *Mahabharata*, and King Bharata is a character in the *Mahabharata*. Through selection and juxtaposition of words and images, Burney simultaneously referenced three different types of sovereign power (Hindu, Muslim and modern), which coincide with the periodisation of Indian history established in colonial historiography. This form of 'composite

[15] This blog used to be available at http://www.azizburney.com/ (accessed 23 July 2017). This domain name is now for sale (when accessed on 11 March 2019), but Burney continues to maintain an active online presence via his social media accounts.

nationalism' was pitched at the state and the official record, and overdetermined to the point of absurdity.

Questions about the intention and effect of this exorbitant nationalism were further encouraged by the content of these editorials. Like Azad, Burney's writings not only crossed borders between genres, formats and languages, the written and the spoken word, but also between the sayable and the unsayable. Most controversial was a series of editorials he wrote implicating a Hindu nationalist paramilitary organisation, the Rashtriya Swayamsevak Sangh (RSS), in the 2008 Mumbai attacks. On 26 November 2008, gunmen attacked various landmarks in Mumbai, including Chhatrapati Shivaji Terminus and the Taj Mahal Hotel, killing 174 people over the course of three days. The attacks were at least partly planned from Pakistan and badly affected relations between the two countries.

Burney's editorials on the incident were collected and published as a book, with both Hindi and Urdu editions, in December 2010. The compilation attracted media attention because of the presence of Congress politician Digvijaya Singh at its New Delhi and Mumbai book launches. During these events, Singh controversially claimed that Hemant Karkare, head of the Maharashtra Anti-Terrorism Squad, had rung him a few hours before his death in the Mumbai attacks to say he feared for his life because of threats from Hindu extremists. (Karkare had been heading an investigation into the 2008 Malegaon bomb blasts, in which Hindutva organisations had been implicated.) The resulting uproar forced an apology from Burney, which was published in both the Hindi and Urdu editions of *Sahara*.

On the front page of the 28 January 2011 Urdu-language edition is a short text in Hindi titled: '*Aziz Burney ki taraf se saphai aur maphi: RSS ki Sajish 26/11 pustak ke sandarbh main*' ('A clarification and apology from Aziz Burney with regards to his book *RSS Conspiracy, 26/11*'). The fact that the apology was written in Hindi emphasises the impression of accommodation, especially in the heavily Sanskritised Hindi of its closing lines: '*hridya se ksama chahta hun*' ('I seek forgiveness from my heart'). The apology was removed from the e-edition of *Roznama Rashtriya Sahara*, although it did appear in the Hindi online edition. Staff in the Sahara Group's Noida office told me that this editorial decision had come from above, but it was arguably equally an answer to feared and actual responses from below. Both its inclusion and removal were facilitated by new technology that makes it easier to produce multilingual layouts and edit e-editions. (Something similar was seen during the colonial period, when a multilingual readership and Azad's use of the latest printing technology made it easier to censor *al-Hilal*.)

The 13 February 2011 edition of the RSS English language publication *The Organiser* claimed that Burney wrote his apology because of a lawsuit filed on 7 August 2009 by a social worker with RSS connections.[16] But given the delay in publishing the apology and the fact that the book compiling his articles was published in the meantime, it seems unlikely that this was the only reason. Other reports speculated that Burney was made to publish it on the front page of both the Hindi and Urdu editions of *Rashtriya Sahara* in an attempt to appease his Hindu patron, Sahara India Group chairman, Subrato Roy, who was keen to maintain working relations with all political parties and to avoid antagonising a powerful organisation such as the RSS.

Roy had started his para-banking business in 1978 with a modest capital investment of Rs. 2000. By 2008 it had grown into India's largest residuary non-banking company, with 4512 offices across seven Indian states, employing 1.1 million workers (Bandyopadhyay 2014: 6). Sahara's unconventional business model and opaque accounting systems had encouraged suspicion that it was a 'parking space for politicians' ill-gotten gains', whose media outlets were a mouthpiece for these same parties (ibid.: 89).[17] Subrato Roy himself described his company as a 'family' (*pariwar* in Hindi), based in a corporate philosophy of 'collective materialism', which harmoniously blended emotional, spiritual and material interests.[18]

In compliance with this ethos, Burney had named his son Subrat after Roy. The dedication of a previous collection of his editorials also featured a family

16 Pramod Kumar, 'Burney Apologises for His Vicious Canard against RSS Will Digvijay Follow Suit or Face Trial?', *The Organiser*, 13 February 2011: http://organiser.org/archives/historic/dynamic/modules4df7.html?name=Content&pa=showpage&pid=384&page=8, accessed 23 September 2015).

17 Bandyopadhyay describes how, when asked by the Income Tax department to furnish a list of MPs and MLAs who kept money with the group in December 1996, Sahara responded by claiming it was impossible to do so because the company had a computerised accounting system based on unique numbers and not names (ibid.: 89–93). Roy was later imprisoned in February 2014 on a Supreme Court warrant for failing to refund the 240 billion rupees he owed to investors.

18 See the statement of philosophy on the Sahara India Pariwar website: https://www.sahara.in/heritage.html (accessed 7 May 2020). It is expounded at greater length in Roy's self-published book: *Shanti, Sukh: Santushti* [Peace, Happiness: Contentment] (2010).

tree, with Mahatma Gandhi in central place and Burney's father and Roy on the left and right branch (2003: 3). Even after leaving Sahara to start his own newspaper, Burney insisted that he maintained a close relationship with Roy. The relationship between the two men would last forever, Burney proclaimed. At first, there was a relationship between an employer and an employee; now there was a love that was not limited to the period that he remained on the Sahara payroll. The volatile patron–client relations evident in such displays of loyalty contrast with Azad's own relatively secure financial position, made possible by the strength of *pir–murid* ties that bound descendants of the disciples of his father, Sufi *pir* Shaikh Muhammad Khairuddin Dehlavi.[19] Resulting from external compulsion, and with reference to state-sanctioned forms of secularism, this accommodation to Hindu nationalists was also distinct from Azad's experiments with revolutionary politics in Calcutta.

The contrast was starkly evident in a series of editorials Burney wrote about the controversial 2010 Allahabad High Court judgment on the Ayodhya land title case. Disputes over who owns this plot of land, reputedly the site of a temple marking the birth of the Hindu deity Ram, came to a violent culmination in the 1992 destruction of the Babri Masjid, built on this spot in 1528. On 30 September 2010, the Allahabad High Court declared that Ayodhya was the birthplace of Ram. The site was divided three ways between two Hindu organisations, the Hindu Mahasabha and the Nirmohi Akhara, and the Sunni Waqf board. As an infant, Ram's claims could be represented by the Hindu Mahasabha, and as a god, any claims made on his behalf were not subject to time constraints, unlike those by the Sunni Waqf board, which were dismissed on this basis even though the board was allocated a third of the land. The judgment was met with both shock and relief as anticipated communal clashes did not occur, but there were soon criticisms of it as irrational.[20]

Aziz Burney had been in the habit of writing emotional editorials on the anniversary of the destruction of the Babri Masjid, and it was anticipated that

19 *Al-Hilal's* chief patron was Haji Nur Muhammad Zakariya, son of Haji Zakariya, a wealthy merchant and disciple of Azad's father (Minault 1982: 39–40).

20 On 9 May 2011, the Supreme Court stayed the judgment on appeal, describing it as "something strange" given that no one had requested division of the land. 'Supreme Court stays Allahabad High Court Verdict on Ayodhya', *The Hindu* (9 May 2011) http://www.thehindu.com/news/national/supreme-court-stays-allahabad-high-court-verdict-on-ayodhya/article2003448.ece, accessed 1 September 2015.

he would issue a strong response to the 2010 High Court judgment. A few days later, on 2 October 2010, he duly wrote an editorial titled '*Kya zaruri hai, suprim kort jana ... zara ghor karen*' ('What need is there to go to the Supreme Court ... please reflect on this'). In this editorial, Burney acknowledged that 30 September 2010 was a difficult day for the Indian people and the Indian state and expressed gratitude that there had been no communal incidents. He respectfully asked those Muslim leaders and members of the *ulama* who wanted to appeal the judgment whether, given that it is the state's responsibility to maintain peace and unity, it would actually be possible for a mosque to be built on the site. He offered a scenario in which Muslims would ask their Hindu brothers to build a splendid Ram temple, whilst they themselves would build a mosque on the land allotted to them by the High Court. The two buildings would then become an internationally renowned symbol of Indian traditions of communal harmony for coming generations. These editorials sharply differed from Azad's editorials on the Kanpur mosque incident not just in their 'moderation', but also in their relatively narrow frame of reference. In these texts, the international merely figured as an imagined audience for the resolution of a local conflict, rather than as a site for strong comparisons and connections.

Over the following days (4, 8–15 October 2010), Burney wrote more editorials on this theme. In these texts, he presented himself in the role of a mediator between the concerns of the Muslim community and the needs of the Indian state, but with one eye on the proprietor of his newspaper and another on the political parties, particularly the ruling Congress Party, which was preparing to contest the 2012 Assembly elections in Uttar Pradesh. Many Indian Muslims believe that Congress played a dishonourable role in the Ayodhya land title case. From the placement of Hindu idols inside the masjid in 1949 and the unlocking of its gates in 1986, to its destruction in 1992 and the 2010 High Court judgment, some of the most notorious episodes in this controversy have occurred when Congress was in power at the centre. Despite Congress's proclaimed secular identity, the correlation encouraged speculation about a Hindutva strain in Congress politics. The party has periodically sought out figures who could mediate between Muslims and Congress to allay such fears. During the independence struggle, this role had been performed by Abul Kalam Azad, but Burney's stance here more closely recalls that of the former

Congress Party politician, Arif Mohammad Khan, who had cited Congress 'saffronisation' as a reason for his decision to quit the party and join the BJP in 2004.[21] There is something of the self-dramatising tone of Arif Khan's pledge to 'surrender' himself to the BJP in Burney's editorials.

The archetypal performance of the loyal Muslim subject would be Sir Syed's pamphlet on the 1857 rebellion. This was written in Urdu for what he claimed was an exclusively British readership, and he is said to have offered a reward of Rs. 1000 to anyone who could prove it had been read by an Indian (Akhtar 2015: 24). Five hundred copies were printed in 1859, the Government of India kept one copy and all others were sent to Britain. Sir Syed's elaborate precautions and strenuous denials, alongside the decision to write in Urdu and publish the text in India, encourage questions about his motive in writing, printing and distributing this text. Similar questions are encouraged by Burney's and Arif Khan's professions of loyalty. Arif Khan specifically referred to Sir Syed's pragmatic accommodation to British rule when urging Muslims to learn from and befriend Hindu nationalists after the Gujarat pogrom of 2002.

These loyalties would prove harder to sustain in an era of volatile electoral politics as opposed to a period of regime change. Arif Khan had previously left another political party, the Bahujan Samaj Party, for entering a coalition with the BJP following the Gujarat pogrom, and this encourages doubts about the sincerity of his words here. Rather than being addressed to fellow Muslims, they seemed designed to attract the attention of the ruling Bharatiya Janata Party. But the provocative wording of his statements also registered his unease at representing a Hindu nationalist version of a 'good Muslim', and Aziz Burney's editorials expressed a similar discomfort.[22] His proposal to his co-religionists reads as ingenuous as his apology to the RSS.

Because Aziz Burney's editorials were written in both Hindi and Urdu, they were widely accessible, and in a June 2011 interview, he stated that he was aware that Congress politicians were reading them. During our first meeting

[21] '"I want to surrender to the BJP": The Rediff Election Interview/Arif Mohammed Khan', *rediff.com*, 24 February 2004, http://www.rediff.com/election/2004/feb/23inter.htm (accessed 26 February 2018).

[22] See Hilal Ahmed's, 'How to be BJP's version of a "good Muslim" – A guide by Arif Mohammad Khan', in *The Print*, 4 September 2019, https://theprint.in/opinion/how-to-be-bjps-version-of-a-good-muslim-a-guide-by-arif-mohammad-khan/286321/ (accessed 12 February 2020).

in 2010, he had shown me a letter in Hindi from Sonia Gandhi thanking him for his support in the 2009 national elections.[23] Rumours were circulating that Congress was planning to re-launch its Urdu newspaper, *Qaumi Awaz*, in order to reach Muslim voters in time for the 2012 Uttar Pradesh legislative assembly election, and that Burney would be its editor. Rumours were also circulating that he had ambitions for a seat in the Rajya Sabha (upper house) on a Congress Party ticket. His efforts, if that is what they were, seem to have been unsuccessful. *Qaumi Awaz* did not resume publication; no Rajya Sabha seat was in the offing; and in November 2011, Burney was transferred to the corporate relations department at Sahara Group and his editorials ceased to appear.

Soon after leaving Sahara, Burney realised his ambition of becoming a 'one man media house' with his self-published daily newspaper, *Azizul Hind*. Following the launch of his paper in 2013, he expressed excitement at the possibilities offered by new technology.[24] Newspapers used to reach only a limited circle, he said, but now social networking and websites had considerably broadened their reach, bringing him closer to his readers. Previously, he had had to tour the country from Kanyakumari to Darjeeling in order to address hundreds of thousands of people, but today, even a journalist shut up in a room was capable of being discussed in every part of the country and having the government worried about what he might publish in the morning. Burney said he wrote his editorials at 10.00 pm and two hours later they reached 130 countries, with people running them through translation software and reading them in various languages. What need was there now for him to go anywhere?

By means of the latest communications technology, Burney evoked ancient forms of inscription, a writing 'without Paper, without Pen', which does much more than attempt to represent speech (Mignolo 1998: 76). Through his online editorials, he aimed to both recover the authority of the spoken word and avail of the insurrectionary possibilities of writing. He even attempted to expiate what Sheldon Pollock has described as 'the guilt of Babel' by reaching readers in distant countries speaking other tongues through the medium of this ur-language (2006: 504). Again, comparison could be made with Azad's

23 Interview with Aziz Burney, Noida, 22 June 2011.

24 Interview with Aziz Burney, 4 September 2014, Noida.

ambitions in *al-Hilal*, with the prophetic pretentions of his Urdu and especially his Arabic editorials, where being read seemed to be less of a concern than transmitting a message and literally *creating* an audience.

But this attitude of unconcern for sales and profit margins would be much harder for Burney to sustain. As well as being excited by the possibilities of electronic media, Burney seemed to have been caught out by what Rancière has described as the '*onto-technological trick*' (2010a: 78, italics in original). Namely, the over optimistic prognosis of an actually existing 'communism' created by de-territorialised and de-materialised forms of capitalist production, based in communication networks rather than goods for private appropriation. In short, Urdu e-papers seemed to be based in an unsustainable business model. *Azizul Hind* made much of its internet presence but did not reveal its sales and circulation figures. The banner on the front page of the 1 May 2015 edition boasted that it reached 150 countries and 1,809 cities and gave an estimated readership of 3,705,616 on the dubious basis of the number of 'hits' on its website.

The paper edition was also unusually expensive for an Urdu daily (Rs. 5 compared with *Roznama Rashtriya Sahara* at Rs. 3). Subrat Burney claimed this was because of the value of and interest in his father's editorials, which continued to be published under the title 'Azad Bharat ka Itihas' and numbered in a sequence starting from their first appearance in *Roznama Rashtriya Sahara*. He told me *Azizul Hind* received both central and state government advertising, but the editions I saw only contained small-scale private adverts for Unani medicines and larger more prominent ones for the Samajwadi Party. (*Azizul Hind* started publication the year prior to the 2014 national elections and took a strong pro-Samajwadi Party line.)[25] Direct appeals for reader donations, with Aziz Burney's bank account details listed, seemed to reflect its poor financial condition.

On 1 May 2015, a front-page editorial appeared justifying a doubling of *Azizul Hind*'s cover price to Rs. 10. Like Azad, Burney addressed his readers directly to justify this decision, and in similar terms. *Azizul Hind* was a

[25] See the March 2017 article by Afaque Haider, 'My First Brush with Urdu Journalism', on the political pressures he faced whilst working at *Azizul Hind* . https://cafedissensus.com/2017/03/19/my-first-brush-with-urdu-journalism/ (accessed 5 December 2017).

movement and not just a newspaper, he explained. But it cost Rs. 10 to produce the paper: Rs. 3.6 for paper, Rs. 2.32 for printing and Rs. 3.18 for editorial expenses.[26] Only through advertising revenue and the co-operation of those who keep the pain of the *qaum* in their hearts would the paper be able to cover these costs. He emphasised his principled line in refusing advertisements from substandard or communal elements. He pointed out that the *qaum* needed its own media at a time when communalists had bought Urdu media in an effort to reach Urdu-knowing people. This was a reference to the daily newspaper *Inquilab*, which had been bought by the Dainik Jagran press group, an organisation with a strong Hindu nationalist association. Dainik Jagran's former managing director, Narendra Mohan, was a BJP Rajya Sabha member.

Burney stated that he had started *Azizul Hind* in order to represent the *qaum* and its interests at national and international levels, but now he was faced with the choice of either shutting *Azizul Hind*, increasing its price or switching to a weekly format. He asked readers to continue buying the paper at the increased price so that the *Azizul Hind* movement could remain alive. His decision to increase the price had not been taken lightly, he wrote. There were cheaper newspapers available, but when one looked at *Azizul Hind*'s larger purpose, the cost became meaningless. If it had been his aim to get other kinds of benefits from producing a newspaper, then perhaps it would be possible to sell it for Rs. 1, but this would not be true to the requirements of the *qaum* and of journalism. He ended by asking readers to advise him whether they would prefer the paper to be produced weekly or fortnightly, and gave his phone number and email address. Burney's appeal appears to have been unsuccessful. *Azizul Hind* subsequently ceased publication and no further editions have been uploaded onto its website.

Impossible speech

Both Azad and Burney attempted to be a one-man media house, involved themselves in all aspects of periodical production and directly addressed their readers, transgressing various boundaries as they did so. Both men also made

[26] Rs. 18.3 is actually given for editorial costs, but I assume this is an error.

use of different Perso-Arabic and Sanskrit registers of Urdu in order to assert their ambitions to be Muslim *and* national-level leaders. In their work, *qaum* implicitly meant Muslims in India, but writing in a multilingual South Asian context they addressed a much wider audience than Urdu-knowing Muslims. *Al-Hilal*'s difficult language signalled Azad's double consciousness of the colonial censor, whose attention he wished to avoid, and the *ulama*, whom he sought to impress with his piety and erudition. Post-independence, when Hindi was the official vernacular of the Union, Burney used Nagari script and Sanskrit vocabulary to write on issues of national significance.

At other times, Azad's and Burney's efforts went beyond language choice and code switching to encompass the 'open temporality' of the speech act, slippages between meaning and intention, addressee and target, as a message moves from sender to receiver (Butler 1997: 15). But in their testing of the limits of what it is possible to say and near-parodic renderings of official positions, Burney's utterances more closely resembled what Judith Butler describes as 'impossible speech': 'asocial ramblings' that are produced by the very rules that govern 'the domain of speakability' (ibid.: 113). *Giz giz giz* and *buk buk buk* as Sir Syed expressed it a century earlier. Neither emanating from a coherent subject nor addressed to a particular audience, such speech is easily discounted within this domain, hence the infelicitous speech acts of Burney's apology to the RSS and appeals to his co-religionists to respect the High Court decision on the Ayodhya land title case.

Burney's words and actions may have often been opportunistic, but they rarely seemed opportune. By contrast a dyadic relationship between speaker and audience had informed Sir Syed's speeches and texts, as he played up to the prejudices of his elite Indian audiences and the fears of his British readers. Similarly, Azad's understanding of the *qaum* evolved in relation to different audiences, media, languages and contexts: from the dense, allusive prose of *al-Hilal* to the simpler language and more accessible references of his speeches and writings for popular audiences. Burney's attempts to create a sense of a living, impinging audience in his speeches and texts seemed less convincing because his sights were clearly trained on a target above and beyond his ostensible addressee. This was partly because he faced more severe financial pressures than Azad, who chose to publish a weekly magazine rather than a daily newspaper and was financially independent. But it was also an indication of the relatively limited possibilities available to Burney as he attempted to work within the confines of state-sanctioned forms of nationalism and secularism, with strong Hindu-nationalist undercurrents. A crudely instrumentalist approach to power and print led him to dead-end forms of patronage politics and self-publishing, whereas Azad's sensitivity to the context within and audience for whom his messages were transmitted enabled him to get a better handle on their contingent and changeable nature. And, as I describe in the final chapter ('Fearless speech'), this capacity to respond to changing contexts and audiences continues to lend resonance to his words.

3

Emergency pedagogy

The Indian internal emergency of 1975–7 occurred during a particularly febrile period in South Asian history, a decade that commenced with the Bangladesh War of 1971 and was characterised by authoritarian regimes, mass movements, coups and assassinations. One way to reconcile the combination of authoritarianism and greater participation in the political process, social movements centred on charismatic individuals, is a particular type of populist politics encouraged by the intersection of new forms of mass media and ideas of democratic representation. This is how David Page and William Crawley, for example, understand it when they describe the heyday of populism in South Asia as coinciding with a boom in radio ownership, which enabled political leaders to integrate new classes into politics by allowing them to speak to them directly (2001: 52).

Other scholars have emphasised the historical context and structural dynamics and been sceptical about claims to radical transformation and direct communication (Jalal 1995, Jaffrelot and Anil 2020). In her comparative study of democracy in India, Pakistan and Bangladesh, Ayesha Jalal casts doubt on these appeals to the downtrodden and dispossessed (1995: 89). She describes them as part of a balancing act between the need for a new covenant to maintain the legitimacy of the state and old alliances with dominant groups. The contradictory requirement for change and stasis is said to have given the 'populist era' in South Asia its 'duplicitous character' (ibid.).

By dealing with an event in Bangladesh, the assassination of President Sheikh Mujibur Rahman (1920–1975), through its reception in neighbouring India, this chapter advances a different understanding of the movement of power and information within and across national boundaries. Proceeding from the technopolitical understanding of communication outlined in the introduction, I take on board both the transformative impact of new media and the enduring significance of historical dynamics. Further developing the discussion of ignorance and power in the preceding chapters, I describe how obstructions, gaps and misunderstandings in an information matrix brought together previously antagonistic groups in opposition to an authoritarian regime.

My starting point for this discussion is a series of essays on the encoding and decoding of messages in broadcast media that Stuart Hall published contemporaneously with the emergency (1972, 1973 and 1980). His description of the way in which 'a 'raw' historical event' assumes a 'message form' that enables it to pass from source to receiver offers directions for how a particular event might be used to understand a broader process (1980: 129). His encoding and decoding model also usefully highlights key assumptions behind sender-receiver models of communication. Hall dismisses the ideal of perfectly transparent, unilateral communication as something that 'can only exist in the (extremely rare) limiting case of the perfectly censored medium' (1973: 13), but he is also critical of the 'residual pluralism' which underlies the concept of 'selective perception' (1980: 135). Whilst there will always be variant readings, these are never as 'random or privatized' as the concept suggests (ibid.). Individual readings exhibit 'significant clusterings' (ibid.). The process of encoding is said to construct the limits within which such decodings operate. A politically significant moment is said to be reached when events start to be subjected to oppositional reading, but this, too, exists within the parameters established by encoding: 'If there were no limits, audiences could simply read whatever they liked into any message' (ibid.: 135).

In 'External influences on broadcasting', Hall specifies these limits as being defined by the state:

> The broadcasting institutions exercise a wide measure of editorial autonomy in their programmes: but ultimately they operate within the mode of reality of the state, and their programme content is, in the last instance, governed by the dominant ideological perspective and is oriented within its hegemony.
>
> (1972: 1)

This description of the role of broadcasting institutions draws upon the theory of hegemony outlined in Gramsci's *Prison Notebooks*, with its account of indirect domination exercised through a complex of superstructures in which intellectuals serve as functionaries (2003). But Gramsci is more attuned to historical contingencies and local contexts – to how the role of the intellectual played out in different epochs and settings. His description of the 'glimmer' of class consciousness in the 'semi-feudal' hatred of the Italian peasant for the civil servant also offers a basis for opposition to its hegemony through a 'basic, negative, polemical attitude' that exceeds the modern state's mode of reality (ibid.: 273).

This aspect of Gramsci's work is taken up by Ranajit Guha in his work on peasant insurgency in colonial India (1999). These are said to be paradigmatic of all previous and subsequent revolts, and he mentions resistance to the emergency as a recent example in the book's closing passages. Guha pays due respect to the role of consciousness and agency in these earlier rebellions, whilst arguing that their movement was highly structured. He, too, locates the 'organizing principle' for rebel communications in a common and external source of oppression (ibid.: 225). But in the 'semi-feudal' context of colonial India, this was trifurcated between the *sarkar*, *sahukar* and *zamindar* (state, moneylender and landowner) rather than emanating from a single place. The 'very first glimmer' of peasant political consciousness was said to arise when all three came to be viewed as interchangeable (ibid.: 27).

These movements also sought to achieve their aims with an eclectic range of verbal and non-verbal media available to what Guha describes as a 'preliterate' culture slowly transiting to literacy (the arrow of war, the messenger bough, the anonymous threatening letter). The transmission of these messages transformed their form and meaning, and the position of those involved in their exchange. For example, through the 'deverbalistion' of texts as illiterate peasants drew upon the authority of the printed material they came across to legitimise their claims, in the process transforming a verbal sign into a visual one (Guha 1999: 247–9). Or through the transitivity of rumour, as a message passed from a teller to a hearer who became a teller in turn. This logic of circulation looks forward to the role of remediation and intermediality in resistance to the emergency, which this chapter will explore.

Hall's essays were written during a period of global expansion of broadcast media, but they overlook this capacity for messages to reach audiences who are subject to different ideological perspectives, across various formats. The monolithic operations of power he describes also do not speak to emergency-era censorship, which, as Shiv Vishvanathan put it, both 'leaked like a sieve' and was of such a smallness and pettiness that it pervaded social relations and individual consciousness (1998: 45). Despite his scepticism about transparency, Hall's encoding/decoding model more closely resembles the mathematical theory of communication systems developed by Claude Shannon at Bell Telephone Laboratories, in which messages move from source to intended destination through a channel that is 'merely the medium used to transmit the signal from transmitter to receiver' (1998: 33–4).

In this chapter, I outline an alternative model of political communication by considering an event occurring in one context through its reception in another, whilst remaining attentive to the various media in which it was transmitted all the while. Specifically, through reception of the assassination of the President of Bangladesh, Sheikh Mujibur Rahman (Mujib hereafter), in the prison writings of two political leaders arrested in connection with the emergency in India, who learnt of the event through foreign broadcast media – Jayaprakash Narayan (1902–1979), former hero of the independence struggle and leader of the anti-Congress movement for Total Revolution, and L. K. Advani (1927–), Jana Sangh and later Bharatiya Janata Party politician. These well-informed and well-connected figures, who between them spanned the entire period of post-independence politics, had privileged access to information because of their social status and political connections. Their books therefore offer valuable insights into both the workings of repression and censorship and the acts of 'selective perception' that allowed Indians to resist it.

Both Advani's *A Prisoner's Scrap-Book* (1978) and Narayan's *Prison Diary* (1977b) are presented as a day-by-day response to events as they unfold. The books in which they recorded their reflections were in fact published at a later date, had been edited and contain additional content. But their accounts are relatively free of retrospective justification for actions at the time in light of subsequent events that are a feature of other first-hand accounts of the emergency. For example, books by Narayan's doctor (Chhuttani 1995) and jailor (Devashayam 2006) and also B. N. Tandon's *PMO Diary* (2003). The last claims to be a diary kept during this period by a member of the Prime Minister's secretariat but was published decades later.

Narayan's *Prison Diary* was mostly written in English, except for short passages in Hindi expressing patriotism and religious faith. It covers the period from 21 July to 4 November 1975, and according to its editor was minimally edited. Advani's book is written exclusively in English and called a 'scrapbook', but its first part takes the form of a diary. By embedding their reception of Mujib's murder in mundane details of prison life, Advani and Narayan deployed what Daniel Elam, writing about Bhagat Singh's jail notebooks, describes as 'the common and the revolutionary present', which 'refuses the status quo of future realization' (2016: 594). In this instance, official versions of Mujib's murder emanating from state media. But their choice of language and selection of material also indicates that they were writing for specific audiences in both the present and the future, and with reference to previous examples of the prison literature genre. As I will go on to detail, both men benefited in practical and literary ways from colonial-era precedents.

The chapter begins with an overview of the conditions of reception for Mujib's murder in India generally and for the prison writers Advani and Narayan in particular, with special focus on the ideological underpinnings and unintended effects of differential treatment of print and broadcast media. I then go on to analyze the way their books deal with this event and conclude by describing how power and information were disseminated during this period through a process of 'emergency pedagogy'. This term is not used in its usual sense, as a description of trauma relief, but to describe a process of knowledge transmitted will-to-will rather than brain-to-brain, in response to state repression and through the spatiotemporal disordering induced by combinations of new and old media. I describe how in contradiction to 'the old liberal paradigm of civic pedagogy' (Chatterjee 2011: 145), the pedagogic operations of the state taught the populations so addressed something that the state did not itself know, and as a result coalesced them in ways it did not anticipate.

Chaos in the air

News of Mujib's assassination was initially withheld in India, occurring as it did on Indian Independence Day, when Indira Gandhi was due to make her first public address since the proclamation of emergency. Full details of the massacre (the killing of most members of Mujib's immediate family) were also censored. But attempts to withhold news of it within India were rendered futile by unimpeded foreign radio broadcasts. Some of these international radio broadcasts were in regional languages and Urdu, and therefore capable of reaching mass audiences.

The important role played by international radio has been overlooked in accounts of the emergency. Even Weiner's first-hand account of the 1977 election does not mention it, choosing to focus instead on more visible manifestations of dissent: large public meetings, graffiti and handbills (1978). He argues that in a country with low literacy rates and a radio and television network that is controlled by the government and only reaches a fraction of the population, election campaigns mainly take the form of public meetings (ibid.: 21). Page and Crawley, in their book on broadcasting in South Asia, describe the 1977 election result as occurring despite censorship of the press and tight regulation of All India Radio and Doordarshan, the two state-controlled broadcasters (2001: 53). Both analyses ignore the significance of international media and the way various formats intersect, particularly in a context of low literacy levels but high levels of 'literacy awareness' (Bayly 2007: 39), access to literate people and awareness of the power of writing.

There was a historical precedent to this in the role radio had played during the independence struggle and the Second World War. In the first listener research survey conducted by All India Radio (AIR) in 1940, it was discovered that Indians were listening to news from Germany that was hostile to Britain and that the Hindustani news bulletin from Berlin was 'widely listened to' and regarded as 'more truthful' than the English version (Gupta 2001: 469). On another front, there was the threat to empire posed by Radio Moscow. An Intelligence Bureau report from 16 March 1932 described how Indians were picking up its English language broadcasts on favourable conditions in the USSR, and expressed concern about what would happen were it to start broadcasting in other Indian languages (ibid.: 460–1).

The political potential of radio was even greater following the arrival of 'the transistor revolution' that occurred in the 1960s, when radios became ubiquitous even in remote and rural areas. The Indian government had attempted to control foreign radio by subjecting the work of its local correspondents to pre-censorship and, when this did not work, by expelling foreign journalists. Mark Tully, who was the BBC correspondent for India at the time, described having to submit broadcasts for monitoring to the censors at All India Radio, who would interpret 'virtually anything that was not effusive praise as criticism'.[1] Following complaints about the erratic nature of this censorship, journalists were presented with a list of rules. When the BBC and other foreign broadcasters refused to comply with these, they were duly expelled. Despite these expulsions, foreign radio stations continued to broadcast into India for the duration of the emergency, gathering news from local sources by telephone and telex. Tully reported that listenership for the BBC service went up during this period when official media in India was heavily censored.

Getting foreign broadcasters stationed abroad to comply with Indian regulations and submit their material for censorship might not have been possible, but it would have been technically feasible to jam their broadcasts. During the colonial period, this appears to have been attempted with Congress Radio in Bombay. An article by one of the broadcasters described 'the mischief played by the A.I.R (Anti India Radio)', which would jam their broadcasts.[2] However, limitations in the technology available prevented it becoming a general policy, with an engineer in the colonial administration warning that British communications being 'strung out all over the world', they stood to lose more than they would gain by creating 'chaos in the air' (Gupta 2001: 470). Later, during the Cold War period, the USSR adopted a policy of jamming foreign radio broadcasts, but it remained an ineffective technology despite the fact that the Soviets apparently spent the equivalent of billions of US dollars on it.[3] It was reportedly most effective in densely populated urban areas and, even there, easily circumvented by listeners who would take their shortwave radio sets out of city limits to pick up broadcasts in areas where jamming was less intense. Jamming was particularly ill-suited to a large country with

1 Interview with Mark Tully, New Delhi, 13 September 2014.

2 'Congress Radio Calling', copy of an undated and unattributed article relating to the 1942 movement, Nehru Memorial Museum and Library, Miscellaneous Items, Accession No. 99.

3 Serge Schemann, 'Soviet Union Ends Years of Jamming Radio Liberty', *The New York Times*, 1 December 1988: https://www.nytimes.com/1988/12/01/world/soviet-union-ends-years-of-jamming-of-radio-liberty.html (accessed 18 March 2023).

a predominantly rural population and several international borders such as India.

One effect of this was to encourage a form of circulation in which print, radio and the word of mouth were imbricated – most strikingly, in the format of the underground news sheet: handwritten, typed or cyclostyled documents containing on-the-fly translations and transcriptions of foreign newspapers and radio broadcasts, distributed by hand or post, and bearing the slogan 'Read, reproduce and circulate'.[4] The logistics at work in this underground form of circulation were made explicit in an Independence Day address sent out on the same day that Mujib was murdered. In a public letter addressed to 'comrades', located 'somewhere underground' and dated 15 August 1975, the union leader George Fernandes laid out his instructions for the conduct of media *satyagraha* (Anon 1978: 13–14). These included appeals to boycott 'All Indira Radio', as AIR came to be described during the emergency period, and listen to BBC, Voice of America, Pakistani and Peking Radio instead; to duplicate, copy and translate underground news bulletins, and to encourage others to do these things (ibid.: 14). The logic of circulation was concentrated in the formula 'three raised to the power of eighteen', whereby if three people tell a story to only three others 'in eighteen operations the whole country will have heard the story' (ibid.). He ended with the injunction: 'Learn the power of the spoken word' (ibid.).

In its dialogism, Fernandes's 'spoken word' closely resembled what Bakhtin designates as 'the living word', the smallest linguistic unit of his theory of heteroglossia or 'social diversity of speech types' (2006: 263). Whereas a code, according to Bakhtin, is merely 'a technical means of transmitting information', and without any 'cognitive, creative significance', 'live speech' is 'created in the process of transmission' (1986: 147). Context enters the speech that frames it in a 'chemical union' rather than a 'mathematical bond' (2006: 340). It therefore cannot be studied in isolation from its 'contextualized (dialogizing) framing' (ibid.). On this basis Bakhtin distinguishes between semiotics, the transmission of ready-made codes, and live speech. The living word participates in what Bakhtin describes as 'the social life of discourse … discourse in the

[4] Nehru Memorial Museum and Library, Jayaprakash Narayan Papers, IIIrd Instalment, Subject file no. 315.

open spaces of public squares, streets, cities and villages' (ibid.: 259). But in the closed spaces of emergency-era India, the power of the spoken word was underlined by the attempt to silence it and acquired greater potency through being dispersed, translated and mixed with other media, notably print and broadcast media, both of which are technically mediated rather than social in the sense of involving face-to-face interaction.

Dissemination of underground literature was also encouraged by the flat-footed operations of state censorship, which in a period of low literacy levels was disproportionately concerned with print. (The 1971 census recorded an overall literacy rate of a mere 34.45 per cent.) Indira Gandhi even claimed that opposition to her rule came from the newspapers alone:

> While explaining the reasons for the imposition of Emergency, Smt. Gandhi had said that it was the newspapers which were inciting the people and creating a terrible situation. According to her, the agitation was only in the newspapers and once the newspapers were placed under censorship there was no agitation.
>
> (GI 1978, Vol. I: 33)

According to this view, it was readers who possessed a critical intellect and were therefore capable of threatening state projects, whereas in a September 1975 address to Directors of AIR, V. C. Shukla, Minister of Information and Broadcasting, described radio as 'the most potent medium that the Government has at its command' (GI 1977, Appendix 7: 15).

In contrast to the way in which Indira Gandhi worried about the unruliness of print, broadcast media was viewed as an instrument over which the state had control. The Indian government notoriously offered transistor radios as an inducement for men to undergo sterilisation during the emergency, and there is a similar kind of logic to this. Both initiatives configured listeners as passive ('silent') recipients of state programmes and messages. State censorship was informed by a standard theory of communication, which privileges the spoken over the written word because of its immediacy and a hierarchy that places speakers and writers over readers and listeners. Those who opposed the emergency benefited from the resulting inconsistencies in implementation of state censorship, compounded by the interface between the spoken and written word in a multilingual context. (This, for example, is how George

Fernandes's Independence Day message came to be widely disseminated through the written and spoken word in various languages.) Moreover, in an age of broadcast media dissent did not have to remain local. Reaction was rendered ineffective on a national scale by international radio working in conjunction with modern telecommunications and the simple cyclostyle duplication technology of the local underground press. By these means, it also elided Bakhtin's distinction between the living word and technical means by combining the properties of both.

Prison writers

Prison conditions varied widely during the emergency, even within a single jail. Prisons were a regional rather than central state subject, meaning that detention conditions differed from state to state, in accordance with classifications established in colonial-era legislation on the categorisation and separation of prisoners. Specifically, the 1894 Prisons Act and colonial prison manuals that divided prisoners on the basis of social and educational status and ethnicity. *The Maintenance of Internal Security (Conditions of Detention) (Mysore) Order, 1971* (MISA), under which L. K. Advani was detained in Bangalore, stated that 'security prisoners' would be divided into two classes, 'Class 'A' and Class 'B' having regard to the state of health, education, status and mode of living of such security prisoners prior to detention'. The race bar may have been lifted (categories such as European and Indian which were a feature of colonial manuals), but the reference to education and social status remained – 'habit of life' as it was expressed in the early jail manuals.[5]

In many ways Narayan and Advani appear to have received preferential treatment from the prison authorities. Fear of the repercussions of his dying in custody led to Narayan being shifted to hospitals in Delhi and Chandigarh and eventually released on 12 November 1975. Conditions seem to have been

[5] In the 'The Maintenance of Internal Security (Conditions of Detention) (Mysore) Order, 1971' this was expressed as 'mode of living'. Security prisoners were divided into class A and B on the basis of 'health, education, status and mode of living' prior to detention. (National Archives of India, Home List No. 180; 1287 5. 41011/9/KNT/77-T-4 – 'Replies received from Karnataka on Questionnaire reg. treatment in Jails'.)

particularly favourable for Advani, who was arrested as part of a parliamentary delegation and kept in Class A conditions in the south Indian state of Karnataka for the most part. In Bangalore jail, he was allowed regular family visits, able to send and receive letters and telegrams and had the use of what he described as 'the best jail library I have ever seen', containing English and Hindi books as well as a wide range of Kannada literature (1978: 16). Unlike other categories of MISA detainees, there were no restrictions on his use of the library and a transistor radio.

Even when Advani was briefly transferred to Rohtak jail in Haryana (15 July to 23 September 1975), where there was only one class of MISA prisoner, he continued to have company and access to media. In Ahmedabad, where he was briefly transferred in March 1976, he was able to receive news reports and to convey information about his movements to family members and party workers through a co-detainee, who maintained 'a very active communication link with those outside' (ibid.: 131). Both Advani and Narayan could send and receive letters, access national and international media, and write about their response to unfolding events. Advani mentioned not being able to use a typewriter when in prison but experienced no other restrictions on writing materials.[6] Having been arrested under MISA, Advani and Narayan were being held in preventive rather than punitive detention and therefore 'detenus' rather than convicts. Although this, too, was inconsistently applied with the Shah Commission observing in its state-wise survey of jail conditions that except for food, clothing and reading material, those detained under MISA were often lodged in the same conditions as other inmates (GI 1978, Vol. III: 135).

With Narayan and some of the other senior movement leaders, there was the additional awkwardness that many of them had been heroes of the independence movement. The last time they had been imprisoned was by the colonial state. The Shah Commission pointed to the irony of the situation:

> At no time since Independence was such a large scale detention of senior and respected leaders ordered simultaneously all over the country and no notice whatever was given to the authorities concerned for being prepared to receive the large influx of respected leaders as detenus. A large number of those who were detained, were fairly advanced in age and many of them

[6] Interview with L. K. Advani, New Delhi, 20 September 2014.

> were in need of constant and specialised medical attention for which the jail hospitals were totally ill-equipped.
>
> (GI 1978, Vol. III: 135)

Unsurprisingly, those opposed to the emergency made comparisons with this earlier period of repression and situated their publications in relation to independence-era precedents. Anti-colonial prison literature had become a familiar genre by the mid-seventies, and examples such as Narayan's *Inside Lahore Fort* (1959), his record of detention by the Punjab Government in 1944, were well known. In his preface to *A Prisoner's Scrap-Book*, Moraji Desai, the then Prime Minister, described its title as an example of 'Shri Advani's modesty', and said he was sure it 'will prove to be an important addition to the Library of our second liberation' (Advani 1978: vi).

Both Advani and Narayan drew historical analogies with colonial repression in their emergency-era prison writings, describing Indira Gandhi as even more tyrannical than the colonial state. Narayan observed that it was only in independent India that he had experienced 'tear gas, lathi blows' and solitary detention (1977: 6). Advani claimed that nothing 'the British did in 1936 in the matter of civil liberties can match the crimes against democracy by the present government' (1978: 77). Parallels between the emergency and earlier periods in Indian history underlined the significance of the moment both men were living through. As Advani noted, these analogies were a common feature of journalism during the emergency. Precluded from criticising the government directly, writers took to 'historical narratives and references which have a moral for the present' (1978: 51). But prisoners, who were not submitting their private writing for censorship, were operating from different imperatives when drawing parallels and making comparisons. Through comparison and contrast, they attempted to discern rather than conceal the outlines of their current experience and also to assert its world-historical significance. In this way, they also drew upon what Elizabeth Grosz describes as 'the virtual relevance of the past' in order to reconfigure the present (2004: 252).

The virtual and the past were both available to them because of the storage capacities of the media through which the messages they received were transmitted. From his emergency-era writings, it is clear that Advani was particularly attuned to changes wrought in the scope, reach and form of messages disseminated by new technology, and able to place these changes internationally. Familiar with the ways of modern-day politics and media, Advani drew parallels between Indira Gandhi's actions and those of Richard Nixon. He observed that the new style of politics in India was based on the same principles, with 'political manipulation becoming the substitute of political policy, and invention of bogeys to mobilise mass support' (1978: 268).

In making the comparison with Nixon, Advani was also possibly thinking of his televised appeals for support for the Vietnam War from what he famously described as 'the great silent majority of my fellow Americans'. By writing about his response to media and distributing this writing through the underground press, Advani established voice and set himself apart, asserted a capacity to both know and act despite his consumption of censored media and confinement in a state jail. Reflecting on Indira Gandhi's audacity in 'lying' in her first formal address to the nation since the emergency, he wrote that 'this outright lie … must have given to the thinking sections of our people a measure of the deceit and untruth which marked Indira Gandhi's campaign of calumny against the opposition' (1978: 38). As a journalist and politician, someone professionally qualified to decode state messages, he implicitly included himself in this category.

Narayan's account also demonstrated his awareness that he was writing a historically significant document, not just responding to the exigencies of the moment in producing documents for the underground press. Both men were transmitters *and* receivers of emergency-era messages. Rather than being a passive audience for news of a 'raw' event, they constructed meanings from information they received from a variety of media, which they interpreted through their awareness of a host of Cold War and postcolonial contexts. The information they received only became knowledge through slippages between the time of the killing and dissemination of news of the event, collective and internal discussion about its significance, and the solitary process of writing.

But whilst their position and location may have been special, far from being unique it was shared by many Indians both within and without the walls of emergency-era prisons. This was sweepingly expressed in the RSS history of this period, which declared 'Mrs Gandhi transformed the whole country into a huge jail by proclaiming the emergency' (Sahasrabuddhe and Vajpayee 1991: 89). During the emergency, Ranajit Guha cited the continued use of colonial-era preventive detention legislation as evidence that "the world's largest democracy' was a sham from the very outset' (1976: 52). For nearly all twenty-eight years of its postcolonial existence, Indians had lived in fear of imprisonment, meaning the Indian state was effectively a police state (ibid.: 43–4). Congress's defeat in the 1977 election has also been described as something of a 'jail break' in its apparent affirmation of liberal, democratic values (Rudolph and Rudolph 1978). The cases of these 'prison writers' are therefore presented with a view to understanding the wider dynamics of repression and resistance during this period, leading up to a consideration of the 'reader voters' who participated in the 1977 election.

'Back to the barbaric feudal days'

Narayan was kept in solitary confinement, and his jail dairies often lament the fact. Every day there is something in the papers that upsets him, he wrote, usually Indira Gandhi's 'half-truths and lies', and he wished that there was another prisoner with him with whom he could talk and vent his feelings (1977b: 14). This would be worth 'many tablets and sedatives and tranquillisers' (ibid.). Solitary confinement seemed to induce a state of solipsistic introspection in Narayan. The very first entry in his *Prison Diary*, dated 21 July 1975, established the tone of self-recrimination and regret that pervades the book: 'My world lies in a shambles all round me … I must bear the full, the whole, responsibility' (ibid.: 1). Later he went on to describe how 'every nail driven deeper into the coffin of Indian democracy is like a nail driven into my heart' (ibid.: 4), which was not an empty simile given the state of his health.

His visceral response to politics recalls a period when the emperor's physical person was the locus of the state. From the controversy over purchase of his dialysis machine (Narayan 1977a: 97–8), through to postmortem examinations to determine whether he had been medically injured in jail by not being given appropriate treatment, his imprisonment during the emergency and death soon after became a part of 'socio-political-medical history' (Chhuttani 1995: viii). Narayan himself drew these parallels in his response to the account of Aurangzeb's death in Ishwari Prasad's *History of Muslim Rule*, which he described reading on the eve of Mujib's murder. In the entry for 14 August 1975, he compared his own situation and Prasad's account of Aurangzeb's lonely final days: 'What the Emperor felt, a humble person like me could be allowed to feel' (1977b: 15).

But the example of Aurangzeb, under whose rule the Mughal empire reached its greatest extent before falling apart, also encouraged more impersonal reflection on the emergency. He observed that there had never been a successful attempt to govern India from a single centre and heavily centralised states had not lasted long. The borders of various empires expanded and shrank with the passing of time and all of them eventually disintegrated. This was the case even when there was 'no concept of democracy based on adult franchise, or of civil liberties and rights of every common citizen' (ibid.: 16). Thinking about Indira Gandhi's actions in stark historical perspective, without reference to specific rulers and periods, allowed Narayan to abstract out the dynamics that he perceived to be at play. From this he drew the hopeful lesson that the emergency period would also be short-lived.

In less general terms, this response fit within Narayan's long-standing interest in nationalism and federalism. His attitude changed over the decades from hostility to states reorganisation to participation in peace missions in Nagaland and Kashmir, which led him to advocate for smaller and more autonomous states. But he remained concerned with how to reconcile the right to self-determination and the need for overall unity throughout. With reference to events in Bangladesh, this is evident in his entry for 18 August 1975, which expressed relief that Bangladesh would retain the name of the 'People's Republic', that there would not be 'any constitutional links forged with Pakistan – confederation, association or anything else like that' and 'Bangladesh is not going to become anyone's satellite' (1977b: 19–20). Despite his empathy with Aurangzeb, there is evidence here of unease at the prospect of a latter-day example of 'Muslim rule', another Islamic state on India's borders.

Narayan's reference to satellites expressed the same concern in the idiom of geopolitics. At the international level, his support for national self-determination was part of his support for non-alignment, which led him to view both the USSR and United States with suspicion. This attitude was manifest in an elaborate conspiracy theory about the emergency being a Soviet take-over plot. In the entry for 22 July 1975, he predicted a time would come when 'having squeezed the juice out of Mrs Gandhi, the Russians through the CPI and their Trojan horses within the Congress will dump her on the garbage heap of history and install in her place their own man' (ibid.: 3–4). He also wrote of the role of the Americans in spreading disinformation. False rumours that Bangladesh would be renamed the Islamic Republic were revealed to originate from a US news agency, leading him to wonder why the Americans are 'always up to this kind of mischief' (ibid.: 20).

Narayan's awareness of a range of competing perspectives during the Cold War era informed his analysis of the international coverage of the event, which he received prior to the Indian press commentary. Because of the wide variety of media from distant countries that he referred to, some in languages he could not read or even understand, I assume he came across their contents through news digests on international radio, but this is not specified. He mentioned coverage in Russia, France, Yugoslavia and the United States specifically, and made vaguer references to the European and Western press in general (ibid.: 20). Russia and the Russian press were said to be predictably silent or noncommittal, whereas the communist press in Europe saw the hand of the CIA in the event, *L'Humanité* being the most explicit in making this claim. Non-communist European papers were apparently divided, some viewing it as a US-backed rightist coup, others discerning the support of China. Only Yugoslavia regretted the eclipse of the policy of non-alignment for which Mujib stood.

All these readings were ultimately rejected as Narayan decided that the 'affair was a domestic event' (ibid.). When further details of the killing emerged on 22 August 1975 (ibid.: 27–8), he identified it as an assertion of oligarchic power in accordance with a familiar pattern. The precautionary murder of all available members of Mujib's family was said to be a return to the 'barbaric feudal days … when brother killed brother to seize the crown' (ibid.: 27). Nevertheless, he struggled to reconcile the barbarity of this act with the military regime's continued espousal of the tenets of 'Mujidabad' (nationalism, socialism, secularism and democracy): 'His (Mushtaq Ahmed) taking over supreme martial law power while still talking of democracy, I can understand. All dictators talk like this. We have our own Mrs Gandhi. But why destroy the entire Mujib family?' (ibid.). He left open the possibility of third-party involvement and concluded, 'the truth will only emerge from the passage of time' (ibid.). In a context of censorship and distortion of information, all received accounts were refused, past, present and future elided.

Although Narayan may have been sensitive to both 'the literal and connotative' levels of the accounts he received, he did more than simply engage in an 'oppositional reading' along lines delimited by the process of 'encoding' (Hall 1980: 137–8). By reading various hegemonic codes *against* one another, he effected something like the 'contraction or distention of temporalities', which Rancière specifies as necessary for thinking and writing democratic history (2011c: 65). With reference to the novels of Virginia Woolf, Rancière speaks of the 'liberating political possibilities' of modes of individuation and the interlinking of sequences, which challenge 'the formatting of reality' of state-controlled media (ibid.). By 'undoing the relations between the visible, the sayable, and the thinkable', they establish a grid that makes it possible to think of 'political dissensuality' (ibid.).

This grid was outlined in one of the J.P. movement's most famous slogans: '*sampoorna kranti ab nara hai, bhawi itihaas hamara hai*' (Narayan 1977b: 128 – 'total revolution is now the slogan, future history belongs to us'), conveying a sense of what would be the retrospective historical significance of this 'second independence struggle'. In Narayan's prison writings, it seemed to be expressed in two registers. Listening to radio reports of the massacre brought up the suggestion of eternal recurrence and even regression – back to the 'barbaric feudal days … when brother killed brother' – puncturing the progressive pretensions of the new regime. Reading about those days allowed him to invoke the future anterior, to kick the traces of the present to reveal the pattern of the past, to evoke a different distribution of power and demarcation of territorial boundaries.

'We, representing the entire political spectrum in the country'

Unlike Narayan, Advani was always in the company of other detenus, and at various points in his book, he referred to the political leaders with whom he had been arrested as friends and colleagues, a comradeship that extended across party lines. This was of a piece with the composition of Janata itself, which was formed out of a combination of parties opposed to Indira Gandhi's Congress. Advani described all party discussions on what stance to take towards Narayan, whose call for the police and army to revolt alienated some detenus (1978: 50–1), and of how and to what extent to form a coalition with left parties that opposed the emergency (ibid.: 48). These ties would be stretched to the limit in later discussions over whether it was possible to be a member of the party and the Hindu nationalist paramilitary organisation, the Rashtriya Swayamsevak Sangh (RSS). Arguments over dual membership of the RSS would eventually lead to the break-up of the Janata Party, but during this unusual time, and in these extreme circumstances, affiliations seemed to extend across ideological lines.

Both the Jamaat-e-Islami and the RSS were banned during the emergency, and in his diaries Advani recounted strategic political alliances and improbable friendships formed in the common space of the jail. In an entry for 5 July 1975, he described how the jail authorities had separated the RSS members from 'the Jamaat people', who were being detained alongside those held on smuggling charges, 'obviously prompted by considerations of religious homogeneity', the smugglers presumably being Muslim (ibid.: 17). The Jamaat members were said to have protested against the classification, which led to 'political prisoners' (an unofficial but respected status) being housed with those suspected of criminal activity (ibid.: 17–18). Advani reported that 'adjustments were accordingly made' and remarked upon the hypocrisy of an ostensibly secular government perpetuating 'religious and other denominations by every one of its acts' (ibid.: 17). It was during the emergency itself that the word 'secular' was added to the preamble of the Indian Constitution in a rebuttal of the religio-political forces that had opposed Indira Gandhi. These forces were to meet in emergency-era jails and unite in opposition to Indira Gandhi's rule, in a manoeuvre that recalls the cross-denominational alliances encouraged by colonial repression during the Khilafat movement.

Another similarity with the Khilafat movement was the cosmopolitan aspect to this reaching beyond the confines of given identities and political positions. Advani described reading media in various languages, and coming from national and international sources, against each other, and doing so in the company of other prisoners who acted as a fact-checking and critical chorus. Early in his book, Advani described how censorship of the press meant 'the Indian student of public affairs has no option but to tune in to foreign broadcasting media. I took it upon myself to keep track of reports regarding India relayed by the BBC, Voice of America, Voice of Germany and Radio Australia … Radio Moscow, Peking Radio and Radio Pakistan' (ibid.: 17). On a previous occasion, in the entry for 4 August 1975, he described an instance when someone in the News Services Division of All India Radio had 'bungled' and allowed the Punjabi and Urdu divisions to report on proposals to amend the Representation of the People Act, information that had been removed from the English bulletin (ibid.: 32).

Both aspects of his reading practice came together in his account of Indira Gandhi performing the flag hoisting ceremony on Independence Day, which he was able to watch on a television set kept in the canteen of Rohtak jail. Advani described how 'we, representing practically the entire political spectrum in the country', could not comprehend an allusion in Indira Gandhi's speech to an opposition ruler who had ridiculed the tricolour as a 'rag' (ibid.: 38). This led to an excursus on Dalit politics in Maharashtra by Socialist Party leader Madhu Dandavate, who explained that this remark had been made by a member of the Dalit Panthers. The detainees also commented upon the otherwise mellow tone of the speech and Indira Gandhi's unconvincing performance of anger. She was said to be 'making a special effort to look enraged' when referring to the opposition at the beginning of her speech, but her 'worked-up wrath' failed to impress (ibid.). (With a television broadcast there is also the possibility to read a speaker's physical expressions against his or her words.)

The mystery was resolved when Advani listened to the Voice of America morning news bulletin and heard about the military coup in Bangladesh and the assassination of Sheikh Mujibur Rahman. He shared the news with the other inmates, who reacted with shocked disbelief. A few days previously, Dandavate had heard a radio broadcast announcing the resignation of eight cabinet ministers and relayed the information to the other prisoners, who only realised later that this had occurred in Argentina and not India. The others met Advani's report of a coup in Bangladesh with scepticism, and this made him wait for confirmation of what he had heard. Advani began trying to get reception of a medium wave radio station to see if any regional language broadcast might be available. He finally got a Marathi news bulletin, which declared that Mujib had sent an Independence Day greeting to the Indian

President. But he soon came across Voice of America and BBC reports on 'the gory events in Dacca that morning' (ibid.: 39). He also listened to Dacca Radio, which broadcast the swearing in of the new Head of State (ibid.: 40). All India Radio, meanwhile, took five hours to report that a coup had taken place (ibid.), and a full account of the killings did not appear until much later.

'Clog the openings and you run the risk of explosions', Advani concluded (ibid.: 39), referring to events occurring in both Bangladesh and India. But all the above suggests that repression also encouraged a search for news sources in other media and various languages, alliances across previously existing lines, and critical reception of both official and unofficial information. As with the 'first' independence movement, this was a volatile process. By linking individual readers and writers through illicit circulation of media and particular modes of reading and writing, censorship produced a sense of community that was provoked by but outside the direct control of state regulation. Groups and subjects coalesced in this way were hard to fix, a difficulty that went beyond individual reader response or linguistic indeterminacy – the necessarily incomplete task of subjectification. Censorship articulated subjectivity and sociality, but in ways unintended by the censor and not fully determined by either reader or writer.

Because of its incorporation of elements from across the political spectrum, from Naxalites to Hindu nationalist organisations, around the amorphous goal of 'total revolution' and under the charismatic leadership of Narayan, the J.P. movement has sometimes been labelled fascist. (A pamphlet collected in part two of Advani's *Scrapbook*, 'Anatomy of Fascism', reversed this accusation [ibid.: 249–69].) Even those who participated in it have subsequently expressed the possibility that it was regressive. In an interview given in 2000, Socialist Party politician Dandavate questioned the inclusion of the Jana Sangh.[7] He claimed Narayan believed that only the total mobilisation of forces opposed to the emergency could bring about its revocation, and given the 1977 election results, Narayan may well have been justified in his belief. But, speaking to an interviewer in the Jawaharlal Nehru Memorial Museum and Library during a time when a BJP government was in power at the centre, Dandavate regretted

[7] Madhu Dandavate. (interviewee), recorded by Smt. Usha Prasad (interviewer), 12 December 2000, Nehru Memorial Museum and Library, Oral History Project (778).

the long-term repercussions of this move. He argued communal forces such as the Jana Sangh gained respectability during the Janata Party period, whilst the Socialists fell into decline.

Dandavate may well have been thinking about the career of former prison-mate L. K. Advani, who had risen to the position of Home Minister in the BJP government. Advani had come to political prominence a second time in the 1990s, as one of the leaders of the campaign to build a temple on the site of the Babri Masjid, culminating in the violent destruction of the mosque in 1992. Advani had launched the campaign to rebuild the temple with a procession from Somnath, site of a temple repeatedly destroyed by Muslim rulers and controversially renovated by the Congress government in 1951, to Ayodhya, the north Indian town in which the Babri Masjid was located. Coming from someone as avowedly secular as Advani (a Sindhi Hindu unassociated with the north Indian Hindu identity at work in the Ayodhya movement), the opportunism of his actions seemed blatant.

It also seemed to contrast with Advani's liberal emergency-era politics, which in his prison writings was expressed in a concern with civil liberties and human rights. Opposition to the death penalty in India was occasioned by inspection of a gallows (Advani 1978: 58). Discussion of a UN General Assembly resolution prohibiting torture, unlawful arrest and detention followed a meeting with a schoolteacher who had been badly beaten by police officers (ibid.: 88). The resolution had been supported by the Indian representative at the UN during the emergency itself, and in the English translation of the RSS history of the period, in a heavily illustrated chapter titled 'Atrocities', this was likened to 'the Devil quoting the scriptures' (Sahasrabuddhe and Vajpayee 1991: 242). Advani's account was drier. Displaying a stronger sense of the international, of history, and with an eye on future and foreign readerships, he left out the detail that India had signed the resolution and focused instead on the role played by Greece in sponsoring the motion (1978: 88).

Across the *Scrapbook* as a whole, Advani's references were often non-Indian (Thomas Jefferson, Cesare Pavese, Solzhenitsyn), and the political ideology that comes across most strongly is a liberalism that contrasts with his later politics. The single extended religious reference stands out because of its incongruity. The 'sins' of the past few months are not Indira Gandhi's alone, he wrote, but the 'collective guilt' of all Congressmen, regardless of whether they actively supported her or merely acquiesced: 'Bhishma and Drona were as much responsible for the outrageous disrobing of Draupadi as were Duryodhana and Dushasana' (ibid.: 78). This is footnoted as an allusion 'to an episode in the Mahabharata' (ibid.), which says something about whom Advani imagined his readers would be. These liberal attitudes were no less of a performance than his later actions in Ayodhya, but aimed at a future Anglophone readership rather than a national electorate.

Religious references returned in his next book, *The People Betrayed* (1979), which dealt with the disintegration of the Janata Party on the, in his view, pretext of joint membership of the RSS. Advani described the RSS as the 'hobgoblin' of Indian politics, a scare figure that other parties could draw upon to frighten Muslim voters (ibid.: 80–1). He elaborated on this insight with reference to the war diary of Joseph Goebbels, Minister of Information and Propaganda of National Socialist Germany, which he described as one of the 'precious documents' recovered from post-war Germany:

> Analysts of Nazi propaganda techniques are all agreed that one of the cardinal principles of their strategy was: there must always be an enemy for the people to identify as the cause of all their problems; all propaganda must be keyed to ensuring that hatred against the enemy does not sag. The Bolsheviks and the Jews were favourite hate-objects of Nazi propaganda.
>
> (Ibid.: 80)

During such moments, Advani demonstrated an awareness of what Laclau, in his work on fascism and ideology, describes as the importance of 'an antagonistic relationship with a dominant bloc' in the process of popular-democratic interpellations, which produce the subject known as 'the people' (1979: 107). These are independent of any precise class content and therefore available to 'quite distinct political discourse', including fascism (ibid.: 111). Hence the difficulty in identifying the politics of the J.P. movement on a left–right spectrum because of its use of such a wide range of popular-democratic interpellations to oppose Indira Gandhi's regime. The movement variously appealed to liberal principles, socialist ideals, histories of anti-colonial struggle and religious beliefs. Even with reference to a single figure, Advani, affiliations seemed to shift according to audience and context. When in prison, in the company of prisoners from across the political spectrum, writing for an international audience and the historical record, Advani's politics were ostentatiously liberal and secular. When in power as a BJP minister and seeking to mobilise a national electorate through the televised spectacle of the Ayodha campaign, he invoked a much narrower vision of the people.

Reader voters

One of the notable features of the emergency was the apparently comprehensive but transitory nature of its acceptance, making it hard to tell how state messages were being read. In their essay on the period, Lloyd and Susanne Rudolph note how 'opportunism and fear, joined with conventional prudence and apathy', combined with state and party influence on the economy and associational life to produce 'many of the outer signs of totalitarianism' (1978: 386). Congress's defeat in the March 1977 election is said to have revealed this to be a 'temporary adaptation rather than adherence based on conviction' (ibid.). But if the 1977 election result was, as they claim, an endorsement of 'a liberal state and a democratic regime' (ibid.: 399), what to make of Indira Gandhi's re-election just a few years later in 1980, which aroused concerns in the minds of political analysts that Indians were 'indifferent to the dangers of authoritarianism and more concerned with the price of onions' (Weiner 1983: 134)?

The period has also provoked larger questions about Indian democracy. Writing at the time, Ranajit Guha claimed the emergency revealed that democracy in India had 'long been dead, if it was ever alive at all' (1976: 52). More recent literature has also reflected on the extent to which it was an exceptional event and its relationship to subsequent forms of authoritarianism (Jaffrelot and Anil 2020, Prakash 2019). As discussed earlier, the emergency was pivotal in bringing Hindu nationalists to political prominence and power. Narendra Modi, who made his reputation during this period, published his own emergency-era writings as part of the 2014 election campaign (Modi 2014). He also repeatedly refers to the period in his speech and writings as evidence of Congress's dictatorial tendencies. The return of BJP rule under his leadership has, in its turn, provoked fears that India is transitioning into a 'Hindu Raj' (Jaffrelot 2021). Nevertheless, an emergency on the scale of that proclaimed in 1975–7 has not been attempted since. As well as revealing authoritarian strains in the postcolonial Indian state, the period offers insights into how this has been resisted, and the relationship between repression and resistance.

In a book on liberalism in India, published a couple of years before the 2014 BJP election victory, Christopher Bayly had attributed Indians' apparent resistance to totalitarian ideologies to the radical individualism of certain forms of Hinduism. This was said to have prevented 'the creation by the state or political leaderships of an Indian 'socialist man' or 'fascist man'' (2012: 24). But rather than being the preserve of any particular religious or cultural community, as with earlier insurgencies, the 'organising principle' for this response seems more likely to have been the oppressive actions of the state (Guha 1999). Resistance was shaped through a dialectical relationship with its hegemony. In his work on nineteenth century peasant rebellions, Guha described their increasingly national, transnational and systematic nature as the colonial state outgrew its 'predatory and mercantilist beginnings' to mature into a regulated empire (ibid.: 25). During the emergency period, resistance responded to the double-edged instrumentality of the developmental state: closely intertwined processes of education and control. Hence the progressive agenda that was the ostensible justification for the emergency, as expressed in Indira Gandhi's Twenty Point Economic Programme.

There were also continuities between the two forms of hegemony. The avowedly socialist Indira Gandhi's autocratic actions resembled those of British liberals during the colonial period who espoused the principle of liberty but believed it did not apply to childlike barbarians 'in need of direction by benign imperial authority' (Bayly 2012: 13). Despite different 'core notions' regarding the relationship between individual and community, they shared what the political theorist Michael Freeden, in a discussion of eugenics and liberal thought, has described as an 'idea environment' (1983). Specifically, a developmental concept of history rather than a cyclical or accumulative one. The developmental mandate for emergency-era repression has come to be judged as spurious and to have been based on a faulty pedagogic model encapsulated in the first point of Sanjay Gandhi's Five Point Programme, 'each one teach one'. This slogan resembled George Fernandes's 'media satyagraha' manifesto in phrasing but differed from it drastically in being disseminated by official decree. The failure of Indira Gandhi's wider Twenty-Point Programme has been attributed to the 'quixotic' nature of its attempt to establish 'grass-roots organization for popular mobilization by fiat from above' (Frankel 2005: 549).

The self-contradictory nature of this top-down pedagogic model is particularly clear in countries such as India, where historically it had been both justified by racial hierarchies and based in enlightenment-era faith in mutability. In both the colonial and postcolonial period, progressives' complacency about their own civility and reasonableness made them resistant to extending political rights to those who were not yet ready to represent themselves. As well as being grounded in faith in their own superiority, this was informed by a theory of learning in which the movement from ignorance to understanding is brought about through external intervention. This chapter has described how those who opposed the prevailing order engaged in a particular type of counter-pedagogy. Narayan and Advani's intellectual activities recalled those of Indian liberals during the colonial period, who attempted to 'excavate, appropriate and cannibalise' Euro-American thought in their search for freedom (Bayly 2012: 11). This involved both looking to the liberalism of other European countries and American republicanism and also picking and choosing the aspects of British liberalism that resonated with them. Say, in adhering to the principle of liberty, ignoring the fact that many of its western advocates believed it did not apply to colonial subjects.

But similar acts of oppositional reading could also be perceived in the 1977 election result delivered by a mostly illiterate electorate. This saw Muslims support the Janata Party in large numbers despite the party's incorporation of former members of the Hindu nationalist Jana Sangh. The Janata Party and its allies won 328 seats out of 542 in the 1977 election whilst Congress gained only 153 (Weiner 1978: 67). Almost all the leaders of the Janata Party were elected, and often by large margins. The union leader George Fernandes won his seat with a margin of 330,000 despite being in jail during the entire election campaign (ibid.). Congress won only two seats in north India (ibid.: 69), historic centre of Congress Party power, but also the site of some of the worst violence of the emergency, much of which targeted Muslims.

In his book on the 1977 election, Weiner described scenes in the streets of Delhi as the results came in:

> People seemed elated by the knowledge of what their votes had done. At the large billboard on Parliament Street a group was asked who they thought would be India's next prime minister. Did they prefer Morarji Desai, Jagjivan Ram, or Charan Singh? 'It doesn't matter,' said one of the men. 'If we don't like the prime minister we can always replace him.'
>
> (Ibid.: 60)

Voters seemed to be voting not so much for a particular party or programme, but against an autocratic regime and in affirmation of democratic anarchy, government based in the 'drawing of lots', with its scandalous revelation that 'the government of societies cannot but rest in the last resort on its own contingency' (Rancière 2006b: 47). A non-exclusionary form of the people was momentarily coalesced through the anonymity of the voting process and the shared experience of reading competing hegemonic articulations against the grain. These reading practices involved subversive combinations of audiovisual media that recall Guha's account of the negation and inversion of the prevailing order in nineteenth-century rural insurgencies ('the world turned upside down') – but with the significant addition of the electoral mechanism and electronic media. The next chapters will further explore the impact of these new technologies of representation.

4

The model code

In its report on the 1962 Indian general election, the Election Commission of India (ECI) mentioned a code of conduct that had evolved just prior to the 1960 legislative assembly elections in 'the politically conscious State of Kerala' (GI [Government of India] 1965: 58-61). The code covered campaigning activities, and its emphasis was on maintaining public order and respecting 'the right of every individual for peaceful undisturbed home life'. Meetings and processions had to be planned and approved well in advance, with a view to avoiding disruption to members of the public and clashes with other political parties. Speeches and slogans delivered from public platforms were required to observe a 'high standard of decency and decorum'. Derogatory remarks about 'the private lives, personal habits or physical peculiarities' of individuals, or their 'religion, caste or community', were to be avoided. Likewise posters and placards that sought to humiliate individuals or ridicule 'the beliefs and practices of the followers of any religious or political thought'. The burning of effigies of political rivals would not be countenanced.

Judging the exercise to have been a success, the ECI decided to circulate this code to political parties and state governments during the 1962 election, and in 1968 framed its own Model Code of Conduct for the guidance of Candidates and Political Parties.[1] The Model Code has non-statutory force, is dependent upon the cooperation of the political parties. But over the years its purpose has moved beyond an original emphasis on preserving public order to creating a level playing field of political competition. Situated at the crossroads of law, politics and society, the Code offers a useful vantage point

1 The text of the Model Code of Conduct is available from: https://ceo.uk.gov.in/files/pdf/ModelCodeofConduct%20.pdf (accessed 5 October 2024).

for exploring tensions between the principle of popular sovereignty and the practice of conducting elections.

These tensions are often thought to be particularly acute in postcolonial states such as India. In their introduction to a special edition of *Election Law Journal*, Gilmartin and Moog attribute the difference in the way 'the "voice of the people"' is conceptualised in the American and Indian systems to their different histories and social structures (2012: 147). In the United States, this concept is said to be rooted in a market model of society according to which the people's voice emerges from a marketplace of choices made by individuals between 'competing ideas and interests' (ibid.). As a result, regulation of elections is viewed as necessary but limited in scope. In post-independence India, on the other hand, voting has been linked to a vision of national citizenship, which seeks to transcend the structures of an authoritarian colonial state and a society segmented by 'caste, region, religion, community, and patronage' (ibid.). Electoral regulation is seen as more than a necessity, and the constitutionally established ECI, positioned apart from government and above politics, is tasked with and authorised by realisation of this vision.

In this chapter, I argue against the myth of authentic democracy that underlies this vision, based in an impossible speech situation in which decision-makers and citizens are co-present and to which any general election would fall short. As political theorists have observed, this deliberative model does not apply in contexts ranging from hierarchical caste societies with 'lordly' modes of communication (Burghart 1996) to mass democracies (Young 2000), as well as postcolonial states such as India which combine both. None of these settings lend themselves to the ideal of un-coerced and un-biased participants freely evaluating one another's statements.[2] Hence the recourse to a complementary myth of regulatory impartiality, based in an equally 'impossible political optic', in which certain bodies are configured as all-seeing and disinterested judges of the public interest (Latour 2024).

[2] For critical responses to Habermas's notion of an ideal speech situation and John Rawls' drama of consent, theories which inform much political science literature on deliberative democracy, see Mouffe (1999) and Cavell (1991) respectively.

Proceeding from a technopolitical and aesthetic view of politics as a 'system of a priori forms determining what presents itself to sense experience' (Rancière 2011c: 13), in this chapter, I work towards an alternative understanding of democratic representation. I begin by considering the metropolitan precursors for and colonial precepts of electoral regulation in India. I then look at the BJP's campaign during the pivotal 2014 general election, drawing upon observations collected during fieldwork in the state of Uttar Pradesh from December 2013 to May 2014. This election was fought in a lofty presidential mode nationally, but with shrewd accounting of communal equations at the local level. I describe how during the 2014 general election, the BJP was able to profit from the unfixity of ascriptive identities, slippages between the local, regional and national levels of the election, and election officials' inability to span them. Both the elections in UP and the communal riots that preceded them attest to the power of not seeing and not acting. I argue that rather than being a failure of a state-instigated process of rationalisation and modernisation, this was an effect of an attempt to regulate into existence a level playing field, informed by a narrow view of what constitutes that field and the elements that could potentially skew it.

I conclude by suggesting a different basis for electoral regulation and democratic representation, one that does not sacralise the people and the electoral process. Instead of focusing on a narrowly defined field of electoral competition and set of actors, this would proceed from a stronger understanding of representation as a set of relations between 'the visible and the invisible, the visible and speech, the said and the unsaid' (Rancière 2009b: 93–4). By being attuned to the absence of any single legitimising principle of political community, it would be better placed to oppose appeals to primordial ties and oligarchic concentration of power, which in India and elsewhere threaten to result in ethnic democracy.

The sacred space-time of popular sovereignty

In an essay on the history of election law in India, David Gilmartin quotes a Supreme Court judgment on an appeal case presented in Andhra Pradesh and published in 1981:

> In a democracy such as ours the purity and sanctity of elections, the sacrosanct and sacred nature of the electoral process must be preserved and maintained.
>
> (Quoted in Gilmartin 2007: 78)

He emphasises that this is not a reference to sanctity in a strictly religious sense but an appeal to the concept of a sovereign authority located outside state and society. A sacred space, founded in the free will and conscience of the individual voter, is the locus of the people. This sacred space and the 'powerful, sovereign fiction' of the people it contains, lie at the heart of India's electoral system (ibid.: 77). Gilmartin observes that the conceptual distinction between state, society and the people on which it is based originates in eighteenth- and nineteenth-century Britain. He also describes numerous contradictions in the application of electoral law in India. But for him these contradictions are inherent to the electoral system developed in Britain rather than the result of an unsuccessful transplantation of European ideas onto non-European soil. The image of the electorate is said to be a substantiation of the concept of the people, which is central to the 'universalist imaginings of modernity', the idea of 'a community of equal human beings living in what Anderson calls homogenous empty time' (2007: 55). Gilmartin argues that viewing this concept more 'concretely', through the law and the vote, reveals an internal tension 'critical to the structuring of sovereignty' in electoral democracies (ibid.: 56). He describes this paradox in an image no less abstract than Anderson's invocation of empty homogeneous time:

> Only by standing apart from both state and society, could the people serve as sovereign. And yet, only by making their voices heard through elections, could the people rule.
>
> (Ibid.)

Significantly, in a later work, Anderson does deal with what Gilmartin describes as two concrete manifestations of the concept of the people, the law and the vote. His ideas on these topics suggest new directions for thinking about this concept through the numerical and temporal properties of elections. The relationship between the notion of popular sovereignty and practice of majoritarian democracy, between empty homogeneous time and electoral time, suggests not that one is more concrete than the other, or even that they are in contradiction, but that both are imbricated. A metaphysical concept runs through a normative framework.

In *The Spectre of Comparisons* (1998a), Anderson reiterates the importance of seriality in the modern imagining of collectivity, expressed as a distinction between two types of serialisation describing different kinds of political practice. One, 'figured by the newspaper', is 'unbound and unenumerated', and the other, by the census, 'bound and numerated' (ibid.: 40). In his description of 'electoralism', he consigns the practice of elections to the latter, describing the ballot as 'isomorphic' with the census in its anonymity and 'finite numerology' (ibid.: 42). For Anderson, the consequences of this for the development of collective subjectivities are twofold: proportional entitlement based on the total number of those entitled to vote leads to a reinforcement of ethnic politics on the basis of this entitlement. This starkly numerical mode of representation is said to both harden ascriptive identities and lend them political efficacy, as a result opening them up to contestation. But he also notes that as the notion of popular sovereignty spread and the suffrage widened, and the state acquired a welfare-and-development mission, voters began to influence the categories of census enumeration (ibid.: 39). This suggests the categories are in fact porous and the numbers multivalent.

On closer inspection, empty homogeneous time also seems to closely resemble what American political scientist Dennis F. Thompson describes as 'the special character of election time' encouraged by the practice of simultaneous voting (2004: 51):

> In an ordinary election, each voter acts as if he or she is voting at the same time as every other voter. No voter knows how others have voted until everyone has voted. No one can change a vote in response to how others have voted. And everyone votes with at least potential access to the same information.
>
> (Ibid.: 57)

Simultaneity is said to have a normative rationale with two different aspects. Firstly, to the extent that they take place simultaneously, elections allow for the expression of the will of a 'determinate majority', allowing the outcome to be seen as the result of a single decision rather than a series of decisions made by different majorities (ibid.: 58). This helps create 'a more coherent popular sovereign' (ibid.). Secondly, by ensuring that voters make their choice with equal access to information, it rests upon 'the democratic value of fairness' (ibid.). The origins of this ideal would probably be John Stuart Mill's 'one man, one vote; one vote, one value', but there are also echoes of Anderson's evocation of the unbound serialities and universal consciousness produced by the daily reading of a newspaper written in a single language describing events happening all over the world. Both activities are characterised by periodicity, simultaneity and finality.

As with Anderson's account of monolingual mass reading publics, most aspects of this description run contrary to actual practice in India. The 2014 Lok Sabha election was particularly long-drawn-out. The entire polling process, from announcement of the election dates on 5 March 2014 to the announcement of the election result on 16 May 2014, lasted sixty-three days. Polling itself took place in nine phases over thirty-six days, from 7 April to 12 May, and all of this was done in the interests of fairness. 'The integrity of elections is paramount', former election commissioner, SY Qureshi, was quoted saying in a BBC interview on the 2014 election: 'Since we've had phased elections, they have definitely become freer and fairer'.[3]

Perceptions of police partisanship necessitated the deployment of federal forces and led to 120,000 paramilitary troops being moved about the country to secure polling stations, counting centres and electronic voting machines. This was a costly and time-consuming process, especially in large states with fragile infrastructure and poor law and order such as UP. Whereas in Kerala and Gujarat polling occurred on a single day, in Uttar Pradesh it was carried out in six phases from 10 March to 12 May 2014. The polls swept across the state in a roughly west to east direction. This was the opposite direction to the 2009 polls and ended up favouring the BJP. Polling began in a part of the state where the BJP had made inroads through post-riot communal polarisation, and ended in the east, where there was a much-publicised contest between Modi and the Aam Aadmi Party candidate Arvind Kejriwal in the symbolically important seat of Varanasi.

[3] Soutik Biswas, 'Why does India's election take so long?', BBC News, 2 May 2014, http://www.bbc.co.uk/news/world-asia-india-27233843 (accessed 18 December 2014).

As I travelled across the state during the elections, visiting Muzaffarnagar, Lucknow and Varanasi in turn, I heard plenty of speculation about the outcome of elections in UP and other parts of India. Under the Model Code of Conduct, results of exit polls could not be released prior to 12 May, but opinion polls were not so tightly restricted and there was sometimes an overlap between the two forms.[4] Intimations of the results also came via party workers who moved across the state to canvass in different areas after polling had finished in their own constituencies. Reports of BJP successes in the earlier phases of the election and predictions of its success in subsequent ones certainly seemed to affect the morale of workers belonging to all parties. In a first-past-the-post system, where candidates win by a simple plurality of votes, these reports are also likely to have affected the choices of voters. Pre-election discussions conducted in party offices, on the streets and in private homes, centered on which parties were in front, the electoral preferences of different caste and religious groups, and therefore which candidate was a good bet in that particular seat. A fug of rumour and speculation shrouded these deliberations, which created talk of a Modi 'wave' and even a Modi 'tsunami' long before results were out.

The implications of all of this might seem to be grave. However, Thompson himself acknowledges that his description of what he describes as an 'ordinary election day' runs contrary to actual practice in the United States (2004: 57). The drawing up of electoral districts, scheduling of polls and loose separation between elections and other periods of political activity often violate this norm (ibid.: 51). Like Anderson, he is untroubled by these discrepancies. They are anomalies rather than counterevidence and result from an incorrect understanding of 'the special character of election time' (ibid.). The main difference in the two systems therefore seems to be one of inflection rather than category. Both are founded in the ideal of a level playing field of political competition; in the United States this is the starting point, in India, something yet to be achieved. Significant differences are encouraged by that 'yet', notably

4 ECI Guidelines for Publication and Dissemination of Results of Opinion Polls/Exit Polls (1998): http://eci.nic.in/archive/instruction/recent/media/pnxitpoll_FINAL.html. ECI Communication dated 16 April 2014 on 'Opinion Poll & Exit Poll – Distinction Between – Commission's advise [sic] regarding', observes that news channels have been broadcasting opinion polls on the basis of concluded polls, and requests them to desist from this practice: http://eci.nic.in/eci_main1/current/Exit%20Poll%20&%20Opinion%20Poll%2016_4_14.pdf (both accessed 21 September 2015).

the pedagogic function of a body such as the ECI, but the ideal remains the same. Thompson's description of the special character of election time in the US electoral process does not fundamentally differ from Gilmartin and Moog's description of the 'strong cyclical, temporal structure' of Indian election administration (2012: 146). The idea of election time as distinct from 'the 'normal' temporal realm of everyday politics', requiring 'special rules' so that 'the free voice of the individual can be heard', is familiar from democratic theory in both India and the United States. Ultimately, the rationale behind mundane details of election procedure in both countries rests upon the 'sacred' space-time of popular sovereignty.

Gilmartin makes this explicit in a subsequent essay, when he uses Carl Schmitt's assertion that all major modern theories of the state are secularised theological concepts as the first step in his own global history of voting, albeit acknowledging limits to its universal applicability given that it is 'deeply embedded within the specific history of European Christianity' (2012: 409). Whether it be the concept of kingship in premodern India, sovereignty in the Safavid and Mughal empires or the divine right of kings in Europe, the same underlying tension between worldly politics and a divine seat of authority is said to characterise them all. This tension is said to provide the background for the modern idea of popular sovereignty.

However, the paradoxical nature of sovereign power seems to be heightened when it is vested in the people rather than a king, especially when indirectly expressed in an anonymous voting process or located in impersonal institutions. In the eyes of Carl Schmitt, it transforms it completely:

> The sovereign, who in the deistic view of the world, even if conceived as residing outside the world, had remained the engineer of the great machine, has been radically pushed aside. The machine now runs by itself. The metaphysical proposition that God enunciates only general and not particular declarations of will governed the metaphysics of Leibniz and Nicolas Malebranche. The general will of Rousseau became identical with the will of the sovereign; but simultaneously the concept of the general also contained a quantitative determination with regard to its subject, which means that the people became the sovereign. The decisionistic and personalistic element in the concept of sovereignty was thus lost.
>
> (2005: 48)

Again we come across an image of a 'machine' of state, mindless in its operations ('the machine now runs by itself') and unspecific in its authority ('the people'). In the face of this loss, the only solution is 'decisionism', which in a post-monarchical age is best represented by 'dictatorship' (ibid.: 66) – Schmitt's theories also being embedded in his active support for National Socialism.[5] His constitutional theory is informed by a radically inegalitarian understanding of politics as based in the making of distinctions, in which even the democratic concept of equality, like all political concepts, is founded upon 'the quality of belonging to a *particular people*' (2008: 258, italics in the translation). According to Schmitt, the 'equality of everything "that bears a human face"' is incapable of providing a foundation for a state, a state form or a form of government, because it allows for no distinctive differentiations and delimitations (ibid.: 257).

For those who do not view democracy as a state form this would be a virtue. In ironic allusion to notions of both legality and sacrality, Rancière describes democracy as founded upon the seventh title to rule, referring to the seventh qualification to govern enumerated in Book III of Plato's *Laws*: '"the choice of God" or, otherwise said, the "drawing of lots"' (2010a: 31) – that is, based in the absence of *any* entitlement to govern. As a result, it is opposed to the principle that those who rule do so by virtue of some special qualification. For Rancière the '"figure of the people" is the enactment of the capacity that does not belong to any particular group … but rather to the capacity of everybody, of anybody' (quoted in O'Connor 2015). This power is irreducible to a state-sanctioned representative model precisely because it does not refer to 'a mass of people united by a homogenous will' (ibid.). Democracy is therefore distinct from, and not always congruous with, the practice of elections. In this anti-foundationalist account of democracy, human agency is both de-centred and made possible by non-human intervention – through technical mediation, by the intercession of 'divine' chance. These interventions have the salutary effect of preventing power from being the preserve of those who want it.

However, as discussed in previous chapters, oligarchic power can operate impersonally, through a lack of accountability ('the rule of nobody') and

5 See Richard Mehring's *Carl Schmitt: A Biography* (2014), which describes Schmitt's 'resistible rise' to the position of Crown Jurist for National Socialism.

processes of ideological misrecognition ('méconnaissance') as much as by direct rule and overt propaganda. Many aspects of the BJP's populist campaign in the 2014 Indian general election seemed to bear out political theorist Ernesto Laclau's criticism of the assumption that 'the 'people' as a historical actor will be constituted around a progressive identity' (2007: 246). Rather than embracing emancipatory politics, this identity may well take what he describes as a 'fascist' direction. 'To explore the system of alternatives', Laclau suggests, we need to examine the forms of representation which give rise to the impossible but necessary figure of 'the people' (ibid.: 247).

In the next sections, I pick up on this suggestion with reference to the history of elections in India, and the position of the constitutionally established and ostensibly politically independent ECI. I focus on its struggle with executive power and also to enforce its Code through officials who are subject to local influence. I argue that these strains result from the absence of a single principle of community legitimising the Indian nation-state and a multiplicity of possible identifications, which are porously bounded and therefore open to contestation. I look in particular at how the demos (the people), the void at the fulcrum of democracy, comes into definition through the calculus of numerical politics ('the numbers game') and the perlocutionary force of communal rhetoric ('social engineering'). I then describe how a concern with 'ethical' campaigning enabled the manipulation of these identities during the 2014 Indian general election.

The numbers game

The history of elections in Britain and India are of course very different, but a similar dynamic can be discerned in both: extension of the suffrage in a context of severe inequality inadvertently producing new political actors. In nineteenth-century Britain, the cautious nature of the 1832 Reform Act catalysed a militant reform movement, which radically transformed perceptions of politics. Limiting the vote to property owners and those who earned more than £10 per year excluded the mass of wage labourers, ensuring that any movement to extend the franchise would 'divide the country on class lines' (Thompson 1984: 5). The resulting assumption of an interest in politics by a 'hitherto non-political crowd' was the most alarming aspect of Chartism for conservative members of the upper classes (ibid.: 12).

There was obviously no movement equivalent to the Chartists in India, but the growth of the Congress Party was viewed with similar alarm by some members of the indigenous elite. In a speech delivered in Lucknow in 1887, Syed Ahmad Khan focused his attention on the demand of its National Conference that there should be elections to a section of the Viceroy of India's Council:

> And let us suppose first of all that we have universal suffrage, as in America, and that everybody, *chamars* [a Dalit caste] and all, have votes. And first suppose that all Mahomedan electors vote for a Mahomedan member and all Hindu electors for a Hindu member, and now count how many votes the Mahomedan member has and how many the Hindu. It is certain that the Hindu member will have four times as numerous. Therefore we can prove by mathematics that there will be four votes for the Hindu to every one vote for the Mahomedan. And now how can the Mahomedan guard his interests? It would be like a game of dice, in which one man had four dice and the other only one.
>
> (Khan 1888: 12)

Ahmad Khan's words expressed an age-old horror of democratic anarchy – horror that *everybody*, 'Chamars and all', should have the vote and decide the distribution of places. But he also spoke of a second scandal, that in a context such as India communal loyalties would load the dice, making the outcome of elections anything but arbitrary. His anxieties anticipate the ambiguous position of Muslims within majoritarian political forms such as nationalism and electoral democracy.

The colonial state responded to the push-pull of centrifugal and centripetal impulses with the Indian Councils Act of 1909, also known as the Morley-Minto reforms, which introduced elections to posts in Imperial and local legislative councils, but with distinct representative mechanisms for Muslims. Through reserved seats and separate electorates (seats in which Muslims would vote for Muslim candidates), they would be represented beyond their numerical proportion.[6] The Liberal government elected to office in 1906 provided the main impetus for the Councils Act, just as the Whig government

6 Separate electorates had been used in provincial governments since the 1880s, as following the 1857 rebellion, the British sought to include more Indians in government through 'carefully measured

had been for the 1832 Reform Act in Britain. But it did so in response to the unrest provoked by the partition of Bengal, not least the Congress-led *swadeshi* (home rule) movement, and also as a result of pressure from *ashraf* Muslims, those of 'noble' birth, who were uneasily watching these developments.

The historian Farzana Shaikh has argued that 'weightage' for *ashraf* Muslims was introduced to spare these 'gentlemen of the East' the humiliation of having to seek the consent of the peasantry and the proletariat before taking part in government deliberations (1991: 159). By these means, colonial officials were able to propound a view of representation as a 'descriptive activity', a matter of 'accurate correspondence between a representative and his constituency' and avert the possibility of 'representation as a substantive, creative activity' (ibid.: 138). But a novel basis for representation was opened up with the introduction of *non-territorial* representation. Representation in England and America may have been justified as a means for different economic and social interest groups to have a voice in government, but in practice it had been based on geographically defined communities.[7] This innovation was born of what Laclau describes as an ancient concern to balance '*arithmetical* equality' against '*geometrical* harmony', with the aim of preserving stability, which in practice exposes something 'essentially uncountable' that 'distorts the very principle of counting' (2007: 244–5, italics in the original). In his work on populist reason, he identifies this as 'the *demos* – the 'people' – which, while being a part, also claims to be the whole' (ibid.: 245). Indian Muslims were well placed to understand the risks of numerically and territorially based forms of political representation, and to seek new ways of forging sociopolitical community, which registered this paradox.

At the time this innovation was not seen as particularly radical. The more militant section of the Congress Party rejected the Morley-Minto reforms for falling short of the goal of independence and was particularly hostile to separate electorates, viewing them as a continuation of the divide-and-rule policy it believed had motivated the 1905 partition of Bengal. They were only

doses of nomination and election' (Bajpai 2011: 32), but these reforms were notable for introducing them at the national level.

7 Even when, in seventeenth-century England, special seats had been created in the House of Commons for 'gentlemen' who lacked the means or status to get a seat in the House of Lords, these were based on locality rather than class (Morgan 1989: 41–2).

adopted much later by members of Depressed Class groups, now known as Dalits or Scheduled Castes, when they advocated for separate electorates on a caste basis in their testimony to the Simon Commission between 1928 and 1929 (Zelliot 1972: 84). Pouring new wine into old bottles they attempted to fill out the colonial understanding of descriptive representation to allow for it to become a substantive, creative activity, to transform a mechanism designed to protect an elite minority into a means to allow for the fuller participation of Scheduled Castes in political life.

This demand was taken up and pushed through by Bhimrao Ramji Ambedkar (1892–1956), the Dalit leader who drafted the Constitution of India. Ambedkar had originally supported universal suffrage; when the British rejected this, he changed his position to promote separate electorates for members of the Depressed Class along the lines of those provided for Muslims. His stance hardened as a result of clashes with Gandhi on this issue, but his attitude to what Anderson describes as numerical politics remained ambivalent. In the early 1940s, Ambedkar had complained of how politics in India had 'become a matter of numbers' advantaging one community over another on a numerical basis, resulting in the census being 'deliberately cooked for securing political advantages which numbers give' (1943: 9). Members of the Scheduled Castes, or Untouchables as he called them, were 'quartered, cooked and served' at every decennial census as various caste and religious groups sought to incorporate them (ibid.). Although this might render the census unreliable, Ambedkar argued, it does not invalidate its findings: 'one cannot be far wrong if it was said that the present number of the Untouchables in British India is round about 60 million people' (ibid.: 10).

His reasons for accepting this figure are not hard to guess – 60 million was a lot. According to census findings, Scheduled Castes made up about a sixth of the then total population of British India, enough to make a difference to electoral arithmetic in areas such as Bengal and the Punjab where Hindus and Muslims were closely balanced. The category 'Scheduled Caste' was also a product of colonial processes of classification, enumeration and representation. Subordination predated British rule, but it was colonial taxonomy that transformed highly varied and widely dispersed groups into a unitary and trans-regional category, and electoral reform that gave it political clout. From what Anderson, in his criticism of diaspora identity politics, diagnoses as a lack of 'universal grounding' (1998a: 45) comes the potential of these categories to move and to galvanise. These shifts reflect the existence of multiple, changing and conflicting principles of community, which result from the entanglements of numerical politics. In this numbers game, the counting mechanism, those who operate it and those who are subject to its operations, all cross-influence and transform one another.

Social engineering

The very first rule of the Model Code of Conduct states that no party or candidate should engage in any activity that might encourage communal disharmony. Yet even though the 2014 election in Muzaffarnagar district was openly fought on the basis of communal polarisation resulting from riots that took place there the previous summer, only a single instance of inflammatory speech was reported during it. Amit Shah, head of the BJP's campaign in UP, was criticised by the Election Commission for describing the election as an opportunity to exact revenge for riots that had occurred the previous year, during meetings in Muzaffarnagar, Shamli and Bijnor districts, and temporarily barred from campaigning in UP under the Model Code of Conduct.

On one reading the election could be seen as another example of the perverse effects of normative frameworks that exceed real-world conditions, as a return of the primordial repressed, with electoral appeals on the basis of religion, region and caste. A theory of action in which certain inputs (words, formulas, images) produce definite outcomes underlay Shah's own '*badlaa*' (revenge) comments, in which a motor response was invoked and an emotional appeal was made. Most notoriously, during an address he made to an audience in Shamli district on 3 April 2014:

> The honour of Western Uttar Pradesh is in question. The time for taking revenge has now come. This is not the Mughal-era, when revenge would be taken with swords and arrows. The 2014 election is facing [us]. By pressing a button [on an electronic voting machine] you can take revenge.[8]

[8] From the ECI notification against Shah dated 7 April 2014, quotes from his Hindi speech translated by me. http://eci.nic.in/eci_main1/current/Notice_07042014.pdf (accessed 23 September 2015).

Wielding a sword, shooting an arrow and casting a vote were here presented as equivalent activities. The weapon changed according to the political system prevailing at the time, democracy as opposed to feudalism, but the cause and outcome sought remained the same: to avenge an outrage against female honour and therefore that of the whole community.

However, it is significant that the age of swords and arrows was said to be over, confined to the Muslim past – the 'Mughal-era'. The electronic voting machine was proposed as an appropriately modern means for Hindus to take revenge. As well as playing upon Hindu nationalist notions of Muslims as barbaric, his words referenced a modern understanding of popular sovereignty as expressed through the reference to an electoral mechanism. This anonymous and quantitively determined sovereign power bore little resemblance to Schmitt's account of the 'personalistic' and 'decisionistic' quality of monarchical rule. In practice, the BJP made use of deception and delay rather than direct action and transparent speech during the UP phase of the 2014 general election – from disseminating 'fake news' to profiting from various oversights by the regional government and ECI.

Far from reflecting long-standing ethnic tensions, these riots were also seemingly without precedent in this part of rural and semi-rural western Uttar Pradesh. Close cooperation between the different ethnicities had long been encouraged by agricultural labour and organisations such as the Communist Party and the Bharatiya Kisan Union.[9] Locals that I spoke to mentioned disturbances in Muzaffarnagar town during emergency-era sterilisation drives, anti-Sikh violence after the assassination of Indira Gandhi in 1984, and

The Mughal reference seems to have been tailored for the Jat *mahasabha* that he was addressing. In popular histories, Jats are depicted as bravely resisting Mughal invasions.

9 In his ethnography of this farmer's union, Dipankar Gupta describes a striking example of modern forms of political action deploying traditional symbols, which offers an instructive contrast to the BJP's election campaign in 2014. In 1989, the farmer's union had led an agitation to recover the body of a young Muslim woman, Nayima, believed to have been abducted and murdered with the connivance of local police officers (1997: 82–3). When her body was eventually recovered, her corpse was draped in the union flag and carried to an offshoot of the river Ganges by Hindu union members. The incident made national news and was still well-remembered in the area in 2014. Both the 'Nayima lao' (bring back Nayima) protests and Amit Shah's '*badlaa*' speech were concerned with female and community honour. The earlier protests had mobilised wide-ranging support against state corruption. In the hands of a political party seeking power on a Hindu nationalist platform, these same concerns were deployed to quite different, divisive ends.

communal tension in the 1980s and 1990s during the campaign to construct the Ram temple, but nothing on the scale of the riots of 2013. At least 51,000 people were displaced over the course of them and 48 killed according to the district administration.[10]

The cause of the riots was disputed, but the most widespread accounts centred on the harassment of a young woman from one community by a youth from another. Shahnawaz, a Muslim from the village of Kawal, had reportedly been harassing Ritu, a Hindu belonging to the Jat caste, from the neighbouring village of Malikpura. A confrontation between Shahnawaz and the brother and cousin of this woman, Sachin and Gaurav, eventually resulted in the deaths of all three men. Prior to these events communal tensions had been stoked by talk of 'love-jihad', an alleged Muslim conspiracy to marry and convert Hindu women, which was somehow conflated with rapes that had recently taken place. The BJP and organisations associated with it were active in publicising this so-called conspiracy and protesting against these crimes.[11]

Amit Shah's words of revenge and violence also carried extra force because of his close relationship with Narendra Modi, Chief Minister of Gujarat during the 2002 anti-Muslim pogrom in that state. Shah was entrusted with overseeing Modi's defence in cases relating to the 2002 massacres and 21 encounter killings (extrajudicial killings by police or armed forces) that occurred between 2003 and 2006. Shah himself was arrested in July 2010 for his involvement in an encounter case and charged with three counts of murder. Opponents of the BJP therefore viewed Shah's appointment to head of the BJP's election campaign in Uttar Pradesh on 12 June 2013 with apprehension. Alongside the announcement that Narendra Modi would be contesting from Varanasi, it indicated that the BJP would be making a concerted effort to win the key state of Uttar Pradesh.

These fears were borne out in the results of the 2014 elections. Within a year of Shah's appointment, the BJP's ailing party organisation had revived and its declining vote share reversed to the tune of seventy-one out of eighty seats

10 From an interview with Kaushal Raj Sharma, Muzaffarnagar District Magistrate, 31 April 2014. NGOs and Samajwadi Party workers claimed that twice as many people had been displaced.

11 The Vishwa Hindu Parishad, a Hindu nationalist organisation with close ties to the BJP, had apparently been campaigning against 'love-Jihad' in the surrounding towns and villages for a year before the incident. Sreenivasan Jain, 'The Muzaffarnagar Model'. *NDTV*, 4 September 2014, http://www.ndtv.com/article/opinion/the-muzaffarnagar-model-586892 (accessed 5 January 2015).

in UP, a big improvement on its performance in the 2009 polls (ten seats and fourth place). Shah's electioneering skills were cited as reasons for the success of the campaign, but his expertise in poll booth management was also part of a wider BJP policy of 'social engineering'. The term is associated with the rise of the Bahujan Samaj Party (BSP), a party representing the interests of Dalits and other socio-economically disadvantaged groups, which had come to power in the state of Uttar Pradesh through cross-caste and religious combinations. But the term has also been used to describe a BJP policy dating back to the late 1990s of extending the scope of its membership beyond its traditional upper-caste north Indian constituency. This involved making incursions into other parts of India, electoral alliances with the BSP, and also inclusion of a group identified as Other Backward Class (OBC) in the 1980 Mandal Commission report on extension of caste-based reservations. This amorphous category, encompassing both the 'traditional' category of caste and the 'modern' one of class, and as much as half the population of India, would be impossible for any political party with national ambitions to ignore.[12]

By the 2014 Lok Sabha election, the BJP had overcome its previous opposition to reservations to such an extent that it was using Modi's OBC status for electoral purposes. This was a steady undercurrent of its campaign, in which he was pointedly contrasted to the Congress prime ministerial candidate, *yuvaraj* (young prince) Rahul Gandhi. The success of this tactic, or at least the irritation it caused Congress, was reflected in its attempts to question his caste status. Modi was a fake OBC, party spokesmen claimed. He in fact belonged to a prosperous, upper-caste, business community and had abused his position as Chief Minister to shoehorn this caste into the OBC category upon assuming office.[13]

[12] See 'OBC count: 52 or 41%?', *The Times of India*, 1 November 2006: http://timesofindia.indiatimes.com/india/OBc-count-52-or-41/articleshow/263918.cms (accessed 10 September 2015). The Mandal Commission Report had reported that OBCs made up 52 per cent of the population of India. The National Sample Survey Organisation in 2006 calculated this as 41 per cent, a lower percentage even though total numbers of OBCs had increased by 6.5 per cent.

[13] This prompted the Gujarat government to release a two-decade old notification, proving that OBC status had been conferred on the Modi-Ghanchi caste before Modi had become elected CM: 'Narendra Modi belongs to Modh-Ghanchi caste, which was added to OBCs categories in 1994, says Gujarat government' in *DNA*, 9 May 2014: http://www.dnaindia.com/india/report-narendra-modi-belongs-to-modh-ghanchi-caste-which-was-added-to-obcs-categories-in-1994-says-gujarat-government-1986389 (accessed 25 October 2014).

Beyond discussion of Modi's caste, BJP overtures to OBC voters included criticism of a Congress proposal to extend reservations to religious minorities within the OBC category. This extension was announced on December 2011, in what was seen as a bid to win Muslim votes in upcoming assembly elections, and soon became known as the Muslim quota even though it referred to religious minorities generally.[14] The sub-quota proposal was struck down by the Andhra Pradesh High Court in June 2012 on the basis that reservations on religious grounds are unconstitutional.[15] The Congress government appealed the decision in the Supreme Court, and the case was ongoing at the time of the 2014 Lok Sabha election, during which opposition to the measure formed a key part of the BJP's 'social engineering' strategy in UP. In opposing the sub-quota, the BJP was able to draw upon Hindu anger at Muslim 'appeasement' without explicitly referring to particular communities.

Calls for voters, implicitly Hindu, to forget their caste differences and unify in supporting the BJP contained a strong anti-Muslim subtext. This was very close to the surface during elections in western UP, where there was resentment of compensation packages for Muslim riot victims and what was perceived to have been unjust treatment of Hindus who had been implicated in the violence. Politicians from all parties also made incendiary speeches and distributed images of the killings during large public meetings. But they again did so most effectively by indirect means – through the circuitous networks of social media, which allowed them to both reach a wide audience and escape censure.

Sangeet Som, a BJP local member of the legislative assembly from the western UP constituency of Sardhana, shared what purported to be a video of the murders of Sachin and Gaurav on his Facebook page. The clip in fact depicted the mob killing of two brothers in Sialkot, Pakistan, in August 2010. By the time the video had been blocked by police and Som booked under the National Security Act, it had been widely viewed and continued to circulate via the mobile phone application, WhatsApp.[16] BlackBerry phones had been

14 'Minorities 4.5% sub-quota as good as dead?' *The Times of India*, 28 May 2014: http://timesofindia.indiatimes.com/india/Minorities-4-5-sub-quota-as-good-as-dead/articleshow/35644660.cms (accessed 1 November 2014).

15 Non-Hindus are included in the existing OBC lists, but on account of their caste status rather than religion. The Central list of OBCs for UP includes Muslim subsets of the mostly Hindu Teli and Kayastha castes.

16 See Satendra Kumar's discussion of the expansion in internet use in rural western UP facilitated by cheap mobile phones and internet (2018).

banned by the Indian government because of the role they had played in coordinating the 2008 Mumbai terror attacks.[17] No such restrictions had been imposed on the far more ubiquitous WhatsApp, whose use of end-to-end encryption has also been accused of threatening national security.[18] Neither the image nor its circulation could directly be attributed to Som or indeed to anyone. The case against him was eventually closed in 2021 due to lack of evidence, and Facebook refused to supply the Indian Central Bureau of Evidence with the names of those who had originally uploaded the video onto social media.[19]

The administration, and by extension the ruling Samajwadi Party, was also criticised for its mishandling of the violence – but for passivity and the ill effects of its policies rather than purposeful action. Perceived derelictions included the transfer of the Superintendent of Police and District Magistrate at the beginning of the riots, creating an administrative vacuum; failure to prevent and control the large public meetings that triggered them, despite the fact that a curfew had officially been declared; and a policy of offering compensation to the displaced on condition that they not return to their original homes. Because most of those who had fled were Muslim, this condition was particularly controversial, and it was quashed in a Supreme Court judgment issued just before the election.

These failings were rumoured to have resulted from more than incompetence, from a compact between the BJP and SP. Both parties stood to benefit from Hindu–Muslim polarisation. Dividing the electorate between themselves on religious lines would bring electoral dividends in a region characterised by cross-caste and religious voting patterns. Specifically, the combination of Muslim and Dalit votes that had elected a Muslim BSP MP in Muzaffarnagar

17 This ban was lifted in 2013 after BlackBerry agreed to let the Indian government intercept data sent over BlackBerry devices. See 'BlackBerry gives Indian government ability to intercept messages' in *Wired*, 11 July 2013: https://www.wired.co.uk/article/blackberry-india (accessed 21 October 2021).

18 See 'Supreme Court rejects PIL for WhatsApp ban, but encryption debate is just beginning' in *The Indian Express*, 21 September 2021: https://indianexpress.com/article/technology/tech-news-technology/supreme-court-rejects-pil-for-whatsapp-ban-but-encryption-debate-is-just-beginning-2885121/ (accessed 21 October 2021).

19 See 'Court accepts SIT closure report against BJP's Sangeet Som in 2012 Muzaffarnagar riots case', *ThePrint*, 9 March 2021: https://theprint.in/judiciary/court-accepts-sit-closure-report-against-bjps-sangeet-som-in-2013-muzaffarnagar-riots-case/618270/ (accessed 21 September 2021). The case was also closed because the case inspector, Subhodh Kumar, had been killed during mob violence following rumours of illegal cow slaughter in Bulandshahr district in 2018.

district. Talk of a split Dalit vote bank and Muslim disaffection from the BSP seemed intended to both weaken the standing of that party and allow the BJP to appeal to lower caste voters.[20] By these means, the BJP was able to shake off its reputation as the 'Brahmin party' and win both Muzaffarnagar constituency and the majority of seats across Uttar Pradesh, a state with one of the highest proportions of Scheduled Caste voters in India. The BJP also won all seventeen seats reserved for Scheduled Caste candidates in UP. An electoral mechanism designed to protect Muslims and Dalits from majoritarian rule was successfully captured by a Hindu nationalist party. Meanwhile, the Bahujan Samaj Party, which claimed to represent this constituency and Ambedkar's legacy, failed to win a single seat anywhere in India.[21]

The results were interpreted by critics of the BJP as evidence of the party's manipulation of identity politics and the first-past-the-post electoral system.[22] But there was no direct and discrete relationship between means and ends at work in this outcome. A tangle of historically embedded instrumentalities and logics led to this decisive result. Both the contours of these identities and the BJP's appeals to them had been shaped by new forms of electoral representation and media technology, many of which predated the BJP. The history of categorisations such as Dalit and OBC also attest to how the weakness of an identification can lend it political strength. Such identities can be all the more powerful because they lack taxonomical precision, do not invariably evoke a positive sense of belonging, which does not preclude them from ever doing so. The post-riot elections in UP highlight how the most effective appeals to these identities can be made by indirect means, through slurs and insinuations and mediated rumour.

[20] Given the pervasiveness of these rumours of Muslim electoral disaffection from the BSP, it is worth noting that SP did not do much better in the 2014 polls than it had in 2009. The party once again came in third place and only increased its vote share by 0.20 per cent (in 2009, the SP had won 14.32 per cent of the vote, and in 2014, 14.52 per cent). The main difference was massively increased support for the BJP, who had not even fielded a candidate in 2009 and won in 2014 with a 59 per cent vote share to BSP's 22.78 per cent.

[21] This was despite the BSP winning 19.6 per cent of total votes in UP and coming third nationally with a vote share of 4.1 per cent. See the breakdown of statistics demonstrating SC support for the BJP in Prabhu Mallikarjunan 'What Have the Reserved Constituencies Voted For?', *india together*, 21 July 2014: http://indiatogether.org/bjp-sweep-in-scheduled-caste-and-tribes-reserved-constituencies-2014-government (accessed 22 December 2014).

[22] See a more skeptical view on SC support for BJP and criticism of the effects of first-past-the-post in Nirmalangshu Mukherji, 'A Stolen Verdict', *Kafila*, 23 May 2014, http://kafila.org/2014/05/23/a-stolen-verdict-nirmalangshu-mukherji/ (accessed 27 February 2014).

The ethics of electoral regulation

During the UP phase of the 2014 elections, instrumentalisation of ascriptive identities was also made possible by bureaucratic blindness to less easily quantified infringements – what was said and done by candidates and their supporters in plain sight of election observers. Amit Shah's words only came to the attention of the Election Commission because of an article filed by the journalist Neha Dixit for an Indian news website.[23] The report was picked up by national print and electronic media and eventually reached the attention of the ECI itself, which requested that election officers in the relevant districts pass on video recordings of the speeches. Dixit herself confirmed that in all her time covering the elections in UP, she had never seen anyone reprimanded for provocative speech.[24] Monitoring teams seemed more concerned with measuring the decibels emanating from loudspeakers than moderating the words coming out of the mouths of politicians.

All of this encouraged speculation about the role of political influence in allowing obvious infringements of the Model Code. However, immediate pressure from political parties and the government was combined with a historically derived understanding of the role of the ECI and its Code. This made influence easy to intuit but hard to locate. Sensing that the BJP were likely to win in Muzaffarnagar and being aware that a Samajwadi Party government would remain in power in UP until at least 2017, local election officers may well have chosen the path of least resistance. But I also heard much grumbling in the Muzaffarnagar BJP office about the pedantic requirements and unsympathetic attitude of the local District Magistrate, who was also the constituency's Election Officer. In this country there are '3 Ms', an RSS worker volunteering there informed me, the DM, the CM and the PM. The DM was subject to the influence of the other two, neither of whom were BJP.

Nevertheless, when I asked the local DM himself why he had not forwarded the videotapes of Shah's speech to the ECI, he responded that he and his team 'did not perceive any violation' in them.[25] Referring to the riots was

[23] Neha Dixit, 'This Election Is a Fight for Honour and Revenge, Amit Shah Tells Jat Audience in Riot Areas', *Scroll*, 4 April 2014, http://scroll.in/article/660535/This-election-is-a-fight-for-honour-and-revenge,-Amit-Shah-tells-Jat-audience-in-riot-areas (accessed 5 January 2015).

[24] From email correspondence with Neha Dixit on 24 December 2014.

[25] Interview with Kaushal Raj Sharma, Muzaffarnagar, 3 May 2014.

not a violation in itself, he claimed. The 'sentiment it creates in the people' and 'the vote appeal it creates through caste and community bias' might be, but in assessing this, 'there is a very thin line that we have to observe, and there comes the experience and there comes basically the judgment'. This line might be hard for an outsider to judge because, in Muzaffarnagar, 'the way of talking of the people, it's [a] little bit aggressive in nature'. But if one looks at the context of the entire speech, at its after-effects, if it in fact contains no communal charge, as evidenced by there being no law-and-order disturbances after it has been given, then it is possible to say that there has not been any violation. This consequentialist understanding of communication, in which it was judged by its immediate outcomes, absolved the election office of any responsibility for moderating politicians' words. No notices for inflammatory speech were issued at the instigation of the DM's office.

This lack of oversight allowed the election to be openly fought on the basis of post-riot communal polarisation. Ambiguous appeals to ascriptive identity and seeming bureaucratic blindness to them were in evidence at the grassroots level soon after Amit Shah's visit. The riots figured large in a tour of rural parts of Khatauli by the BJP candidate on 5 April 2014. The tour was partly a warm-up event for a rally held in Khatauli town the following day, during which the father of Gaurav, one of the Jat youths whose murder was their ostensible cause, was a guest speaker. Khatauli had been badly affected by the violence and fell within the electoral boundaries of Muzaffarnagar.

Sanjeev Baliyan, the BJP candidate for Muzaffarnagar, a vet from a prominent Jat Hindu family, was new to party politics. He seemed to have been selected as an antipode to the sitting BSP MP, Kadir Rana. Rana belonged to a wealthy, politically well-connected Muslim family. His CV included an extensive criminal record (five criminal cases, including charges for murder, attempted murder and criminal intimidation); recorded assets of Rs. 135,202,262; and political experience in both the Samajwadi Party and the Rashtriya Lok Dal prior to joining the Bahujan Samaj Party in 2009.[26] Both candidates had been involved in the riots, and in selecting them, their parties played upon communal divisions. The BJP was seeking to attract Hindu voters across castes

[26] Information from the page on Kadir Rana compiled by the Association for Democratic Reform: http://myneta.info/ls2014/candidate.php?candidate_id=226 (19 February 2014).

and classes, the BSP, to reassure Muslims. Baliyan had been arrested and briefly imprisoned after a *mahapanchayat* (great village assembly) organised by a Jat-dominated farmer's union on the theme of *bahu, beti bachao* (save our daughters-in-law and daughters), which took place the day after the riots broke out. Rana had been charged for inciting violence during a speech to a gathering outside a mosque in Muzaffarnagar city after Friday prayers on 30 August 2013.

The riots were an open and carefully modulated feature of speeches Baliyan delivered to a selection of villages during his tour of Khatauli. In a village with, I was told by BJP volunteers, a large 'Harijan' (Dalit) population, a tightly packed crowd gathered around a tree to hear him talk about the importance of *man samman* (respect), without which a man would be unable to live although he might be able to go some days without food and water. This segued into talk of the necessity for *dharam-yuddh* (religious war), in the context of Hindus, including some of our Harijan brothers, being jailed after the riots on false charges. His words closely resembled those uttered by Shah in his speech to a Jat *mahasabha* two days earlier, although the themes of honour and respect may have had a different meaning for this audience. The speech was harsher in tone than that delivered in the Gujjar caste locality we had just left, where other women had been present and there had been signs of relative prosperity (expensive farm machinery, well maintained roads and houses).

I then accompanied the BJP convoy to a village with a mixed population, where Muslim families watched the proceedings from the back of the square and the rooftops of surrounding buildings. Here Baliyan spoke of how the BJP would bring about communal harmony and peace. Once in power it would be much more vigilant than the SP government in preventing riots from happening, he assured the audience. The District Magistrate of Muzaffarnagar insisted that a monitoring team had been filming and recording the speeches, but I saw no evidence of this.[27] Although police were present throughout, they did not intervene until the end of a long day of campaigning when they prevented the convoy of twenty-one SUVs from driving into a built-up urban area after dark.[28] The candidate and a small group of his supporters walked to

27 Interview with Kaushal Raj Sharma, Muzaffarnagar, 5 May 2014.

28 On the day I accompanied them, the convoy visited twenty-one villages, but I was told the candidate could visit up to forty villages a day because of good communications in this part of western UP.

a gathering in a side street in Jansath instead. From conversations with police officers at this event and others, I got the impression they saw their role as limited to protecting people and property.

The Muzaffarnagar Election Office's interpretation of the Code might seem like a deviation from the ECI's understanding of it, according to which the mere presence of an outsized election poster was enough to exert 'undue influence' upon a voter. But, in their own way, both referenced the ideal of a level playing field of political competition over which the ECI and its officers presided as umpire and arbiter, alongside a preoccupation with decorum in public speech focused on balance rather than content. There is 'some ethics involved in democracy', the District Magistrate of Muzaffarnagar explained to me.[29] In order to do our duty to the nation and preserve 'clean democracy', we should avoid 'tilting towards one candidate' thereby 'disfavouring' another. Given the wider context, this focus on decorum and balance seemed counterproductive, to enable all kinds of 'dirty' politics, and to be a holdover from more heroic periods in the ECI's history.

The Election Commission's reputation was established by its success in administering the first Indian general election in 1951–2 and augmented by the role it had played during the 1977 election.[30] The Congress Party's surprise defeat in the latter seemed to prove that they had been free and fair. Afterwards, in 1979, the ECI added an extra section to the Code, curtailing the power of the ruling party to use state resources for electioneering purposes. Building on a post-emergency vision of the Election Commission as protector of the voice of the people, the Code was further strengthened following the appointment of T.N. Seshan as Chief Election Commissioner in 1990, who introduced new restrictions on campaign expenditure and publicity. His efforts often involved him in direct confrontations with the government, politicians and the press. The Model Code of Conduct was an important weapon in these battles against what he described as the scourge of 'the three Ms', 'Minister-Power, Muscle-Power and Money-Power' (Seshan 1995: 264).

These mini rallies, usually lasting no more than fifteen minutes, were made possible by a combination of physical infrastructure and telecommunications, by metalled roads and mobile phones.

29 Interview with Kaushal Raj Sharma, 31 March 2014.

30 For an account of the immense and complex nature of the task of administering the first election, see Shani (2018).

Ironically these rules designed to curb the misuse of power and resources advantaged a large and well-financed party during the 2014 general election. The BJP benefited from the circumscribed view of communication and inability to span the different layers of its campaign, encouraged by the ECI's narrow focus on expenses. At the local level, an unconcern with unquantifiable offences allowed the election in Muzaffarnagar district to take on a communal tone, which worked to the benefit of the BJP candidate. Nationally, the Model Code favoured a national, non-incumbent party above the ruling Congress, smaller and regional parties.

Whilst individual candidate's expenses were monitored and limited to Rs. 5.4 million or Rs. 7 million during these polls, general party expenses were self-reported and unrestricted. By this expedient the BJP was able to circumvent restrictions on candidate's expenses, resulting in ECl statistics that suggested Modi had spent less on his election campaign in Varanasi than the two main opposition candidates, Arvind Kejriwal (Aam Aadmi Party) and Ajay Rai (Congress). This calculation, which derived from how much money was spent in the district during the official campaign period, overlooked the fact that it began much earlier than the given start date and was not confined to Varanasi. Modi's nomination was only confirmed on 15 March 2014 but rumours that he would stand from there were in circulation from August 2013 onwards. Modi's prominence in the BJP election campaigns also made it hard to distinguish its various layers. Was he campaigning for the BJP nationally through his public appearances? For whichever BJP candidate he was supporting in his capacity as BJP leader? For himself as prime ministerial candidate? As an MP contesting seats in both Gujarat and UP? Set against the context of the BJP's well-resourced and well-organised nationwide campaign, focused on its 'star campaigner', there seemed something irrational in the idea that a level-playing field could be maintained through the avoidance of excessive expenditure by individual candidates in a single district.

This impression was enhanced by the singular way in which these rules were enforced. Despite the importance of social media in the election campaigns, the Muzaffarnagar election office's media monitoring practices were mostly concerned with print. The DM told me that although the focus of their attention was newspapers, they did monitor Facebook accounts and were aware of mobile phones. Two notices had been issued to candidates who had used lists of the mobile phone numbers of voters provided by private companies to send pre-recorded messages.[31] Again the emphasis was on the expense involved. The content of the messages and the way in which these phone numbers had been obtained was not a concern.

Every morning, the media monitoring team in the Muzaffarnagar election office would go through the local press and editions of national papers, whilst keeping an eye on two small television sets positioned at opposite ends of the room. When they detected an article that looked like 'paid news' (party propaganda presented as a news item), they would calculate how much it cost to purchase and the amount would then be deducted from candidates' expenses. Occasionally they would do the same when they detected a 'paid' item on local television. The form they were required to fill out also contained a section on radio, but I was told that this was 'pro forma'. They did not bother to monitor radio because hardly anyone listened to it. The entire exercise seemed to be pro forma given that Indian newspapers were carrying front-page advertisements for Narendra Modi throughout this period, to say nothing of the omnipresence of the BJP on electronic media. This response also overlooked the role of the Model Code of Conduct itself in encouraging these violations. Government adverts are restricted whilst the Code is in force, the idea being that they could become propaganda for the party in power. As discussed in the first chapter, these ads are the mainstay of the vernacular press. Restricting them leaves newspapers even more susceptible to the placement of paid news by political parties.

The BJP was rumoured to have spent 50 billion rupees on advertising alone during the 2014 Indian general election, not far behind the $1 billion (or 60 billion rupees) the Democrats spent on the United States presidential election in 2012.[32] After some prodding by the ECI, in January 2015 the BJP eventually declared a total election expenditure of Rs. 714,28,57,813, but this self-reported and un-itemised figure was met with great scepticism.[33] When

31 Interview with Kaushal Raj Sharma, Muzaffarnagar, 31 March 2014.

32 Siddharth Varadarajan, 'The Best Democracy That Money Can Buy', *Economic Times*, 30 April 2014,https://svaradarajan.com/2014/04/30/the-best-democracy-that-money-can-buy/ (accessed 27 February 2014).

33 Nivedita Menon pointed out the anomalies in an article criticising exemption of the BJP from proposed restrictions on foreign funding for NGOs: 'A Hindustan Times premium front page advertisement costs Rs 3950 PER SQUARE CENTIMETER. How many advertisements like this one did you see? In how many newspapers? Over how many days?' Nivedita Menon, 'When Are

I asked the DM of Muzaffarnagar about the role of black money in the election, his understanding of it seemed to be limited to the illegal distribution of arms, liquor and cash.[34] He claimed eighteen flying squads and forty static surveillance teams were sufficient to prevent circulation of these items. Transactions harder to track than the apocryphal chicken and moonshine used to buy votes seemed to evade his attention as a local election officer.

The scandal of democracy

In practice, the ECI and its Code seem to have been most effective when able to function as a means to obstruct oligarchy rather than as a bureaucratic application of electoral ethics, the 1977 election being perhaps the best example of this. At such moments, an anarchic principle has guided a regulatory instrument. The ECI's vaunted solidity of structure and lofty position mean it is paradoxically well placed to protect the principle of democratic anarchy: the 'scandalous' absence of any single principle of community legitimising the actions of those who govern (Rancière 2006b: 297). The ECI has legitimacy precisely because it is set apart from the principal institutions of state – situated beyond the law and above politics. The Model Code can be effective precisely because it has extra-legal force, is non-statutory and administered by an un-elected body. This allows the ECI to make quick judgments and take swift action in response to violations of its Code, without engaging in lengthy legal procedures.

But this is obviously not invariably the case. During the 2014 election, the extra-legal instruments of a non-state body both worked to insidious effect and were ineffective. Far from maintaining a level playing field, the ECI's timing of the polls, regulation of expenditure and monitoring of public speech all advantaged a well-resourced national party.[35] Subsequent elections, with the BJP in power at the centre, have seen increasingly crude use of communal

Foreign Funds Okay? A Guide for the Perplexed', *Kafila*, 13 June 2014: http://kafila.org/2014/06/13/when-are-foreign-funds-okay-a-guide-for-the-perplexed/ (accessed 22 February 2014).

34 Interview with Kaushal Raj Sharma, Muzaffarnagar, 31 March 2014.

35 See Mohsin Alam Bhat's description of how the ECI's non-legal modalities of architecture, nudge and notice-based regulations allows it to have both a pervasive and insidious effect (Bhat 2021).

rhetoric and a weak response from both the ECI and the courts.[36] For critics of the BJP, this was a sign that the ECI had been co-opted by the party, meaning that it was now almost 'unthinkable' for its senior leaders to be punished for making divisive appeals to religious identities in an election campaign.[37] Co-optation of the ECI was a particularly efficient means for the BJP to install ethnic democracy by neutralising public institutions and 'Hinduizing' public space, whilst holding periodic elections for the sake of legitimacy (Jaffrelot 2021).[38] In such a context, calls to strengthen a single institution can arguably only go so far.

Historically, factors beyond the immediate electoral environment and moment seem to have played a decisive role in the direction taken by the ECI and Indian democracy. The ECI seems to have been particularly effective when the ruling party has been fractured or discredited and when it has worked alongside another force: a sociopolitical movement, as during the emergency, or the media. Former Election Commissioner, James Michael Lyngdoh, has vividly described leading a group of journalists into relief camps in Gujarat in 2002, following the anti-Muslim pogroms that took place that year, and of how

[36] See Mohsin Alam Bhat's discussion of the ECI's 'double standards' in moderating provocative speech in the 2019 election, 'ECI Is Not Up to the Task of Sanitising a Chaotic Electoral Process', 4 June 2019, *The Wire*: https://thewire.in/politics/election-commission-model-code-hate-speech-religion (18 May 2024). During the 2024 elections, Modi was reported to have referred to Muslims as 'infiltrators', compared the Indian National Congress to the Muslim League and accused Congress of seeking to loot wealth from Hindus and redistribute it amongst Muslims. 'Narendra Modi increases anti-Muslim rhetoric in India election campaign', 29 April 2024, *The Financial Times*: https://www.ft.com/content/43a6d2b1-ccb2-4f68-b6ab-fe634e6ef546 (accessed 18 May 2024). This language exceeded even his previous insinuations about Congress's anti-Hindu bias during the 2019 general elections, for which he had been exonerated by the ECI. The ECI issued a notice to the BJP president for Modi's comments during the 2024 polls but did not rebuke him directly. This response was strongly criticised by the BJP's opponents, who claimed it revealed that the Model Code of Conduct was now the 'Modi Code'. 'Model Code of Conduct turned into 'Modi code of conduct' under BJP rule: Mamata', 7 May 2024, *The Deccan Herald*: https://www.deccanherald.com/elections/india/lok-sabha-elections-2024-model-code-of-conduct-turned-into-modi-code-of-conduct-under-bjp-rule-mamata-3011874 (accessed 18 May 2024).

[37] Christoph Jaffrelot, 'India: democracy in name only?', April 2024, *Le Monde Diplomatique*: https://mondediplo.com/2024/04/03india (18 May 2024).

[38] This co-optation is said to have been abetted by changes to the process for selecting the Election Commissioner under the terms of the Chief Election Commissioner and Other Election Commissioners (Appointment, Conditions of Service and Term of Office) Bill, 2023. This was controversial for giving overall control of the selection process to the executive and provoked a walkout by opposition parties when it was passed in the Rajya Sabha (upper house). See 'Controversial bill on appointments to Election Commission clears Lok Sabha', 21 December 2023, *India Today*: https://www.indiatoday.in/india/story/bill-to-regulate-appointment-of-chief-election-commissioner-other-top-officials-passed-in-lok-sabha-2478786-2023-12-21 (accessed 20 May 2024).

the combination of ECI officials and press rendered vocal those who had been 'dumbed down' by fear (2004: 184). In response to accusations that he had been complicit in the violence, Narendra Modi had dissolved the Gujarat legislative assembly and initiated the process for an early election. Lyngdoh's decision to disallow polls so soon after the pogroms provoked Modi to condemn what he described as Lyngdoh's 'fatwa' against the election, in slurring reference to Lyngdoh's non-Hindu ethnicity.[39]

Lyngdoh himself claimed it had restored trust in the electoral process amongst politicians from all parties in Kashmir, where elections were being held in the same year (2004: 205). As self-aggrandising as his words may have been, they expressed a nuanced understanding of the electoral field, one which was both sensitive to a particular context and to how news of these elections might play out elsewhere.[40] Lyngdoh's cancellation of the elections could be seen as a truly democratic act in its refusal to shore-up BJP rule. In this way it was similar in effect, if not design, to the role the ECI had played in encouraging Indians to vote without fear during the 1977 elections. Both proceeded from a this-worldly and diachronic perspective on the field of political competition rather than blind faith in an administrative process. In refusing to hold elections and by affirming voter anonymity, they expressed a distinctive view of electoral democracy; one which understood that it is not limited to the simple act of casting a ballot, and that a vote's meaning is not exhausted by its function in this procedure.

During such moments in the ECI's history it is possible to discern an alternative basis for electoral regulation. Rather than sacralising the electoral process, this would understand representation as an aesthetic and technopolitical act. Instead of being primarily concerned with balance and decorum, legislation would be keyed to animating dissensual modes of

[39] 'Some journalists asked me recently, "Has James Michael Lyngdoh come from Italy?"', *Outlook*, 30 September 2002:http://www.outlookindia.com/article/some-journalists-asked-me-recently-has-james-michael-lyngdoh-come-from-italy/217399 (accessed 21 September 2015). The reference to a *fatwa* when speaking of a Christian indicates the extent to which Muslims loom large in the imagination of Hindu nationalists.

[40] Narendra Modi would go on to contest and win legislative assembly elections in Gujarat later that year. But Lyngdoh's actions continue to be cited as an inspiring example of the ECI using its powers against powerful politicians, especially when compared to the recent actions of the ECI. See Monobina Gupta, 'The Legacy of a Different CEC: When J.M. Lyngdoh Stood up to Modi', 6 May 2019, *The Wire*: https://thewire.in/politics/election-commission-jm-lyngodh-modi-model-code (accessed 18 May 2024).

public life, to making the unheard audible and the unseen visible. As with the 1977 general election and the 2002 Gujarat election, this would serve as an obstacle to both oligarchic power and divisive, ethnonationalist appeals. In the following chapter, I consider further examples of democratic action at the interface of formal and unofficial politics, old and new media, by looking at how street protests against a citizenship law and in defence of a constitution enacted new forms of the people.

5

Fearless speech

As a child Azad was never fond of the games children usually indulge in. Even at the age of eight his games were unique. Sometimes, he would line up trunks and boxes and pronounce them to be a train. Then he would tie one of father's turbans round his head and taking his seat on one of the boxes, he would ask us, his sisters, to shout and cry 'Give way, give way, the Maulana from Delhi is on his way.' When we said, 'Brother, there is no crowd here, whom should we push aside or ask to get out of the way', he would remonstrate, 'Can't you follow this simple make-believe? Can't you visualize that a large crowd has come to receive me?' Then he would get down from the box and walk slowly and deliberately, like an elderly person. Sometimes he would climb a raised platform and ask his sisters to surround him and applaud him, imagining that he was speaking amidst thousands of persons who were cheering and applauding his speech.

(Interview with Fatima Begum, sister of Abul Kalam Azad, 1959)

In his overview of the Indian nationalist leader Abul Kalam Azad's career, Aijaz Ahmad presents this account of the child Azad as revealing ambitions and character traits that would persist throughout his life. He is struck by two 'images of desire' for Azad, the role of 'a great theologian and a great orator', and also 'the absence of a role for anyone else beyond that of anonymous parts of the spectacle' (Ahmad 1992: 140). Ahmad claims that this image of the man apart from the crowd, 'deliberate, grave, superior, admired', was to be an enduring aspect of Azad's public persona, creating an unbridgeable gap between him and most Indian Muslims (ibid.). Whereas Gandhi's language was that of a syncretic mass culture, Azad remained rooted in elite Muslim traditions (ibid.: 136–7). Unlike Gandhi, many Indians admired him but few could '*identify* with him' (ibid.: 137, italics in the original).

This sense of distance is encouraged by the equivocal status of a lot of the biographical writing by and about Azad. Much of this work is characterised by what Ahmad describes as 'artifice': from the prison letters collected in *Ghubar-i khatir*, which includes letters written after he had been released; the illustrious family history recounted in *Tazkirah*; the oral fragments pulled together by Humayun Kabir in Azad's English-language 'autobiography'; and the Urdu text *Azad ki kahani khud Azad ki zabani* ('Azad's story in Azad's own words'), whose amanuensis, Ahmad speculates, had never even met its subject (Ahmad 1992: 140–1). Ahmad's own account of Azad describes a life continually remade and 'a *voice*, in his writings, which constantly changes its own timbre and texture' (ibid.: 124). As previously discussed, these shifts were arguably less a result of 'a heart riven by contrary desires and a mind tempted by irreconcilable convictions', as Ahmad claims (ibid.), than Azad's awareness of several audiences from the colonial censor to the *ulama*. This awareness made him an effective politician and journalist, prevented him from descending into 'impossible speech', asocial rantings and ramblings that emanate from an incoherent speaker and fail to reach a target audience (Butler 1997: 133).

Some of that early pleasure in fantasy and oratory can be perceived in his mature speech and writings, during moments when he seemed to be less interested in conveying a message than performing a role. Sometimes this was the role of an Imam ul-Hind, a great statesman and theologian. At other times, his position was more akin to that of truth teller, *parrhesiastes* in Greek, one who takes a risk and faces danger as they disclose a truth that threatens a sovereign power. The intention of the latter mode of speech is less to convince than to criticise either the interlocutor or the speaker themselves, and Foucault describes *parrhesia* as central to the tradition of western critical thought (2001). Unlike 'impossible speech', classical *parrhesia* requires a speaker who knows his own status and presupposes a relationship with an addressee. The former is usually a male citizen and the latter is always more powerful than the speaker: 'when a philosopher criticizes a tyrant, when a citizen criticizes the majority...then such speakers may be using *parrhesia*' (ibid.: 18). Slaves and women cannot participate in the political life of the city and play the *parrhesiastic* game.

In this chapter, I outline another form of *parrhesia* ('fearless speech') informed by the principle of equality on the one hand and an experience of disenfranchisement on the other. I analyse Azad's October 1947 post-Partition address, delivered from the steps of the Jama Majsid in Delhi, berating the *qaum* for not heeding his warnings on the dangers of the Two Nation theory, as an example of the semiotics of this counter-tradition. Namely, an alchemical combination of speaker, audience and context, which both shapes the message and transforms the constituent elements in the communication network. This model of communication is distinct from both the unilinear theory of communication that informs state censorship and the univocality of the 'one-man media house' model described in previous chapters. But in its reflexivity, it also differs from the simple process of inversion and negation at work in more 'elementary' forms of insurgency (Guha 1999). Azad is located within this tradition less as a figure to emulate or with whom to identify than as a repertoire of gestures available to those occupying a similar position, as a vector rather than a role model.

I specifically look at how Azad's words and acts continue to resonate with figures beyond the stereotype of a political Muslim in either a reformist or revolutionary mode: Dalits and women involved in the 2019–20 protests against nationwide extension of the National Register of Citizens and the passing of the Citizenship Amendment Act.[1] The former demanded documentary proof of entitlement to citizenship, which many Indians would struggle to provide, and its imposition on the state of Assam had left 1.9 million people stateless.[2] The latter offered exemption for provisions of documentary evidence for non-Muslim refugees entering India from three Muslim-majority states. This raised the prospect of differential citizenship, with Indian Muslims vulnerable to denaturalisation at the whim of bureaucratic officials in fulfilment of Azad's fears about the consequences of Partition in his Jama Masjid speech.[3] The amendment also threatened to change the character of the Indian

[1] For an analysis of the political purposes of the category of political Muslim, see Ahmed (2019).

[2] For a list of the admissible documents for the NRC in Assam, see http://www.nrcassam.nic.in/admin-documents.html (accessed 4 March 2020).

[3] Exemptions for full provision of documentary proof of residence would be made for Hindus, Jains, Christians, Sikhs, Buddhists and Parsis entering India from the 'neighbouring', Muslim majority

state – exclusion of minorities from the benefits of citizenship being a key feature of *Herrenvolk* democracy (Smooha 1997).

During both interventions, minoritised subjects went beyond possible speech and realpolitik to establish new grounds for collective belonging. Towards this end they made use of a religio-political lexicon of fearless speech and staged their interventions in extra-parliamentary space and on electronic media. But a distinctive form of street politics was at work in their efforts: one shaped by a vernacular knowledge of Delhi cityscapes and also proceeding from an awareness of the law. Through infusions of different styles of anti-imperial protest, the authorial subject position of the Constitution was loosed from that of the colonial-era anxious administrator, called upon to govern a potentially dangerous alien population (Dasgupta 2014: 231–2). Protests against a citizenship law and in defence of a constitution, in turn, enacted novel forms of consanguineous relation and civil contract.

'I hailed you, you cut off my tongue'

Azad's Jama Masjid address was the last in a series of speeches in which he defined his own role and that of the wider community of Indian Muslims in the independence struggle. The most celebrated of these is probably his Presidential Address to the Indian National Congress in March 1940, in which he asserted his pride in being Indian and Muslim and indispensability within the nation ('without me this splendid structure of India is incomplete'). But

states of Afghanistan, Bangladesh and Pakistan. For the text of the Citizenship Amendment Act, see (GI 2019a): http://egazette.nic.in/WriteReadData/2019/214646.pdf (accessed 4 March 2020). Afghanistan can hardly be described as neighbouring India, beyond a disputed sixty-five-mile section of the Durand Line. The BJP's decision to describe it as such was aimed at Pakistani claims to this territory, part of the conflict over the status of Jammu and Kashmir, and is contradicted by official documents produced by the Indian government's own ministries. See Tarun Deol's article, 'On India-Afghanistan border, Amit Shah is right and opposition is not wrong', *ThePrint*, 9 December 2019 https://theprint.in/india/on-india-afghanistan-border-amit-shah-is-right-and-opposition-is-not-wrong/332696/ (accessed 4 March 2020). Mukul Kesavan has described the prejudice and illogic informing this policy of accepting refugees from Afghanistan but barring refugees from neighbouring Myanmar, a Buddhist state in the process of ethnically cleansing its Muslim minority. See his article 'An all-India NRC would turn citizens into supplicants', *The Telegraph* (online edition), 24 November 2019: https://www.telegraphindia.com/opinion/an-all-india-nrc-would-turn-citizens-into-supplicants/cid/1721575 (accessed 4 March 2020).

the strongest expression of his position as an Indian Muslim was arguably contained in *Qaul-i Faisal* (translatable as both 'final judgement' and 'last word'), his statement to the Presidency Magistrate in January 1922 after being imprisoned for his involvement in the non-cooperation movement (Azad n.d. (a)).

In this prison oration, he outlined an Islamic tradition of fearless speech, citing the example of the old woman who in early Islamic days had rebuked the Caliph in public (ibid.: 116). This example may well have resonated with Azad as he broke a policy of silence to make his statement in court. He was not speaking out to defend himself, he insisted, as that would be acceding to the terms under which the British had imprisoned him, but to join a long procession of martyrs to truth awaiting final judgement in the court of God. Azad denied the authority of those who had arrested him by asserting his claims in the eyes of a wider public and higher court. This double manoeuvre highlights what Foucault described as a central paradox of *parhessia* – a form of speech that in the 'Socratic-Platonic' tradition had set itself against rhetoric became 'the zero degree of those rhetorical figures which intensify the emotions of the audience' (2001: 20–1). This is perhaps especially the case for those excluded from 'Socratic-Platonic' traditions of speech, who do not have access to sovereign power, and who must resort to unorthodox modes of expression which appeal to a broader audience.

In keeping with this post-sovereign mode of *parhessiastic* speech, Azad's Jama Masjid speech began with a stirring proclamation of defeat:

> I hailed you, you cut off my tongue; I picked up my pen, you severed my hand; I wanted to move, you broke my legs; I tried to run and you injured my back…I am frozen (*jamud*), I am the child-like helpless cry (*daur-i uftadah sada*) of one who is left to live the life of a stranger in their own land.
>
> (2012: 337–8)

This cry of helplessness looked back to Sir Syed's writings at the time of the 1857 rebellion and forward to Aziz Burney's editorials on the Ayodhya land title case. At different pivotal periods in India's political history, each man had expressed despair at the marginalised position of Indian Muslims, experienced as a falling off from the high period of Mughal rule. But Azad's speech differed in being personally addressed to this group – in the form of the crowd assembled around him on the Jama Masjid steps, whom he had addressed many times before – rather than an attempt to speak on their behalf for an unseen audience. This arguably lent Azad's speech its energy, made fluent and evocative his description of how a failed illocutionary act had immobilised him, reduced him to a childish plaint.

Over the course of the speech, the mood of recrimination and self-pity subsided, and Azad concluded his address with more advice:

> I say again, say repeatedly, keep a grip on your senses. Bring together by yourself your own surroundings, your own existence. This is not a commodity I can buy for you from the market.
>
> (Ibid.: 343)

Even at this low point Azad was asserting the possibility of creative thought and action, beyond the truck and barter of the 'low' politics that he believed had brought about Partition. His comments foresee the practice of vote-bank politics, voting on communal lines, in which the Muslim vote would be sought en bloc by political parties via figures such as Burney and Arif Khan.

Azad emphasised he was not seeking that sort of leadership role here. He directly addressed his audience using the informal subject pronoun *tum*, and *azizon*, a second person plural form of address derived from *aziz*. This usage of *aziz* approximates to dear, precious, respected or beloved rather than great, that is, to a polite or intimate form of address, with the use of the informal subject pronoun *tum* suggesting the latter. He described the occasion as a congress of Muslims (as an *ijtima*) and also implied an elite social background for his audience when he mentioned a shared historic experience of in-migration from Central Asia via the Ganges–Yamuna Doab (ibid.: 340). These are the cosmopolitan origins that Sir Syed asserted to the British in order to distinguish himself as a member of the *ashraf* elite, claim allegiance with the colonial government and separate off from the mass of South Asian Muslims, the *ajlaf* who descend from converts. But this would have been a less romantic reference for Azad, who had actually migrated to India from Mecca as a child.

There was also the significance of the location of the speech. Azad began by referring to the historic Jama Masjid, built by the Mughal emperor Shah Jahan in the mid-seventeenth century and therefore associated with the Muslim royal past (ibid.: 337).[4] But the Jama Masjid is not associated with state power in the same way as the nearby Red Fort. The mosque has long served as a valuable open space in a congested part of the city, featuring high-density housing and non-stop commercial and industrial activity. Locals use its courtyard as a thoroughfare to access different parts of Old Delhi, and its steps are a popular gathering place. The crowds Azad addressed would have been socially diverse and may even have included non-Muslims.

Azad's references to the glorious past also drew upon a distinctive temporal register. His exuberant description of his audience's fallen condition, 'today you fear the earthquake [*zalzalah*], once you were the earthquake' (ibid.: 342), recalls the *surah al-zalzalah* in the Qur'an, which describes the Day of Judgement, and also tales such as the *Alif Laila* (known in English as *The One Thousand and One Nights*) and *Dastan-i Amir Hamza* (*The Adventures of Amir Hamza*), which were performed on the steps of the Jama Masjid. The mixture of the magical and the mundane typical of this story-telling tradition was evident in Azad's speech as he berated his audience: whereas your ancestors leapt into the oceans, rebounded from the mountains, laughed in the face of thunder and lightning, changed the course of the winds and the whirlwinds, you lift your hems to avoid dirty rainwater (ibid.). The powers he described sounded more supernatural than this-worldly, and there may have been some mockery of gentility in his comment about rainwater for the benefit of the popular audience assembled in the Masjid.

In his post-Partition speech, Azad evoked the royal Muslim past to counter Sir Syed's counsel of state loyalty, of which Aziz Burney's brand of performative nationalism was a variant. Azad told his audience that he was not asking them to seek a certificate of loyalty (*wafadari ka sartifakat*) from the powers-that-be (*hakimana iqtidar*) or to adopt the smooth and easy (*salisi*) life they led under foreign rule (ibid.: 342). (This was a dig at pro-British Muslims such as Sir Syed, whose quietism he had ridiculed in *al-Hilal*.) Instead, they should look at the

[4] This built heritage had famously been commemorated by Syed Ahmad Khan in his lavishly illustrated book on Delhi's monuments, *Asar-al-Sanadid* (Traces of the Nobles), published in Persian in 1847 and in Urdu in 1854. Written in the court languages of the time, Syed Ahmad's assertions of the aura and authority of Indo-Islamic architecture is likely to have been intended for a British readership. See Naim (2011). For the postcolonial political legacy of this heritage, see Ahmed (2014).

resplendent lineaments (*ujle naqsh-o-nigar*) of the relics that surround them as proof of their inalienable right to live in the land of their ancestors: 'Do not forget them. Do not forsake them. Remain their custodian. Understand if you are not ready to flee, then no power can make you flee' (ibid.). Azad's use of the word *naqsh* in *naqsh-o-nigar* may have had a special charge at this moment, as *naqsh* can signify the outlines of a map, drawing attention to the recent redrawing of the map of India. He then switched to the first-person plural to declare: 'Come, let us today pledge that this country is ours, we belong to it, and any fundamental decisions about its destiny will remain incomplete without our voice' (ibid.).

A speech that began with an individual profession of inarticulacy moved towards an assertion of collective voice. This voice fell somewhere between the 'We the people' with which the Indian Constitution begins, and the demands made by those speaking on behalf of particular constituencies. As discussed earlier, the grounds for this manoeuvre had been laid out in *al-Hilal*, when Azad's support for restoration of the Ottoman caliphate drew him closer to the nationalist movement, building upon the expanded, trans-regional and cross-denominational notion of the *qaum* at work in Sir Syed's writing for the British. But there was nothing inevitable about this trajectory. The Khilafat movement had also been a key moment in the call for the formation of Pakistan by a newly politically confident *ulama* (Hasan 1981). Positioned differently, and addressing a much wider audience, Azad was impelled towards a different stance.

'I am willing to give my life for my own *qaum*'

More than sixty years after it had taken place, Azad's stance in his post-Partition address was invoked in a speech given by Dalit activist and anti-CAA protestor, Chandrashekhar Azad Ravan, on the steps of the Jama Masjid in Old Delhi on 20 December 2019. The resemblance was noted at the time, with Azad Ravan's presence on the steps highlighting the conservatism of current Muslim leadership and enthusing Muslim youth.[5] Azad Ravan would later

[5] See Maryam Sikander, 'In an era of citizenship debates, recalling Maulana Azad and the fight for India's secular backbone', 18 January 2020, *Scroll.in*: https://scroll.in/article/948058/in-an-era-of-citizenship-debates-recalling-maulana-azad-and-the-fight-for-indias-secular-backbone (accessed 6

claim that he had deliberately chosen this site because it was the location of Abul Kalam Azad's Partition-era speeches:

> During the time of Partition, Maulana Abul Kalam Azad stood there and asked the Muslims of India not to go to Pakistan. The country is yours, he said. The Partition will only harm you. I felt, by imposing the NRC, CAA, another attempt is being made to divide the country on the basis of religion.[6]

There were also practical reasons for this choice of location. Section 144 of the Indian Penal code, usually interpreted as prohibiting public assembly of more than four persons, had been imposed around Jama Masjid, but Friday prayers were allowed to take place.[7] Azad Ravan acted in the knowledge that stopping prayers in one of the largest mosques in India would have been an outrage and restricting access to the mosque hard to police. When asked how he managed to breach the tight security cordon outside its gates, he responded, 'My name is Chandrashekhar Azad. Police cannot hold me captive. I wore a cap and a shawl and entered the masjid easily.'[8] In his speech he also repeatedly asked police stationed outside the mosque to respect the sanctity of this house of God (*khuda ka ghar*).

Like Abul Kalam Azad, Azad Ravan specifically staged his protest in the liminal space of the Jama Masjid steps, which has long served many non-religious purposes and been the site of unorthodox forms of Islamic worship. The shrine of the Armenian-Iranian Jewish mystic, Sarmad, is located at the foot of the east gate of the Masjid, painted bright red for the blood spilt during his beheading on this site. Sarmad had been killed for refusing to recite the full Muslim profession of faith when ordered to do so by the

March 2022). Azad Ravan's actions were also compared to the response of the imam of the Masjid, who had adopted a pro-CAA line and delivered a cautious speech during Friday prayers on 20 December, just before Azad Ravan's intervention. See Mohammed Wajihuddin, "Imam' Chandra Shekhar Azad', *Times of India*, 23 January 2020. 'https://timesofindia.indiatimes.com/blogs/beyond-the-burqa/imam-chandra-shekhar-azad/ (accessed 4 March 2020).

6 Azad Ravan quoted in "Will give my blood, let Modi give his': Bhim Army chief Chandrashekhar Azad', *TheWeek.in*, 17 January 2020: https://www.theweek.in/news/india/2020/01/17/Will-give-my-blood-let-Modi-give-his-Bhim-Army-chief-Chandrashekhar-Azad.html (accessed 16 April 2020).

7 Soutik Biswas, 'Citizenship Act protests: How a colonial-era law is being used in India', *BBC News*, 20 December 2019: https://www.bbc.co.uk/news/world-asia-india-50849909 (accessed 17 May 2024).

8 "My Name Is Azad. Police Cannot Hold Me Captive,' Says Bhim Army Chief', *NDTV*, 21 December 2019: https://www.ndtv.com/india-news/caa-protests-chandrashekhar-azad-bhim-army-chief-says-my-name-is-azad-police-cant-hold-me-captive-2152206 (accessed 7 April 2020).

emperor Aurangzeb. Instead of reciting *la ilaha illa'llah* (there is no god but Allah), he had proclaimed *la ilaha* (there is no god).[9] According to popular lore, after being executed Sarmad had walked up the Jama Masjid steps with his severed head under his arm and ascended straight to heaven. His legend is well known, and his shrine continues to be visited by both Hindu and Muslim worshippers.[10]

The flouting of religious and political authority in Sarmad's heretical reiteration of the first *kalima* had also appealed to the young Abul Kalam Azad, who wrote a text on his transgressive life. Echoes of Sarmad's 'fearless speech' can be heard in the images of mutilation and dismemberment in Azad's Jama Masjid address. More profoundly, Sarmad's defiant stance evoked the power of a violence that exceeds the law not just by breaking its strictures but also in refusing its terms, refusing to be fixed through guilt to the order of law and power. Azad had performed the same rhetorical move in his prison oration.

This purity of position and purpose would be harder to maintain once Azad left prison and was once again actively involved in opposing colonial rule through participation in a mass movement. His text on Sarmad appeared in 1910, soon before he released his weekly journal *al-Hilal* in 1912, and this has encouraged speculation about the political motives behind the sudden and expedient religiosity of *al-Hilal*.[11] Azad himself commented on what he described as the eternal inextricability of politics and religion in Asia when discussing Aurangzeb's real motives for ordering Sarmad's killing (n.d.[b]: 19). In his text, he argued that Sarmad's murder was a result of the tension between religious and political authority inherent in the concept of divine kingship. Through his involvement in the Khilafat struggle, he had attempted to resolve

9 For a particularly florid version of this story, see Hansen's *The Peacock Throne* (1972: 396–412). For a more contemporary perspective on Sarmad's significance, see Saleem Kidwai's entry on 'Sarmad' in his and Ruth Vanita's anthology of literature on same sex love in India (Kidwai 2000: 157–8).

10 See Mayank Austen Soofi's 2014 blog post, which recounts the living history of Sarmad's shrine and includes photographs of shrine literature in Hindi: http://www.thedelhiwalla.com/2014/02/06/city-faith-hazrat-sarmad-shahids-dargah-near-jama-masjid/ (13 April 2020).

11 Douglas notes an abrupt shift in the tone of Azad's writings, from the crisis of faith described in his autobiographical writing to the 'intensely religious' *al-Hilal*, although he dismisses accusations that this was a result of opportunism (Douglas 1988: 102). Datta sees no contradiction between the two phases and has a pragmatic view of Azad's use of religion. When it came to the instrumentalization of religion, Azad, like Gandhi, had no choice. Religion was 'by far the easiest and most effective weapon' to unite people in the fight against foreign rule (Datta 1990: 84).

these tensions by both using religion to mobilise resistance to the colonial state and fostering cross-denominational political alliances to do so on a national scale.

Azad Ravan also attempted to encompass both domains when he couched his protest in sacrificial imagery familiar from various religious traditions, alongside a post-independence addition of a reference to the Indian Constitution. Azad Ravan is named after Chandrashekhar Azad, the Indian revolutionary who gave his life to save a comrade, and he is also a lawyer.[12] These two elements were combined in a tweet he wrote during his speech:

> I am sat here on the steps of Jama Masjid to tell Mr Modi that 'we will not let you kill our Constitution'. This Constitution is ours and to defend it we will fight to the last breath.[13]

A Hindi translation of the Constitution, with the iconic image of a suited and bespectacled Ambedkar on the cover, also featured in Azad Ravan's public interventions. During the anti-CAA protests he often read aloud from this book or held it aloft. In his work on the everyday life of the Constitution, Rohit De describes a dialectical relationship between the Constitution as an English-language product of 'elite consensus' and the document that came alive in popular imagination as 'ordinary people' invested it with meaning, 'took recourse through it, and argued with it' (2018: 9). Azad Ravan's actions highlight how the Constitution has become a living text through its status as a material object and audiovisual rhetorical tool, and how these aspects have become increasingly significant as the text has been translated and remediated.

Azad Ravan's message about the Constitution was re-tweeted '4.6K' times and liked '16.3K' times on his twitter feed. Innumerable versions of his speech were livestreamed and shared online. Two days previously, on 18 December 2019, Delhi police had pressured internet providers to shut down their services in parts of the city, including Jama Masjid. But this had only been imposed

12 Chandrashekhar Azad Ravan was named after the Indian revolutionary, Chandrashekhar Azad (1906–1931), who, like Maulana Azad, had adopted the pseudonym 'Azad' (free). Azad Ravan and his brother, Bhagat Singh, were both named after famous revolutionaries by their schoolteacher father. See the 2017 interview with their mother, Kamlesh Devi: 'My Son a Dalit Revolutionary, Says Bhim Army Chief's Mother', Uday Singh Rana, 19 June 2017, NEWS18.com https://www.news18.com/news/india/my-son-a-dalit-revolutionary-says-bhim-army-chiefs-mother-1437081.html (accessed 30 January 2020).

13 https://twitter.com/BhimArmyChief/status/1207986977636700161 (accessed 20 February 2020).

for a few hours. A longer shutdown would have been difficult to enforce in a location close to the centre of the national capital. (Jama Masjid is just three miles away from the Central Secretariat.) As a result, his words and image were able to circulate freely, both in real time and after the event.[14] This was the combination of intimacy and technological speed that Aziz Burney had aspired to but not quite achieved in his e-editorials, embedded as they were within the infrastructure of a print newspaper and a univocal ('one-man media house') model of communication.

Azad Ravan's intervention had the character of an event rather than a determinate message. The figure of this Dalit activist on the steps of the Jama Masjid brandishing a Hindi copy of the Constitution excited as much attention as his speech, especially as he did not address his audience from a podium but from the midst of a jostling crowd. Azad Ravan was just one of a number of men who had ascended the masjid steps, ostensibly to do *namaz*, and instead turned round to face the assembled television and mobile phone cameras, waving copies of the Constitution and shouting slogans against the CAA. This combination of Muslim and Dalit opposition to authoritarian rule was expressed both visually and aurally in the press of bodies gathered on the Jama Masjid steps. And just as Abul Kalam Azad, when delivering his post-Partition address, would have been aware that his words were being recorded for radio broadcast and would later be printed, Azad Ravan's actions seemed designed to be disseminated through television broadcasts and social media.

In one of the speeches he delivered from the Jama Masjid steps, Azad Ravan, too, spoke of the *qaum*, proclaiming, 'I am willing to give my life for my own *qaum* – those who are standing here – but I will not allow them to be killed'.[15] This was in reference to specific instances of police violence against protestors, but also a broader refusal of necropolitics, the investiture of sovereignty in

[14] When the Delhi police later attempted to prosecute him for inflammatory speech, they only provided soundless images from drone recordings of the protest as evidence. The prosecution was unsuccessful. The Delhi police was 'behaving as if Jama Masjid was Pakistan', Justice Kamini Lau said in her judgement – meaning, presumably, as if it were not part of India. 'Inside the Parliament, things which should have been said, were not said', she observed, 'and that is why people are out on the streets'. 'As If Jama Masjid Was In Pakistan': Delhi Court Slams Police On Chandrashekhar Azad's Arrest', *Outlook*, 14 January 2020, https://www.outlookindia.com/website/story/india-news-jama-masjid-not-in-pakistan-peaceful-protests-can-happen-anywhere-delhi-court-on-chandrashekhar-azads-arrest/345676 (accessed 24 February 2020).

[15] 'Chandrashekhar Azad addresses protestors in Jama Masjid', *Dalit Camera*, New Delhi, 20 December 2019. https://www.youtube.com/watch?v=3oJbxL2xqiw (accessed 8 April 2020).

the right to exclude and kill, and to define certain populations as expendable and killable (Mbembe 2003 and 2019).[16] Abul Kalam Azad had dissented from necropolitical power in both his account of the execution of Sarmad and editorials on the Kanpur mosque riots. There are continuities in argument and imagery in his account of how Sarmad's spilt blood distressed Aurangzeb for the rest of his days, and of the Kanpur riots as part of a global sacrificial offering of Muslim blood, resulting from the break-up of the Ottoman empire.[17]

Anti-Muslim violence also formed the context for Azad Ravan's offers to sacrifice himself for his *qaum*: a wave of riots and killings that had broken out in Uttar Pradesh in the run-up to the 2014 election and spread across India following the BJP's victory in that election. Azad Ravan had come to national prominence through his involvement in the Bhim Army, an Ambedkarite organisation involved in opposing communal violence through direct actions.[18] In offering his own life to combat this violence, Azad Ravan was making use of a power distinct from 'the power to kill, to let live, or to expose to death' (Mbembe 2019: 66), the power to give or lose one's own life. Azad Ravan's words recalled various famous colonial-era examples of the use of this power, from Gandhi's fasts unto death to the actions of his namesake, the revolutionary martyr Chandrashekhar Azad. But as a Dalit he stood at several removes from this tradition of 'sublative self-sacrifice' (Skaria 2016), based in the caste-ordained purity and prowess of the *Kshatriya* (warrior).

Gandhi had claimed a *Kshatriya* genealogy for *ahimsa* and identified Ram as one of its votaries (ibid.: 94). Azad Ravan's home state of Uttar Pradesh is both the site of the Ram temple in Ayodhya and the Ramlila festival, annual re-enactments of the *Ramayana* which culminate in the burning of effigies of Ravan, the demon king who abducts Ram's wife Sita. By appending 'Ravan' to

16 Mbembe's theory of necropolitics combines aspects of Foucault's theory of biopower with Agamben's theory of the state of exception. In a recent monograph (2019), he extends his argument to encompass Bauman on liquidity and Weizman on verticality. Running through all these theories is the conflation of sovereignty with the power to take life.

17 The earlier text placed Sarmad's death in a tradition of Sufi martyrdom, in which Aurangzeb merely served as the instrument of Sarmad's apotheosis. But Azad's lively and detailed recounting of the orally disseminated versions of his death leaves a stronger impression than the more authoritative written sources that he also mentions. These popular versions are often more critical of Aurangzeb (cf. their descriptions of the 'magical' properties of Sarmad's spilt blood).

18 See 'Ambedkarite 2.0: Saharanpur's Bhim Army signals the rise of a new, aggressive Dalit politics', *Scroll.in*, 13 May 2017: https://scroll.in/article/837494/ambedkarite-2-0-saharanpurs-bhim-army-signals-the-rise-of-a-new-aggressive-dalit-politics (13 April 2020).

his birthname, Azad Ravan mocked various Hindu traditions which cite the kingdom of Ram as an example of righteous rule. These include the Gandhian utopian vision of Ram *rajya* and the centrality of Ram and the Ram mandir for Hindu nationalist politics, as well as folkloric 'little traditions' of the non-elite (Ramanujan 1994). In assuming this name, Azad Ravan drew upon a counter tradition of the dissemination of the *Ramayana* across South and Southeast Asia, in which Ravan is a hero (Ramanujan 1999) and more recent worship of Ravan as an expression of Dalit defiance of 'Brahminical ideology'.[19]

Along similar rhetorical lines, his use of this term *qaum* restaged an earlier intra-Islamic debate about the compatibility of Islam and territorial nationalism, which also looked to prior and alternative ways of imagining sociopolitical community. This was part of a global response to the dissolution of the Ottoman and British empires, as Muslims living in various countries considered the possibilities of the nation form. The Citizenship Amendment Act responded to the political fallout from these intellectual discussions, to the creation of India, Pakistan and eventually Bangladesh. The CAA reflected post-independence anxieties about 'terrorist' infiltration from Muslim majority states and Bangladeshi economic migration into the northeast of India.

Azad Ravan rejected the narrow, statist perspective that informed these fears through an assertion of fatal solidarity with all those encompassed within *mera qaum*. His use of the Urdu word was in deference to his surroundings and mostly Muslim audience, also evident in other parts of his speech in which he used Urdu vocabulary. For example, in the earlier respectful reference to its location as *khuda ka ghar* (God's house). But significantly he did not specify the religious identity of the group he was referring to. His *qaum* was minimally qualified as all those standing beside him, which could potentially have been anybody. Like Abul Kalam Azad in his post-Partition Jama Masjid speech, Azad Ravan was impelled towards a notion of the *qaum* absent of any qualification save for an equal stake in and right to the commons ('this country is ours, we belong to it', in Azad's words). Azad, through his concurrent support

[19] See Rajesh Manchal, 'Worshipping Ravan: Snubbing Brahmanical Mythology', *Forward Press*, 2 October 2013: https://www.forwardpress.in/2013/10/worshipping-ravan-snubbing-brahmanical-mythology/ (accessed 27 February 2024).

for the Khilafat movement and the independence struggle, and Azad Ravan in his opposition to the CAA, moved towards a different basis for solidarity.

'I will sit here till blood stops flowing in my veins'

The process by which these non-exclusionary alliances are forged perhaps came to their fullest realisation in protests against the CAA organised by women who occupied a section of a highway in South Delhi in the winter of 2019–20. In the densely populated neighbourhood of Shaheen Bagh, which despite its regal name ('garden of falcons') is lacking in parks and green spaces, large groups of mostly Muslim women coalesced around the slogan: *hum kaghaz nahin dikhaenge* (we will not show the papers).[20] In terms that recalled Azad's Jama Masjid speech, the women of Shaheen Bagh also refused the authority of certificates of loyalty from the powers-that-be and asserted their claim to the commons by taking part in the *parrhesiastic* game. But their intervention was even more radical. Through their use of the pronoun *hum*, which can signify both the singular and plural first-person in colloquial speech, they elided the distinction between individual dissent and collective action. By 'claiming public spaces as an extension of domestic life' (Faisal 2020: 721), they blurred the boundary between bare-life and the political by transforming a highway into an agora, a creche and a kitchen.

As with Azad's and Azad Ravan's Jama Masjid speeches, their protest was all the more resonant because of its location. Shaheen Bagh is in the south Delhi suburb of Jamia Nagar, a locality with a large Muslim population, directly linked to Jama Masjid in the north by highways running east and west

[20] Appropriately enough, the slogan of this leaderless movement was multi-authored, translated and remediated. The slogan had gained currency after featuring in a Hindi poem tweeted by the comedian Varun Grover. In his tweet, he acknowledged the influence of the Urdu poet Rahat Indori and Bengali protest banners bearing the equivalent slogan *kagoj dekhabo na*. See 'Kagaz Nahi Dikhayenge': Varun Grover's Anti-NRC Poem Is Viral', 22 December 2019, *Outlook*: https://www.outlookindia.com/national/india-news-kagaaz-nahi-dikhayenge-varun-grovers-anti-nrc-poem-is-viral-news-344545 (accessed 6 April 2024). The phrasing also recalls the refrain of Faiz Ahmed Faiz's poem against the Zia ul-Haq regime, *hum dekhenge* ('we will see'). This had become famous in Pakistan when performed on Pakistani television by the singer Iqbal Bano, despite a ban on Faiz's poetry, and also when adopted as an anthem of the anti-CAA protests in India. See Kaveri Bamzai, 'Modi's India Unhappy with Protesters Singing Faiz's Hum Dekhenge. Zia's Pakistan Was Too', *The Print*, 2 January 2020: https://theprint.in/opinion/modi-india-unhappy-with-faizs-hum-dekhenge-zias-pakistan-was-too/343560/ (accessed 3 April 2020).

of the Yamuna River. The area had first come to prominence in 1935 as the new site of the Jamia Millia Islamia, a Muslim university founded in 1920 by educators and politicians involved in the independence struggle, including Abul Kalam Azad. Following the first mass exodus of two-thirds of Delhi's Muslim population during the time of Partition, there had been further out migration from the old city to the southern peripheries in the early 1980s. Those escaping the congested inner city and seeking employment during that period were joined by Muslims escaping communal violence across north India in the early 1990s.[21]

In recent years, the area has acquired a new reputation as a centre of 'anti-national' activity. In 2008, it gained notoriety as the site of an 'encounter' killing (extrajudicial police killing) of two Muslim students accused of belonging to a radical jihadist organisation. The local response to this incident helps account for the extraordinary speed and reach of the Shaheen Bagh protests by a community well versed in the workings of the media and the law. Mohammed Sayeed's ethnography of the local response to the killings describes how they provided the impetus for a collective learning of legal procedures by local residents, which in itself changed their meaning and operation (2020). In the hands of locals seeking to protect themselves from police violence, the law was transformed from an external arbiter of justice operating along 'a *vertical* axis' to a set of '*horizontal* procedures' deployed for tactical advantage (ibid.: 53, italics in the original). Media, especially non-mainstream online media, played an important role in 'knowing the event, learning the law'.[22] The Shaheen Bagh protests worked to similar pedagogic effect on a national scale by evoking the Constitution and making adroit use of media to challenge the narrow definitions of citizenship enacted in the CAA. The protests may not have succeeded in annulling the CAA, but in drawing attention to its implications, they arguably played a part in preventing nationwide implementation of

[21] See Laurent Gayer's chapter on the factors behind this migration to Abul Fazl Enclave (2012). Shaheen Bagh is also known as Abul Fazl II.

[22] Sayeed details how official accounts of the killing as relayed on national broadcast media were quickly countered by news websites run by Muslim journalists affiliated with the institute of mass communications in the nearby Jamia Millia Islamia. They collected information about the event using both on-the-ground reports gathered using interviews and mobile phones and by requesting information under the Right to Information Act.

the NRC by a BJP government highly sensitive to criticism, and to foreign criticism in particular.

The protests had become internationally famous after being translated into a modern language of celebrity and rights, as well as an older religio-political idiom of sacrifice as political resistance. In an interview with *Time Magazine*, on being named one of the 100 Most Influential People of 2020, one of the protestors, Bilkis Bano was quoted as proclaiming: 'I will sit here till blood stops flowing in my veins so the children of this country and the world breathe the air of justice and equality'.[23] Bano's sit-in and 'liberty or death' rhetoric spoke to US traditions of dissent, from the Revolutionary War through to the Civil Rights movement, and they were also part of a repertoire of speech and actions available from histories of anti-imperial protest. But resistance was expressed through the performance of everyday activities and with reference to the fact of mortality, rather than as a violent response to a sovereign power. The words attributed to Bano were underscored by her status as an 82-year-old woman speaking of death with the authority of someone approaching the end of her life.

In both India and the United States, the Shaheen Bagh protests attracted attention because of the involvement of women. As discussed earlier, the CAA and NRC require documentary proof of patrilineal ancestry, which many Indians are unlikely to possess. Women who do not work outside the home have even less need to keep these records and may be in the habit of writing their father's or husband's names on official documents. This custom had led to the disqualification of 2.8 million female voters who refused to reveal their proper names to Election Registration Officers during the first Indian general election of 1951–52 (GI 1955a: 72–3).[24]

The Shaheen Bagh protests were an ingenious response to this gridlock of patriarchal strictures and governmental practices, which restrict the exercise of female citizenship. The most prominent group of protestors, the *dadis* (grandmothers), may have resembled a stereotype of a Muslim housewife or *gharelu aurat*. But their self-presentation as senior women

[23] Rana Ayyub, 'The 100 Most Influential People of 2020: Bilkis', 22 September 2020, *Time Magazine*: https://time.com/collection/100-most-influential-people-2020/5888255/bilkis/ (accessed 22 January 2022).

[24] See the detailed discussion of this episode in Shani (2021).

stands in relief set against the paternalism of much BJP rhetoric on women, evident in its campaigns against sexual violence (*bahu-beti bachao*, 'save our daughters and daughters-in-law') and sex-selective abortion (*beti bachao*, 'save our daughters'). The women's infringement of the limits of the home and immediate kin helps explain why seniority and gender did not protect them from violent abuse. In a reprisal of his remarks during the 2014 general election campaign, BJP Party President, Amit Shah, urged voters in the 2020 Delhi assembly elections to 'press the button' on the voting machine 'with such anger that its current is felt at Shaheen Bagh'.[25] As with his earlier comments, voting was presented as a means to punish minorities who had overstepped the boundaries of their given communities.

Protestors countered this view of democracy by expressing faith in the authority of another document – the Constitution – with pictures of Ambedkar, the politician who oversaw its drafting, and the preamble of the Constitution, declaring India a secular, socialist republic, held aloft on banners during the demonstrations. There were multiple layers of irony at work in these invocations. The words 'secular' and 'socialist' had been added to the preamble by Indira Gandhi during the internal emergency of 1975–7, in response to the religio-political movements that had challenged her autocratic rule. Despite his prominence in the anti-CAA campaign, Ambedkar had been an adherent of the Two Nation theory. Like Iqbal, he believed that Islam was incompatible with territorial nationalism, and that Hindus and Muslim were incapable of living together in one nation.[26] In his final speech to the Constituent Assembly, on 25 November 1949, he had also opposed 'the bloody methods of revolution' and urged the abandonment of 'civil disobedience, non-cooperation and satyagraha' (GI 2014: 978).

[25] Rohini Chatterji, 'Press Button With Such Anger That Shaheen Bagh Feels Current, Says Amit Shah', 26 January 2020, *HuffPost*: https://www.huffpost.com/archive/in/entry/delhi-assembly-elections-2020-amit-shah-shaheen-bagh_in_5e2e62d9c5b67d8874b4f4d7 (accessed 22 January 2022).

[26] These views were outlined in Ambedkar's *Thoughts on Pakistan* (1941), a treatise written in response to the Muslim League's Lahore Resolution. It is beyond the scope of this chapter to go into a detailed discussion of this text, which presents a nuanced account of the causes of Hindu–Muslim conflict, seen in historical and ideological context. But in this text, he repeats familiar claims about the inability of Muslims to exist within a non-Muslim polity. See the discussion of Pan-Islamism and the Khilafat movement in the final chapter, chapter XII, 'National Frustration' (Ambedkar 1941: 269–346).

But thinking in terms of a shared aporic position within a discursive field rather than specific beliefs, in many ways Ambedkar seemed an appropriate emblem for this movement. During an earlier period he had also dealt with the position of marginalised groups within majoritarian political forms such as the nation and arrived at similar solutions. In *bahujan*, the Pali word for many or mass, which he had come across in his study of Buddhist scriptures, he found a term capable of representing his Scheduled Caste constituency.[27] As with *qaum*, the meaning of *bahujan* has been transformed as different actors have adopted it.[28] But common to the modern iterations of both terms was an insistence upon the indivisibility of minority rights and national rights.

Building on this legacy, anti-CAA protests were fought on the basis of equality of persons rather than minority rights, with reference to Article 14 of the Indian Constitution, which declares equality before the law and equal protection of the laws to all persons within India's territory a Fundamental Right.[29] In the 1948 Draft Constitution, this was explicitly connected to the right to life and liberty, as what was then Article 15 declared, 'No person shall be deprived of his life or personal liberty except according to procedure established by law, nor shall any person be denied equality before the law or the equal protection of the laws within the territory of India.'[30]

During both periods, the larger context for emphasising this principle were refugee crises that had created large populations of non-citizens and persisting social and economic inequalities. Ambedkar had referred to the latter specifically in his famous closing remarks to the Constituent Assembly, when he forecast a life of contradictions awaiting India upon independence (GI 2014: 979). He therefore seemed an appropriate avatar for a movement that involved an unillusioned assertion of the principle of equality by those

[27] In their Pali-English dictionary, Davids and Stede define the term as, 'Bāhujañña (adj.) [fr. bahu+jana, cp. sāmañña fr. sa- maṇa] belonging to the mass of people, property of many people or of the masses.' (1921–5: 487), from the University of Chicago's Digital Dictionaries of South Asia webpage: https://dsalsrv04.uchicago.edu/cgi-bin/app/pali_query.py?qs=B%C4%81huja%C3%B1%C3%B1a&searchhws=yes (accessed 17 February 2020).

[28] See Badri Narayan's description of the transition from Dalit to Bahujan (Narayan 2006: 33–8).

[29] See 'CAA & Article 14 of Indian Constitution', 29 January 2020, *The Times of India*: https://timesofindia.indiatimes.com/blogs/blunt-frank/caa-article-14-of-indian-constitution/ (accessed 17 February 2020).

[30] *The Draft Constitution* in *The Gazette of India Extraordinary*, New Delhi, 26 February 1948, pp. 137–269, p. 144.

who knew it was more often honoured in the breach. Protestors' actions were in the same spirit as the half-defeated call for national unity in Abul Kalam Azad's post-Partition speech, and Ambedkar's clear-sighted assertion of the principle of political equality in his address to the Constituent Assembly. Their speech acts parlayed the affective force of a tradition of non-violent protest and were also a considered rhetorical move.

The thinking behind the protests was laid out by women interviewed by Indian TV journalist Ravish Kumar.[31] They pointed out that there had been no vocal collective response by Muslims to previous government actions perceived to have targeted them. Specifically, the bifurcation of Kashmir and revocation of sections of Articles 370 and 35(a) of the Indian Constitution, ending the formal autonomy of India's only Muslim-majority state; and the Supreme Court judgement on the Ayodhya land title case, which authorised construction of a temple on the site of a mosque destroyed by Hindu nationalists in 1992.[32] Taking up those issues risked having their claims dismissed as the particular grievances of a minority community.[33] By talking the language of constitutionalism, protestors found a means to escape this double bind, to check executive power and formulate their claims. (Something similar had happened in this locality earlier, with tactical use of the law in the aftermath of the 2008 encounter killings.)

At the same time, little attempt seemed to have been made to avoid 'protesting as Muslim' as recommended by liberal commentators such as Congress politician Shashi Tharoor.[34] Many of the women participating in the *dharna* were identifiable as Muslim by dress. They also openly discussed the

31 *NDTV Prime Time*, 9 January 2020, https://www.youtube.com/watch?v=TQm7nBa49WQ (accessed 3 March 2020).

32 For a discussion of a Kashmiri Muslim response to the anti-CAA protests, see dyuti a (2020). dyuti a describes how even before the abrogation of Article 370 and the introduction of the CAA and NRC, Kashmiri Muslims had viewed with scepticism claims to constitutionally conferred sovereignty and secularism.

33 This accusation had been levelled at earlier, violent anti-CAA protests in Assam and other parts of the Northeast, when Narendra Modi had insinuated that those protesting could be 'identified by their clothes', 'Anti-Citizenship Act protests: Those indulging in arson can be identified by their clothes, says Narendra Modi', *The Hindu*, 15 December 2019. https://www.thehindu.com/elections/jharkhand/anti-citizenship-act-protests-those-indulging-in-arson-can-be-identified-by-their-clothes-says-narendra-modi/article30311723.ece (accessed 3 February 2020).

34 See Manash Firaq Bhattacharjee, *The Wire*, 18 January 2020, 'Debate: Shashi Tharoor and the Liberal Paranoia of Muslims Asserting Their Identity' https://thewire.in/rights/shashi-tharoor-muslims-caa-protests (accessed 10 March 2020).

catalyst for the sit-in, a series of police raids on two historic Muslim institutions of higher education: Aligarh Muslim University and Jamia Millia Islamia. Women interviewed by journalists said they were responding to violence inflicted on their children and grandchildren whilst they were studying in Jamia library, on the pretext that they were involved in anti-CAA protests. Jamia, less than 3 miles away from Shaheen Bagh, was the local university, which meant news of this incident got out quickly.

But in framing their sit-in as fundamentally against the Citizenship Amendment Act, they also positioned themselves as defenders of the Constitution. They did not accept that their particular identities, as Muslims and as women, precluded them from assuming this role. Protestors spoke on both their own behalf and in the interests of a wider community, thereby transforming the outlines of both constituencies. The entry of 'ordinary' Muslim women into public life and national politics expanded existing vocabularies and repertoires of democratic action, and its effects could be seen in subsequent protests, notably in the successful farmers' protests of 2020–1, in which women also featured prominently.

Going beyond the standard languages of nationalism and minority rights in this way, the numbers game of bureaucratic and political representation, allowed for novel forms of popular mobilisation across identity lines. This was evident in the swift response to rumours that the women of Shaheen Bagh would be celebrating the thirtieth anniversary of the forcible expulsion of Hindus from Kashmir in 1989–90. Protestors may well have been motivated by a desire to pre-empt accusations of sedition, which would have resulted in even greater public hostility and further punitive action by the state. But their response was notably thoroughgoing. Within a day of these rumours circulating, a meeting was called at Shaheen Bagh to commemorate the exodus. This featured a two-minute silence in solidarity with those who had lost their homes, performances by Kashmiri Pandit artists, Inder Salim and MK Raina, and even some participation by Kashmiri Hindus who supported the CAA.[35]

[35] See 'Shaheen Bagh protesters express solidarity with Kashmiri Pandits on exodus day', *India Today*, 19 January 2020. https://www.indiatoday.in/india/story/kashmiri-pandits-exodusday-migration-refugees-1638294-2020-01-19, and also 'Shaheen Bagh Observes 2-minute Silence for Kashmiri Pandits in Solidarity Show', *CNN-News 18.com*, 20 January 2020. https://www.news18.com/news/india/shaheen-bagh-observes-2-minute-silence-for-kashmiri-pandits-in-solidarity-show-2464813.html (both accessed 6 March 2020).

By these acts protestors signalled a distance between their movement and those who used a language of violent revenge against them. Like Azad in his prison oration, they were careful to oppose a law and its bureaucratic implementation, rather than a particular person or party, in order to avoid acceding to the terms under which they themselves were charged. In condemning the CAA as antinational, they took part in the effort to save majoritarian political forms from their worst excesses through a continually renamed and re-enacted project of living-in-common. The tenor of these protests therefore seemed clearly distinct from the forging of alliances across an equivalential chain in opposition to a common enemy, as described in Laclau's influential theory of 'populist reason', and whose risks he himself outlined in his earlier work on fascism (2007 and 1979). The equivalential chain, here, was created through a common experience of dispossession. Through the novel juxtaposition of words and images by particular speakers at a specific time and place, this movement folded the *qaum* into the *bahujan* to enact a non-exclusionary form of the people. And this was not articulated by the edicts of a sovereign state or a one-man media house, bearer of a quasi-divine autonomy and authority, but through the multiplicity and multivocality of a collective demand.

Epilogue

On 22 March 2020, the BJP Prime Minister, Narendra Modi, announced a 'people's curfew', which was to run from 7.00 am to 9.00 pm on 22 March 2020 in response to the outbreak of Covid-19 in India.[1] The lockdown emulated those declared in Europe and East Asia and was imposed with four hours' notice to ill effect in a country with a largely informal economy and weak welfare state. Interpreting the lockdown as a law-and-order issue rather than a public health emergency, it was enforced violently and inflexibly. Images of some of the worst instances of this policy circulated widely on broadcast and social media. These included scenes of workers walking hundreds of miles to get back to their home states after public transport had stopped running, waiting in long queues for food from charities because they were no longer earning, and being beaten by police officers for breaking a curfew and doused with diluted bleach by health workers.

Such harsh measures seemed consistent with Giorgio Agamben's contention, in a series of articles on the pandemic, that we he had entered a new, health-based paradigm of governance based on biosecurity (Agamben 2021). He claimed that the mechanism of biosecurity outdid all previous forms of governance in its efficacy and pervasiveness, heralding the end of the era of bourgeois democracy, based on constitutions, rights and parliaments. But in India these measures specifically recalled a colonial legacy of the use of emergency powers to limit democratic self-governance, which had led Indira Gandhi to use constitutional provisions to centralise power in her own hands during the 1970s. Curfew regulations were imposed with reference

[1] 'Take part in "Janata Curfew" and strengthen the fight against Coronavirus', Narendra Modi website, 20 March 2020. https://www.narendramodi.in/take-part-in-janata-curfew-and-add-strength-to-the-fight-against-coronavirus-548855 (accessed 23 March 2020).

to colonial-era legislation, Section 144 of the Criminal Procedure Code, which prohibits the 'unlawful assembly' of more than four people in the case of 'apprehended danger'. As discussed in previous chapters, 'Emergency pedagogy' and 'The model code', both pre- and post-independence the people in whose name public order was maintained by these means were configured as a problem – vectors for crime, disease and violent disruption.

Social distancing regulations were also interpreted by those charged with enforcing them along classist, casteist and ethno-religious lines. State functionaries' actions were in keeping with the high-handed way they habitually treat those they consider socially subordinate. They reflected a specific prejudice towards people who had crossed state borders in search of work coming from the 'BIMARU' states – a punning acronym for the 'sick' (*bimar* in Hindi) states of Bihar, Madhya Pradesh and Uttar Pradesh. The pandemic had itself been blamed on a meeting of the Tablighi Jamaat, a transnational Islamic organisation, which occurred in Delhi in March 2020. Official responses to both this 'super-spreader' event and the 'migrant' workers enacted a classic scapegoating of those beneath regard, beyond the pale and on the move.

The Prime Minister had also recommended a five-minute interval during the curfew. At 5pm, Indians were to stand on their balconies and rooftops, lean out of their windows, and clap hands, beat vessels and ring bells to honour and enthuse health and sanitation workers who were fighting the virus.[2] His words were taken as encouragement for street parties that took place across India that afternoon. This state-sanctioned carnival emulated spontaneous celebrations in Italy and elsewhere, but it also had the character of *jhad phunk* exorcism rituals, which are often presided over by Muslim healers. These celebrations were the obverse of the restrictions imposed because of 'apprehended danger' – an attempt to invoke these same 'dangerous' forces. As discussed in the account of the 2014 Indian general election in Chapter 4, such performances play up to the promise of 'clean' politics, unitary national identity and immediacy, whilst making use of 'impure' religio-political practices, social fissures and technical mediation.

[2] This video has been removed from Narendra Modi's own twitter feed but can be viewed on this Pakistani website: https://propakistani.pk/lens/if-you-have-corona-and-you-know-it-clap-your-hands-modi/ (26 March 2020).

Similar methods have been adopted by popular mobilisations in other contexts, including older democracies such as Britain and the United States. But these incongruities seem particularly clear in India, a country in which liberal norms and institutions seem to have both never fully taken hold and to have had an extraordinary afterlife. The fourth chapter dealt with this paradox in relation to the history of elections in modern India. But across the book, I have described the fallout from the structures and taxonomies of the colonial state as well as how they have been repurposed by those whom they marginalise.

The last chapter dealt with how this was attempted by the anti-CAA protestors, whose disruptive interventions were carried out in the name of the Constitution. Some of the women of Shaheen Bagh responded with similar ingenuity to pandemic-related prohibitions on public assembly. Soon after the curfew was announced on 22 March 2020, a skeleton protest was staged at this site. In compliance with Section 144 and recommendations on social distancing, four women stood two metres away from one another, wearing face masks and protective clothing.[3] Around them stood ranks of empty wooden benches, each bearing a pair of sandals. At 5.00 pm, the remaining protestors shouted slogans against both the coronavirus and the Citizenship Amendment Act. One woman held up a sign proclaiming in English, 'We Support Janta Curfew'.

This woman's statement did not seem to be an expression of faith in the state as guarantor of personal freedom and collective safety. Both the introduction of the CAA-NRC and police handling of protests against them would have done little to encourage such faith. (The site had been petrol bombed on the first day of the curfew, an attack which police dismissed as the result of an internal dispute.)[4] Against this context, there was something pointed in protestors' efforts to be even more scrupulous in observing restrictions than those charged with enforcing them. Rather than being a profession of loyalty, their actions seemed to be an immanent critique of government actions using a repertoire of gestures provided by the state itself. This impression was

3 'Janta Curfew: Only 5 Women at Shaheen Bagh Protest', *ABP News*, 22 March 2020: https://www.youtube.com/watch?v=rvXdzQT-Bkc (17 July 2022). The headline of this YouTube clip possibly also includes the journalist in the count; only four protestors are visible in the video.

4 'As Shaheen Bagh Sticks to 5 Protester Limit, Vigilante Attacks Site With Petrol Bomb', *The Wire*, 22 March 2020: https://thewire.in/communalism/petrol-bomb-shaheen-bagh-janata-curfew (accessed 17 May 2024).

encouraged by the protest's mode of address. As the woman's English language sign indicated, this performance was not exclusively intended for the audience of the Hindi TV programme on which it was broadcast. The use of English, both an international language and a national link language, targeted a much wider audience. They would have known that footage of their protest would circulate even more widely online.

In the second chapter, 'The one-man media house', I described how the Urdu editor-writers Aziz Burney and Abul Kalam Azad had also played with a range of languages and media to address multiple readerships. Aziz Burney wrote his Hindi–Urdu editorials with a view to preferment within existing structures (the Sahara group, the Congress Party, the Indian state) and through the assumption of a well-worn role – that of the loyal Muslim subject. In contrast, and more in keeping with Azad's radical interventions, the women of Shaheen Bagh introduced new political actors and ways of doing politics through creative combinations of old and new representative technologies. Their protests combined the exoskeleton of the Constitution with the attack of a direct action, embodied and situated protest and use of electronic media. This allowed their speech acts to resonate with many different audiences, to travel globally, and to remain known long after the protest site had been demolished by police. This would seem to be less an example of 'impossible speech' than what Butler elsewhere describes as a 'performative contradiction': a claim to enfranchisement by the excluded, which both exposes contradictions within previous formulations of the universal and makes them substantive (1996: 47–8).

These performances were distinct from the ideal of democracy as a reasonable communicative process between citizens and public officials, which Agamben saw as attacked by the forces of biosecurity. Much less did they accord with Agamben's own ideal of 'pure communicability' embodied in the uncovered human face (2021), which, like Bakhtin's 'live speech', describes a speech situation distinct from both the communication of information and the transmission of messages. Agamben had expressed his ideas in an article regretting the adoption of masks during the pandemic. But they emerge from his wider suspicion of all dispositifs (his translators, like Foucault's, translate this as 'apparatuses') that mediate living discourse (2009). Agamben's words were also arguably informed by talk of a threat to western 'values' posed by Muslims in Europe, which have focused on the headscarf. Colonial-era suspicion of the veiled Muslim woman 'who sees without being seen', in Fanon's words, have in recent times boomeranged in Europe and rebounded in India. In all three contexts, this garment became a cathexis for anxieties about the limits of state sovereignty and personal autonomy embodied by subjects belonging to groups viewed as disobedient and disloyal.

All the protestors at Shaheen Bagh on the day of the curfew were masked and some wore hijabs, in compliance with injunctions on both modest dress and social distancing. The sandals laid on a wooden bench, each one standing in for many absent protestors, fell even further short of the ideals of communicability and co-presence. Because they cover the lowest part of the body, the part furthest from the face, shoes are usually removed on entering domestic and sacred space in India. They therefore seemed a fittingly profane symbol for what the political theorist James Martel has described as a 'non-idolatrous' form of representation, which visibly and deliberately fails to offer a true vision of a given community (2012). Acknowledging the non-existence of such a truth, it provides a negative impression or 'empty shell' within which communities can exist in their own variety and ever-shifting political practices (ibid.: 3).

Martel discerns this non-idolatrous form of representation in Walter Benjamin's response to Carl Schmitt's political theology, to which he counters the 'indecisionism' of the sovereigns in German Baroque drama and the *Trauerspiel*'s pervasive air of brokenness and defeat. From an acknowledgement of a common state of ruination, Benjamin derives an account of representation as an act of rearranging the building blocks that form our reality rather than offering a true vision of a community. In this book, I have engaged with social and political theory, including Schmitt, to advance an analogous understanding of representation as an act of reflexive technopolitics. But the starting point for these reflections have been discursive practices by individuals and groups in India, who fit incompletely within various 'given' identities and majoritarian institutions.

This book has explored these ideas across various cross-cutting fields, encompassing intellectual debates in the Urdu press and everyday linguistic practices, underground, electoral and street politics. Across these cases, I have described how those on the sharp edge of these identifications and institutions are well placed to understand how they work, where they fail to work and how they can be undone. From the independence struggle to the emergency and the anti-CAA protests, an experience of subjection, whether it be within the confines of a jail or under the terms of a new citizenship law, has provided the ideal felicity conditions for speech acts that are alive to their own contingency and do not attempt to disguise the conditions for their possibility. This technically mediated form of 'live speech' has opened up the possibility for a non-exclusionary articulation of the people, one that would not be founded upon any transcendent principle or the making of distinctions but made and remade through this-worldly ties.

Bibliography

Abdou, Mohamed. 2022. *Islam and Anarchism: Relationships and Resonances*. London: Pluto Press.

Advani, L K. 1979. *The People Betrayed*. New Delhi: Vision Books.

Advani, L. K. 1978. *A Prisoner's Scrap-Book*. New Delhi: Arnold-Heinemann.

Agamben, Giorgio. 2021. *Where Are We Now? The Epidemic as Politics*. Translated by Valeria Dani. London: Rowman & Littlefield.

Agamben, Giorgio. 2009. 'What Is an Apparatus?', in *What Is an Apparatus? And Other Essays*. Translated by David Kishik and Stefan Pedatella. Stanford, CA: Stanford University Press, pp. 1–24.

Ahmad, Aijaz. 1992. 'Azad's Careers: Roads Taken and Not Taken', in Mushirul Hasan (ed.), *Islam and Indian Nationalism: Reflections on Abul Kalam Azad*. New Delhi: Manohar, pp. 122–75.

Ahmad, Irfan. 2009. *Islamism and Democracy in India: The Transformation of Jamaat-e-Islami*. Princeton: Princeton University Press.

Ahmed, Hilal. 2020. 'Researching India's Muslims: Identities, Methods, Politics', *HAU: Journal of Ethnographic Theory* 10(3), pp. 776–85.

Ahmed, Hilal. 2019. *Siyasi Muslims: A Story of Political Islam in India*. New Delhi: Penguin Viking.

Ahmed, Hilal. 2014. *Muslim Political Discourse in Postcolonial India: Monuments, Memory, Contestation*. New Delhi: Routledge.

Ahmed, Siraj-ud-din. 1920. *The Truth about the Khilafat*. Lahore: Khosla Bros., Electric Printing Works.

Akhtar, Shamin. 2015. 'Sir Syed Ahmad Khan and His Audiences', *Social Scientist* 43(1/2), pp. 23–9.

Alam, Muzaffar. 2023. 'Maulana Azad and His Memory of the Islamic Past: A Study of His Early Writings', *Journal of the Royal Asiatic Society* 33(4), pp. 901–16.

Althusser, Louis. 1977a. 'Ideology and the Ideological State Apparatus', in *Lenin and Philosophy and Other Essays*. London: Monthly Review Press, pp. 127–87.

Althusser, Louis. 1977b. 'Freud and Lacan', in *Lenin and Philosophy and Other Essays*. London: Monthly Review Press, pp. 180–202.

Althusser, Louis. 1977c. 'A Letter on Art in Reply to André Daspré', in *Lenin and Philosophy and Other Essays*. London: Monthly Review Press, pp. 221–7.

Ambedkar, B. R. 2002. 'Conversion (Away from the Hindus)', in Valerian Rodrigues (ed.), *The Essential Writing of B.R. Ambedkar*. New Delhi: Oxford University Press, pp. 219–38.

Ambedkar, B. R. 1943. *Mr Gandhi and the Emancipation of the Untouchables*. Punjab: Bheem Patrika Publications.

Ambedkar, B. R. 1941. *Thoughts on Pakistan*. Bombay: Thacker.

Anand, C. L. 1944. *The Government of India Act 1935: With a Critical Introduction and Commentaries*. Lahore: The University Book Agency.

Anderson, Benedict. 1998a. 'Nationalism, Identity, and the World-in-Motion: On the Logics of Seriality', in Pheng Cheah and Bruce Robbins (eds), *Cosmopolitics: Thinking and Feeling beyond the Nation*. Minneapolis: University of Minnesota Press, pp. 117–33.

Anderson, Benedict. 1998b. *The Spectre of Comparisons: Nationalism, Southeast Asia and the World*. London: Verso.

Anderson, Benedict. 1996. 'Colonial Language Policies in Indonesia and the Philippines: A Contrast in Intended Aims and Unintended Outcomes', in Laura García-Moreno and Peter C. Pfeiffer (eds), *Text and Nation: Cross-Disciplinary Essays on Cultural and National Identities*. Colombia: Canada House, pp. 17–27.

Anderson, Benedict. 1991. *Imagined Communities*. London: Verso.

Anon. 1978. *The Pen in Revolt: Underground Literature Published during the Emergency*. New Delhi: Press Institute of India.

Anon. 1948. 'The Draft Constitution', in *The Gazette of India Extraordinary*. New Delhi, 26 February 1948, pp. 137–269.

Arendt, Hannah. 1969. *On Violence*. New York: Houghton Mifflin Harcourt.

Ashraf, Ali. 2001. 'Appraisal of Azad's Religio-Political Trajectory', in Mushirul Hasan (ed.), *Islam and Indian Nationalism: Reflections on Abul Kalam Azad*. New Delhi: Manohar, pp. 100–21.

Austin, Granville. 2004. *The Indian Constitution: Cornerstone of a Nation*. New Delhi: Oxford University Press.

Austin, Granville. 1999. *Working a Democratic Constitution: The Indian Experience*. New Delhi: Oxford University Press.

Azad, Abul Kalam. 2012. 'Musalman-i Dilli ka Ijtima: Jama Masjid, Dilli, Uktubar, 1947', in *Khutbat-i Azad*. New Delhi: Sahitya Academy, pp. 337–43.

Azad, Abul Kalam. 2010. *Ghubar-i Khatir*. New Delhi: Sahitya Akademi.

Azad, Abul Kalam. 1989. *India Wins Freedom: The Complete Version*. New Delhi: Orient Longman.

Azad, Abul Kalam. 1979. *Tarjuman ul-Quran*. New Delhi: Sahitya Akademi.

Azad, Abul Kalam. n.d.(a) *Qaul-i Faisal: ya'ni Ḥazrat Maulana Abulkalam Azad ka bayan*. Delhi: Caman Book Depot.

Azad, Abul Kalam. n.d.(b) *Hayat-i Sarmad*. Lucknow: Tanvir Pablisharz.

Azad, Abul Kalam (ed.) 2010. *Al-Hilal*. Lucknow: Uttar Pradesh Urdu Academy.

Azoulay, Ariella. 2008. *The Civil Contract of Photography*. New York: Zone Books.

Bajpai, Rochana. 2011. *Debating Difference: Group Rights and Liberal Democracy in India*. New Delhi: Oxford University Press.

Bakhtin, M. M. 2006. 'Discourse in the Novel', in Michael Holquist (ed.), *The Dialogic Imagination: Four Essays by M.M. Bakhtin*. Austin: University of Texas Press, pp. 259–422.

Bakhtin, M. M. 1986. 'From Notes Made in 1970–71', in *Speech Genres and Other Late Essays*. Austin: University of Texas Press, pp. 132–58.

Bandyopadhyay,Tamal. 2014. *Sahara: The Untold Story*. Mumbai: Jaico Publishing House.

Barrier, N. Gerald. 1974. *Banned. Controversial Literature and Political Control in British India: 1907–1947.* Columbia, Missouri: Missouri University Press.

Baruah, Sanjib. 2020. *In the Name of the Nation: India and Its Northeast*. Stanford, CA: Stanford University Press.

Basu, Durga. 2010. *Law of the Press*. Gurgaon: LexisNexis Butterworths.

Bayly, C. A. 2012. *Recovering Liberties: Indian Thought in the Age of Colonialism and Empire*. New Delhi: Cambridge University Press.

Bayly, C. A. 2007. *Empire and Information: Intelligence Gathering and Social Communication in India, 1780–1870*. New Delhi: Cambridge University Press.

Bayly, C. A. 2004. *The Birth of the Modern World 1780–1914: Global Connections and Comparisons*. Oxford: Blackwell.

Bayly, C. A. 2001. *The Origins of Nationality in South Asia: Patriotism and Ethical Government in the Making of Modern India*. New Delhi: Oxford University Press.

Bayly, C. A. 1996. 'Colonial Rule and the "Informational Order" in South Asia', in Nigel Crook (ed.), *The Transmission of Knowledge in South Asia: Essays on Education, Religion, History and Politics*. New Delhi: Oxford University Press, pp. 280–315.

Bayly, C. A. 1975. *The Local Roots of Indian Politics: Allahabad 1880–1920*. London: Oxford University Press.

Bayly, Susan. 1999. *Caste, Society and Politics in India: From the Eighteenth Century to the Modern Age*. Cambridge: Cambridge University Press.

Bhabha, Homi K. 1985. 'Sly Civility', *October* 34, pp. 71–80.

Bharatiya Jana Sangh (BJS). 2005. *Party Documents – 1952–1980: Vol 1. 'Policies and Manifestoes'*. New Delhi: Bharatiya Janata Party.

Bharatiya Janata Party (BJP). 2014. *Election Manifesto*, http://www.bjp.org/images/pdf_2014/full_manifesto_english_07.04.2014.pdf (accessed 30 August 2015).

Bharatiya Janata Party (BJP). 2005. *Party Documents 1980–2005*, Vol-1: Election Manifestoes. New Delhi: Bharatiya Janata Party.

Bhat, M. Mohsin Alam. 2021. 'Governing Democracy Outside the Law: India's Election Commission and the Challenge of Accountability.' *Asian Journal of Comparative Law* 16, pp. S85–S104.

Bourdieu, Pierre. 2000. *Outline of a Theory of Practice*. Cambridge: Cambridge University Press.

Bourdieu, Pierre. 1994. *Language and Symbolic Power*. Cambridge: Polity Press.

Bourdieu, Pierre. 1987a. 'Legitimation and Structured Interests in Weber's Sociology of Religion' in Scott Lash and Sam Whimster (eds), *Max Weber, Rationality and Modernity*. London: Allen Unwin, pp. 119–36.

Bourdieu, Pierre. 1987b. 'What Makes a Social Class? On The Theoretical and Practical Existence Of Groups', *Berkeley Journal of Sociology* 32 (1987), pp. 1–17.

Bourdieu, Pierre. 1984. *Distinction: A Social Critique of the Judgment of Taste*. London: Routledge & Kegan Paul.

Bourdieu, Pierre, Franz Schultheis and Andreas Pfeufter. 2013. 'With Weber Against Weber: In Conversation with Pierre Bourdieu', in Simon Susen and Bryon Turner (eds), *The Legacy of Pierre Bourdieu: Critical Essays*. London: Anthem Press, pp. 111–24.

Bourdieu, Pierre, Loic J. D. Wacquant and Samar Farage. 1994. 'Rethinking the State: Genesis and Structure of the Bureaucratic Field', *Sociological Theory* 12(1), pp. 1–18.

Brass, Paul. 2004. "Elite interests, popular passions, and social power in the language politics of India', *Ethnic and Racial Studies* 27(3), pp. 353–75.

Brass, Paul. 2000. 'Foucault Steals Political Science', *Annual Review of Political Science* 3, pp. 305–30.

Brass, Paul. 1991. *Ethnicity and Nationalism: Theory and Comparison*. New Delhi: Sage.

Brass, Paul. 1989. 'Pluralism, Regionalism and Decentralising Tendencies in Contemporary Indian Politics', in A. Jeyaratnam Wilson and Dennis Dalton (eds), *The States of South Asia: Problems of National Integration*. London: Hurst and Company, pp. 223–64.

Brass, Paul. 1988. 'The Punjab Crisis and the Unity of India', in Atul Kohli (ed.), *India's Democracy: An Analysis of Changing State Society Relations*. Princeton: Princeton University Press, pp. 169–213.

Brass, Paul. 1974. *Language, Religion and Politics in North India.* London: Cambridge University Press.

Burghart, Richard. 1996. 'The Conditions of Listening: The Everyday Experience of Politics in Nepal', in *The Conditions of Listening: Essays on Religion, History and Politics in South Asia.* New Delhi: Oxford University Press, pp. 300–18.

Burney, Aziz. 2010. *RSS ki sazish 26/11*? Noida: Burney Publishing House.

Burney, Aziz. 2005. *Gujarat 2002, the Turning Point of Indian History: India Lose Freedom* [sic]. New Delhi: Indian Publishers' Distributors.

Burney, Aziz. 2003. *Dastan-e Hind.* New Delhi: Farid Book Depot.

Butler, Judith. 2015. *Notes Toward a Performative Theory of Assembly.* Cambridge, MA: Harvard University Press.

Butler, Judith. 1997. *Excitable Speech: A Politics of the Performative.* New York: Routledge.

Butler, Judith. 1996. 'Universality in Culture', in Martha C. Nussbaum (ed.), *For Love of Country: Debating the Limits of Patriotism.* Boston, MA: Beacon Press, pp. 45–52, 47–8.

Carter, Thomas Francis. 1925. *The Invention of Printing in China and its Spread Westward.* New York: Columbia University Press.

Cavell, Stanley. 1991. *Conditions Handsome and Unhandsome: The Constitution of Emersonian Perfectionism.* Chicago: University of Chicago Press.

Centre for Policy Analysis (CPA). 2013. *Muzaffarnagar 2013: Violence by Political Design*, http://cpadelhi.org/papersreports.htm (accessed 19 December 2014).

Chatterjee, Partha. 2011. 'The People in Utopian and Real Time' in *Lineages of Political Society.* New York: Columbia University Press, pp. 129–53.

Chatterjee, Partha. 2004. *The Politics of the Governed: Reflection on Popular Politics in Most of the World.* New Delhi: Permanent Black.

Chatterjee, Partha. 1993. *The Nation and its Fragments* in *The Partha Chatterjee Omnibus.* 2006. New Delhi: Oxford University Press.

Chatterjee, Partha. 1986. *Nationalist Thought and the Colonial World: A Derivative Discourse?* in *The Partha Chatterjee Omnibus.* 2006. New Delhi: Oxford University Press.

Chatterji, Angana P., Thoms Blom Hansen and Christophe Jaffrelot (eds) 2019. *Majoritarian State: How Hindu Nationalism is Changing India.* Oxford: Oxford University Press.

Chhuttani, P. N. (ed.) 1995. *Politicisation of Health: J.P's Documented Medical Profile.* Chandigarh: Tilok Tirath Vidyavati Chuttani Charitable Trust.

Cohn, Bernard S. 1987. 'The Census, Social Structure and Objectification in South Asia', in *An Anthropologist among the Historians and Other Essays*. Oxford: Oxford University Press, pp. 224–54.

Dalmia, Vasudha. 1999. *The Nationalization of Hindu Traditions*. New Delhi: Oxford University Press.

Das, Veena and Deborah Poole (eds) 2004. *Anthropology in the Margins of the State*. New Delhi: Oxford University Press.

Das Gupta, Jyotirindra. 1970. *Language Conflict and National Development: Group Politics and National Language Policy in India*. California: University of California Press.

Dasgupta, Sandipto. 2014. '"A Language Which Is Foreign to Us": Continuities and Anxieties in the Making of the Indian Constitution', *Comparative Studies of South Asia, Africa and the Middle East* 34(2), pp. 228–42.

Datta, V. N. 1990. *Maulana Azad*. New Delhi: Manohar Publications.

De, Rohit. 2018. *A People's Constitution: The Everyday Life of the Law in the Indian Republic*. Princeton: Princeton University Press.

Deleuze, Gilles. 1992. 'What is a *dispositif*?' in Timothy J. Armstrong (ed.), *Michel Foucault, Philosopher: Essays translated from the French and German*. New York: Routledge, pp. 159–68.

Dery, David. 1998. '"Papereality" and Learning in Bureaucratic Organizations', *Administration & Society* 29(6), pp. 677–89.

Deutsch, Karl. W. 1966. *Nationalism and Social Communication: An Enquiry into the Foundations of Nationality*. Cambridge, MA: MIT Press.

Deutsch, Karl. W. 1963. *The Nerves of Government: Models of Political Communication and Control*. London: Collier-Macmillan Ltd.

Devashayam, M. G. 2006. *JP in Jail: An Uncensored Account*. New Delhi: Roli Books.

Disch, Lisa. 2008. 'Representation as "Spokespersonship": Bruno Latour's Political Theory', *Parallax* 14(3), pp. 88–100.

Douglas, Ian Henderson. 1988. *Abul Kalam Azad: An Intellectual and Religious Biography*. New Delhi: Oxford University Press.

dyuti a. 2020. 'Abrogation and assertion: The fault lines of the Indian constitution with regards to Kashmir', *HAU: Journal of Ethnographic Theory* 10(3): 758–66.

Elam, J. Daniel. 2016. 'Commonplace Anti-Colonialism: Bhagat Singh's Jail Notebook and the Politics of Reading', *South Asia: Journal of South Asian Studies* 39(3): 592–607.

Faisal, Syed Mohammed. 2020. 'Shaheen Bagh and the hermeneutics of Muslim identity in South Asia', *HAU: Journal of Ethnographic Theory* 10(3): 767–75.

Farouqui, Ather. (ed.) 2006. *Redefining Urdu Politics in India*. New Delhi: Oxford University Press.

Foucault, Michel. 2001. *Fearless Speech*, Joseph Pearson (ed.). Los Angeles: Semiotext(e).

Foucault, Michel. 1994. 'Le jeu de Michel Foucault' (1977 interview) in *Dits et écrits 1954–1988, Vol. III: 1976–1979*. Paris: Gallimard. pp. 298–329.

Foucault, Michel. 1980. 'The Confession of the Flesh.' (1977 interview) in Colin Gordon (ed.), *Power/Knowledge: Selected Interviews and Other Writings*. Essex: Harvester Press, pp. 194–228.

Foucault, Michel. 1978. *The History of Sexuality Volume I: An Introduction*. New York: Pantheon Books.

Foucault, Michel. 1976. *Histoire de la sexualité: La volonté de savoir*. Paris: Gallimard.

Frankel, Francine R. 2005. *India's Political Economy: 1947–2004*. New Delhi: Oxford University Press.

Freeden, Michael. 2013. 'Liberalism', in Gerald Gauss and Fred D'Agostino (eds), *The Routledge Companion to Social and Political Philosophy*. Oxford: Routledge, pp. 231–42.

Freeden, Michael. 1983. 'Eugenics and Ideology', *The Historical Journal* 26(4), pp. 959–62.

Freeden, Michael. 1979. 'Eugenics and Progressive Thought: A Study in Ideological Affinity', Michael Freeden, *The Historical Journal* 22(3), pp. 645–71.

Fuller, C. J. and Veronique Bénéï (eds) 2000. *The Everyday State and Society in Modern India*. New Delhi: Social Science Press.

Fuller, C. J. and John Harriss. 2000. 'For an Anthropology of the Modern Indian State', in C. J. Fuller and Veronique Bénéï (eds), *The Everyday State and Society in Modern India*. New Delhi: Social Science Press, pp. 1–30.

Gayer, Laurent. 2011. 'Safe and Sound: Searching for a "Good Environment", in Abul Fazl Enclave, Delhi', in Laurent Gayer and Christophe Jaffrelot (eds), *Muslims of Indian Cities: Trajectories of Marginalisation*. New York: Columbia University Press.

Gilmartin, David. 2020. 'Introduction', in *South Asian Sovereignty: The Conundrum of Worldly Power*. Oxford: Routledge.

Gilmartin, David. 2012. 'Towards a Global History of Voting: Sovereignty, the Diffusion of Ideas, and the Enchanted Individual', *Religions*, 3, pp. 407–23.

Gilmartin, David. 2009. 'One Day's Sultan: T.N. Seshan and Indian Democracy', *Contributions to Indian Sociology* 43(247), pp. 247–84.

Gilmartin, David. 2007. 'Election Law and the "People" in Colonial and Postcolonial India', in Dipesh Chakrabarty, Rochona Mazumdar and Andrew Sartori (eds),

From the Colonial to the Postcolonial: India and Pakistan in Transition. New Delhi: Oxford University Press, pp. 55–82.

Gilmartin, David and Robert Moog. 2012. 'Introduction to "Election Law in India"', *Election Law* 11(2), pp. 136–48.

Government of Assam (GA). 2020 'What are the Admissible Documents [for the National Registrar of Citizens]?', http://www.nrcassam.nic.in/admin-documents.html (accessed 4 March 2020).

Government of India (GI). 2022. *Press in India: 2021–22: 66th Annual Report of the Registrar for Newspapers for India.*

Government of India (GI). 2020. *The National Education Policy.*

Government of India (GI). 2019. *Yearly Performance Indicators Indian Telecom Sector (Fourth Edition) 2019.*

Government of India (GI). 2019a. *The Citizenship (Amendment) Act, 2019.*

Government of India (GI). 2018. *Press in India: 2017–18: 62nd Annual Report of the Registrar of Newspapers for India.*

Government of India (GI). 2018a. *Census of India 2011. Paper 1 OF 2018. Language. India, States and Union Territories. (Table C-16).*

Government of India (GI). 2014. *Constituent Assembly Debates. Volume XI. 14/11/1949 to 26/11/1949.*

Government of India (GI). 2011. *Press in India: 2009–10: 54th Annual Report of the Registrar of Newspapers for India.*

Government of India (GI). 1990. *Report on the Implementation of Gujral Committee Recommendations.*

Government of India (GI). 1982. *Report of the Second Press Commission*, in two volumes.

Government of India (GI). 1978. *Interim and final reports of the Shah Commission of Inquiry*, in three volumes.

Government of India (GI). 1977. *White paper on misuse of mass media during the internal emergency.*

Government of India (GI). 1975. *Report of the Committee for the Promotion of Urdu.*

Government of India (GI). 1965. *Report on the Third General Elections in India.* New Delhi.

Government of India (GI). 1955. *Report of the States Reorganisation Commission.*

Government of India (GI). 1955a. *Report on the First General Election in India: 1951–52, Volume 1 (General).*

Government of India (GI). 1954. *Report of the Press Commission*, in two volumes.

Government of Punjab (GP). 1874. *A Manual for the Guidance of Officers of the Prison Department in the Panjab and its Dependencies prepared by order of the*

Panjab Government and Issued Under the Authority of Section 54 of Act XXVI of 1870. Lahore: Central Jail Press.

Government of Uttar Pradesh (GUP). 1962. *Report of the Uttar Pradesh Language Committee.*

Graham, G. F. I. 1974. *The Life and Work of Sir Syed Ahmed Khan*. Karachi: Oxford University Press.

Graham, William A. 1987. *Beyond the Written Word: Oral Aspects of Scripture in the History of Religion*. Cambridge: Cambridge University Press.

Gramsci, Antonio. 2003. *Selections from the Prison Notebooks*. London: Lawrence & Wishart Limited.

Grosz, Elizabeth. 2004. *The Nick of Time*. Durham: Duke University Press.

Guha, Ranajit. 1999. *Elementary Aspects of Peasant Insurgency in Colonial India*. Durham: Duke University Press.

Guha, Ranajit. 1997. *Dominance without Hegemony: History and Power in Colonial India*. Cambridge, MA: Harvard University Press.

Guha, Ranajit. 1976. 'Indian Democracy: Long Dead, Now Buried', *Journal of Contemporary Asia* 6(1), pp. 39–53.

Gupta, Akhil. 2012. *Red Tape: Bureaucracy, Structural Violence and Poverty in India*. Durham: Duke University Press.

Gupta, Akhil. 1995. 'Blurred Boundaries: The Discourse of Corruption, the Culture of Politics, and the Imagined State', *American Ethnologist* 22(2), pp. 375–402.

Gupta, Dipankar. 1997. *Rivalry and Brotherhood: Politics in the Life of Famers in Northern India*. New Delhi: Oxford University Press.

Gupta, Partha Sarathi. 2001. *Power, Politics and the People: Studies in British Imperialism and Indian Nationalism*. New Delhi: Permanent Black.

Hall, Stuart. 1980. 'Encoding/Decoding', in *Culture, Media, Language: Working Papers in Cultural Studies, 1972–79*. London: Hutchinson (in association with the Centre for Contemporary Cultural Studies, University of Birmingham), pp. 128–38.

Hall, Stuart. 1973. 'The 'Structured Communication' of Events', *Centre for Contemporary Cultural Studies Stenciled Occasional Papers Series* 5: http://www.birmingham.ac.uk/Documents/college-artslaw/history/cccs/stencilled-occasional-papers/1to8and11to24and38to48/SOP05.pdf (accessed 22 September 2015).

Hall, Stuart. 1973a, 'A "Reading" of Marx's 1857 Introduction to the Grundrisse', *Centre for Cultural Studies*. University of Birmingham.

Hall, Stuart. 1972. 'External Influences on Broadcasting – "The External-Internal Dialectic in Broadcasting: Television's Double-Bind"', *Centre for Contemporary Cultural Studies Stenciled Occasional Papers Series*, 4: http://www.birmingham.

ac.uk/Documents/college-artslaw/history/cccs/stencilled-occasional-papers/1to8and11to24and38to48/SOP04.pdf (accessed 22 September 2015).

Hansen, Thomas Blom. 1999. *The Saffron Wave: Democracy and Hindu Nationalism in Modern India*. Princeton: Princeton University Press.

Hansen, Thomas Blom and Christophe Jaffrelot. 2000. *The BJP and the Compulsions of Politics in India*. New Delhi: Oxford University Press.

Hansen, Waldermar. 1972. *The Peacock Throne: The Drama of Mogul India*. New Delhi: Motilal Banarasidas, pp. 396–412.

Haq, Abdul. 2007. *Standard 21st Century Dictionary: Urdu to English*. Delhi: Educational Book Publishing House.

Hartung, Jan-Peter. 2013a. *A System of Life: Mawdūdī and the Ideologisation of Islam*. London: Hurst.

Hartung, Jan-Peter. 2013b. 'Who Speaks of What Caliphate? The Indian *Khilafat* Movement and Its Aftermath', in Madawi Al-Rasheed, Carool Kersten, Marat Shterin (eds), *Demystifying the Caliphate*. London: Hurst, pp. 81–94.

Hasan, Mushirul. 1981. 'Religion and Politics: The *Ulama* and Khilafat Movement', *Economic and Political Weekly* 16(20), pp. 903–12.

Haugen, Einar Ingvald. 1972. *The Ecology of Language*. Stanford: Stanford University Press.

Hull, Matthew S. 2012. *Government of Paper: The Materiality of Bureaucracy in Urban Pakistan*. Berkeley: University of California Press.

Iqbal, Muhammad. 1995a. 'The Muslim Community – A Sociological Study', in *Speeches, Writings and Statements of Iqbal*, ed. Latif Ahmed Sherwani. Lahore: Iqbal Academy, pp. 118–37.

Iqbal, Muhammad. 1995b. 'Statement on Islam and Nationalism in Reply to a Statement of Maulana Husain Ahmad, Published in the Ehsan on 9th March, 1938', in *Speeches, Writings and Statements of Iqbal*, ed. Latif Ahmed Sherwani. Lahore: Iqbal Academy, pp. 300–4.

Jalal, Ayesha. 1995. *Democracy and Authoritarianism in South Asia: A Comparative and Historical Perspective*. Cambridge: Cambridge University Press.

Jaffrelot, Christophe. 2021. Modi's India: *Hindu Nationalism and the Rise of Ethnic Democracy*. Princeton: Princeton University Press.

Jaffrelot, Christophe. 2001. 'The Sangh Parivar: Between Sanskritization and Social Engineering', in Hansen, Thomas Blom and Christophe Jaffrelot (eds), *The BJP and the Compulsions of Politics in India*. New Delhi: Oxford University Press, pp. 72–100.

Jaffrelot, Christophe. 2000. 'Islamic Identity and Ethnic Tensions', in Christophe Jaffrelot (ed.), *A History of Pakistan and Its Origins*. London: Anthem Press, pp. 9–38.

Jaffrelot, Christophe. 1998. *The Hindu Nationalist Movement in India*. New York: Columbia University Press.

Jaffrelot, Christophe and Pratinav Anil. 2020. *India's First Dictatorship: The Emergency, 1975–1977*. London: Hurst Publishers.

Jeffrey, Robin. 2000. *India's Newspaper Revolution: Capitalism, Politics and the Indian-language Press*. New Delhi: Oxford University Press.

Jeffrey, Robin. 1997. 'Urdu Newspapers in India: Waiting for Citizen Kane?' *Economic and Political Weekly* 32(13), pp. 631–6.

Jeffrey, Robin. 1994. 'Monitoring Newspapers and Understanding the Indian State'. *Asian Survey* 34(8) (August 1994), pp. 748–63.

Jeffrey, Robin and Assa Doron (eds) 2013. *The Great Indian Phone Book: How Cheap Mobile Phones Change Business, Politics and Daily Life*. London: Hurst.

Kantorowicz, Ernst H. 1981. *The King's Two Bodies: A Study in Medieval Political Theology*. Princeton: Princeton University Press.

Kashfi, Syed M. Abul Khair. (ed.) 2008. *Noori Nastaliq Revolution in Urdu Compositing*. Karachi: Elite Publishers.

Kaviraj, Sudipta. 1992. 'Writing, Speaking, Being: Language and the Historical Formation of Identities in India', in Dagmar Hellmann-Rajanayagam and Dietmar Rothermund (eds), *Nationalstaat und sprachkonflikte in süd und südostasien*. Stuttgart: Franz Steiner Verlag, pp. 25–68.

Khan, Sir Syed Ahmed. 2000. *The Causes of the Indian Revolt*. Frances Robinson (ed.) Oxford: Oxford University Press.

Khan, Sir Syed Ahmed. 1888. *On the Present State of Indian Politics*. Allahabad: Pioneer Press.

Khan, Sir Syed Ahmed. 1872. *Review on Dr. Hunter's Indian Musalmans: Are They Bound in Conscience to Rebel against the Queen?* Benares: Medical Hall Press.

Kidwai, Saleem. 2000. 'Sarmad', in Saleem Kidwai and Ruth Vanita (eds), *Same-Sex Love in India: Readings from Literature and History*. New York: Palgrave Macmillan, pp. 157–8.

King, Christopher R. 1994. *One Language, Two Scripts: The Hindi Movement in Nineteenth Century North India*. Bombay: Oxford University Press.

Kohli-Khandekar, Vanita. 2010. *The Indian Media Business*. New Delhi: Sage.

Kumar, Satendra. 2018. *Badalte Gaon, Badalta Dehat: Nayi Samajikta ka Uday*. New Delhi: Oxford University Press.

Laclau, Ernesto. 2007. *On Populist Reason*. London: Verso.

Laclau, Ernesto. 1990. 'The Impossibility of Society', in *New Reflections on the Revolution of Our Time*. London: Verso, pp. 89–92.

Laclau, Ernesto. 1979. *Politics and Ideology in Marxist Theory: Capitalism-Fascism-Populism*. London: Verso.

Laclau, Ernesto and Chantal Mouffe. 2014. *Hegemony and Socialist Strategy*. London: Verso.

Latour, Bruno. 2024. 'From the Illusions of Democracy to the Realities of its Appearances' in Kristian Bjørkdahl (ed.), *The Problematic Public: Lippmann, Dewey, and Democracy in the Twenty-First Century*. Pennsylvania: Penn State University Press, pp. 45–67.

Latour, Bruno. 2021. 'How to Remain Human in the Wrong Space? A Comment on a Dialogue by Carl Schmitt', *Critical Inquiry* 47(4), pp. 699–718.

Latour, Bruno. 2016. 'Does the Body Politic Need a New Body?' Yusko Ward-Phillips lecture, University of Notre Dame, 3rd of November 2016.

Latour, Bruno. 2014. 'Technical Does Not Mean Material: Comment on Lemmonier, Pierre. 2012. *Mundane Objects: Materiality and Non-verbal Communication*', *HAU: Journal of Ethnographic Theory* 4(1), pp. 507–10.

Latour, Bruno. 2005a. 'From Realpolitik to Dingpolitik: Or How to Make Things Public', in Bruno Latour and Peter Weibel (eds), *Making Things Public: Atmospheres of Democracy*. Karlsruhe: ZKM and MIT Press, pp. 14–39.

Latour, Bruno. 2005b. *Reassembling the Social: An Introduction to Actor-Network Theory*. Oxford: Oxford University Press.

Latour, Bruno. 2003. 'What if we *Talked* Politics a Little?', *Contemporary Political Theory* 2, pp. 143–64.

Latour, Bruno. 1994. 'On Technical Mediation – Philosophy, Sociology, Genealogy', *Common Knowledge* 3(2), pp. 29–64.

Latour, Bruno. 1991a. 'The Berlin key or how to do words with things', in Paul Graves-Brown (ed.), *Matter, Materiality and Modern Culture*. London: Routledge, pp. 10–21.

Latour, Bruno. 1991b. 'Technology is Society Made Durable', in John Law (ed.), *A Sociology of Monsters: Essays on Power, Technology and Domination*. London: Routledge, pp. 103–32.

Latour, Bruno. 1988. *The Pasteurization of France*. Cambridge, MA: Harvard University Press.

Latour, Bruno. 1986. 'The Power of Association', in John Law (ed.), *Power, Action and Belief: A New Sociology of Knowledge?* London: Routledge and Kegan Paul, pp. 264–80.

Latour, Bruno and Steve Woolgar. 1986. *Laboratory Life: The Construction of Social Facts*. Princeton, NJ: Princeton University Press.

Lecker, Michael, 2004. *The 'Constitution of Medina': Muhammad's First Legal Document*. Princeton, NJ: The Darwin Press.

Lelyveld, David. 1993. 'The Fate of Hindustani: Colonial Knowledge and the Project of a National Language', in Carol A. Breckenridge and Peter van der Veer (eds), *Orientalism and the Postcolonial Predicament: Perspectives on South Asia*. Philadelphia: University of Pennsylvania Press, pp. 189–214.

Lyngdoh, James Michael. 2004. *Chronicle of an Impossible Election: The Election Commission and the 2002 Jammu and Kashmir Assembly Elections*. New Delhi: Viking.

Madani, Maulana Hussain Ahmad. 2005. *Composite Nationalism and Islam*. New Delhi: Manohar Publishers & Distributors.

Majeed, Javed. 2007. 'Geographies of Subjectivity, Pan-Islam and Muslim Separatism: Muhammad Iqbal and Selfhood', *Modern Intellectual History* 4(1), pp. 145–61.

Malihabadi, Abdur. 2008. *Azad Ki Kahani Khud Azad Ki Zubani*. New Delhi: Ateqad Publishing House.

Marx, Karl. 2011. 'The Government of India', in Iqbal Husain (ed.), *Karl Marx on India*. New Delhi: Tulika Books, pp. 30–6.

Marx, Karl. 1973. *Grundrisse: Foundations of the Critique of Political Economy*. London: Penguin Books.

Martel, James R. 2022. *Anarchist Prophets: Disappointing Vision and the Power of Collective Sight*. Durham: Duke University Press.

Martel, James R. 2012. *Divine Violence: Walter Benjamin and the Eschatology of Sovereignty*. London: Routledge.

Mathur, Nayanika. 2016. *Paper Tiger: Law, Bureaucracy and the Developmental State in Himalayan India*. Cambridge: Cambridge University Press.

May, Todd., Benjamin Noys and Saul Newman. 2008. 'Democracy, Anarchism and Radical Politics Today: An Interview with Jacques Rancière', *Anarchist Studies* 16(2), pp. 173–85.

Mbembe, Achille. 2019. *Necropolitics*. Durham: Duke University Press.

Mbembe, Achille. 2003. 'Necropolitics', *Public Culture* 15(1), pp. 11–40.

Mehring, Richard. 2014. *Carl Schmitt: A Biography*. Cambridge: Polity Press.

Metcalf, Barbara D. 2005. 'Introduction', in Maulana Hussain Ahmad Madani (eds), *Composite Nationalism and Islam*. New Delhi: Manohar Publishers & Distributors, pp. 23–54.

Mignolo, Walter D. 1998. *The Darker Side of the Renaissance: Literacy, Territoriality and Colonization*. Ann Arbor: University of Michigan Press.

Minault, Gail. 2001. 'The Elusive Maulana: Reflections on Writing Azad's Biography' in Mushirul Hasan (ed.), *Islam and Indian Nationalism: Reflections on Abul Kalam Azad*. New Delhi: Manohar, pp. 17–27.

Minault, Gail. 1982. *The Khilafat Movement: Religious Symbolism and Political Mobilization in India*. New York: Columbia University Press.

Mitchell, Timothy. 2000. 'The Stage of Modernity', in *Questions of Modernity*. Minneapolis: University of Minnesota Press, pp. 1–34.

Mitchell, Timothy. 1991. 'The Limits of the State: Beyond Statist Approaches and Their Critics', *The American Political Science Review* 85(1), pp. 77–96.

Modi, Narendra. 2014. *Abode of Love*. New Delhi: Rajpal & Sons.

Morgan, Edmund S. 1989. *Inventing the People: The Rise of Popular Sovereignty in England and America*. New York: W.W. Norton.

Mouffe, Chantal. 1999. 'Deliberative Democracy or Agonistic Pluralism?', *Social Research* 66(3), pp. 745–58.

Naim, C. M. 2010. 'Syed Ahmad and His Two Books Called Asar-al-Sanadid', *Modern Asian Studies*, 45(3), pp. 669–708.

Narayan, Badri. 2009. *Fascinating Hindutva: Saffron Politics and Dalit Mobilization*. New Delhi: Sage.

Narayan, Badri. 2006. *Women Heroes and Dalit Assertion in North India: Culture, Identity and Politics*. New Delhi: Sage.

Narayan, Jayaprakash. 1977a. *J.P.'s Jail Life (A collection of Personal Letters)*. New Delhi: Arnold-Heinemann.

Narayan, Jayaprakash. 1977b. *Prison Diary*. Bombay: Popular Prakashan.

Narayan, Jayaprakash. 1970. *Nation Building in India*. Varanasi: Navachetna Prakashan.

Narayan, Jayaprakash. 1959. *Inside Lahore Fort*. Madras: Commercial Printing and Publishing House.

National Commission for Minorities (NCM). 2013. *Report on NCM's Visit to Muzaffarnagar (19th September, 2013)*, http://ncm.nic.in/pdf/tour%20reports/Shri%20wajahat/NCM%27s%20visit%20to.pdf (accessed 19/12/2014).

National Institute of Educational Planning and Administration (NIEPA). 2018. *Evaluation of the Implementation of the Scheme for Providing Quality Education in Madrasas: (SPQEM): Report 2018*: chrome-extension://efaidnbmnnnibpcajpcglclefindmkaj/https://www.education.gov.in/sites/upload_files/mhrd/files/upload_document/spemm_report.pdf (accessed 6 April 2024).

Nehru, Jawaharlal. 1959. *The Discovery of India*. New York: Anchor Books

O'Connor, Kieran. 2015. '"Don't They Represent Us?': A Discussion between Jacques Rancière and Ernesto Laclau, *Verso Blog*, 26 May 2015, http://www.versobooks.com/blogs/2008-don-t-they-represent-us-a-discussion-between-jacques-Ranci ère-and-ernesto-laclau (accessed 21 August 2015).

Page, David and William Crawley. 2001. *Satellites Over South Asia: Broadcasting, Culture and Public Interest*. Sage: New Delhi/Thousand Oaks/London.

Piliavsky, Anastasia. (ed.) 2014. *Patronage as Politics in South Asia*. Cambridge: Cambridge University Press.

Pinney, Christopher. 2009. 'Iatrogenic Religion and Politics', in Raminder Kaur and William Mazzarella (eds), *Censorship in South Asia: Cultural Regulation from Sedition to Seduction*. Bloomington and Indianapolis: Indiana University Press, pp. 29–62.

Platts, John T. 2006. *A Dictionary of Urdū, Classical Hindī and English*. New Delhi: Manohar Publishers & Distributors.

Pollock, Sheldon. 2007. 'Literary Culture and Manuscript Culture in Precolonial India' in Simon Eliot, Andrew Nash and Ian Willison (eds), *Literary Cultures and the Material Book*, London: British Library, pp. 77–94.

Pollock, Sheldon. 2006. *The Language of the Gods in the World of Men: Sanskrit, Culture, and Power in Premodern India*. New Delhi: Permanent Black.

Pollock, Sheldon. 2002. 'Cosmopolitan and Vernacular in History', in Sheldon Pollock, Homi K Bhabha, Carol A. Breckenridge and Dipesh Chakrabarty (eds), *Cosmopolitanism*. Durham: Duke University Press, pp. 15–53.

Pollock, Sheldon. 1998. 'The Cosmopolitan Vernacular', *The Journal of Asian Studies*, 57(1), pp. 6–37.

Prakash, Gyan. 2019. *Emergency Chronicles: Indira Gandhi and Democracy's Turning Point*. Princeton: Princeton University Press.

Puri, Balraj. 2005. *JP on Jammu and Kashmir*. New Delhi: Gyan Publishing House.

Quraishi, S. Y. 2014. *An Undocumented Wonder: The Making of the Great Indian Election*. New Delhi: Rupa Publications.

Rahman, Tariq. 2011. *From Hindi to Urdu: A Social and Political History*. Karachi: Oxford University Press.

Rai, Alok. 2001. *Hindi Nationalism*. New Delhi: Orient Longman

Rai, Amit. 1984. *A House Divided: The Origin and Development of Hindi/Hindavi*. Delhi: Oxford University Press.

Rajagopal, Arvind. 2001. *Politics after Television: Hindu Nationalism and the Reshaping of the Public in India*. Cambridge: Cambridge University Press.

Raman, Bhavani. 2012. *Document Raj: Writing and Scribes in Early Colonial South India*. Chicago: University of Chicago Press.

Ramanujan, A. K. 1999. 'Three Hundred Ramayanas: Five Examples and Three Thoughts on Translation', in *The Collected Essays of A.K. Ramanujan*, New Delhi: Oxford University Press, pp. 131–60.

Ramanujan, A. K. 1994. 'Who Needs Folklore? Ramanujan on Folklore', *Indian Literature* 37(4) (162), pp. 93–106.

Ramaswamy, Sumathi. 2009. 'Sanskrit for the Nation', in Asha Sarangi (ed.), *Language and Politics in India*. New Delhi: Oxford University Press, pp. 93–138.

Rancière, Jacques. 2011a. 'Against an Ebbing Tide: An Interview with Jacques Rancière' in Paul Bowman and Richard Stamp (eds), *Reading Rancière*. London and New York: Continuum International Publishing Group, pp. 238–251.

Rancière, Jacques. 2011b. *Mute Speech: Literature, Critical Theory, and Politics*. New York: Columbia.

Rancière, Jacques. 2011c. *The Politics of Aesthetics*. London: Continuum University Press.

Rancière, Jacques. 2010a. *Dissensus: On Politics and Aesthetics*. London: Continuum.

Rancière, Jacques. 2010b. 'Racism: A Passion from Above', *Monthly Review*, 23 September 2010, http://mrzine.monthlyreview.org/2010/Rancière230910.html (accessed 18 January 2015).

Rancière, Jacques. 2009a. 'Contemporary Art and the Politics of Aesthetics' in Beth Hinderliter, William Kaizen, Vered Maimon, Jaleh Mansoor and Seth McCormick (eds), *Communities of Sense: Rethinking Aesthetics and Politics*, pp. 31–50.

Rancière, Jacques. 2009b. *The Emancipated Spectator*. London: Verso.

Rancière, Jacques. 2009c. 'Should Democracy Come? Ethics and Politics in Derrida', in Pheang Cheah and Suzanne Guerlac (eds.) *Derrida and the time of the political*. Durham: Duke University Press, pp. 274–88.

Rancière, Jacques. 2006a. 'Democracy, Republic, Representation', *Constellations*. 13(3), September 2006, pp. 297–307.

Rancière, Jacques. 2006b. *Hatred of Democracy*. London: Verso.

Rancière, Jacques. 2006c. 'Thinking between disciplines: an aesthetics of knowledge', *Parrhesia*, Number 1, pp. 1–12.

Rancière, Jacques. 2004. *The Flesh of Words: The Politics of Writing*. Stanford: Stanford University Press.

Rancière, Jacques. 2004b. 'Who Is the Subject of the Rights of Man?', *South Atlantic Quarterly*, 1 July 2004; 103 (2–3): pp. 297–310.

Rancière, Jacques. 2003. *Short Voyages to the Land of the People*. Stanford: Stanford University Press.

Rancière, Jacques. 2001. 'Ten Theses on Politics', *Theory & Event*. 5(3) (unnumbered online publication).

Rancière, Jacques. 1998. *Disagreement: Politics and Philosophy*. Minneapolis: University of Minnesota Press.

Rancière, Jacques. 1991. *The Ignorant Schoolmaster: Five Lessons in Intellectual Emancipation*. Stanford: Stanford University Press.

Ray, Rajat. 1981. 'Revolutionaries, Pan-Islamists and Bolsheviks: Maulana Abul Kalam Azad and the Political Underworld in Calcutta, 1905–1925', in Mushirul Hasan (ed.), *Communal and Pan-Islamic Trends in Colonial India*. New Delhi: Manohar, pp. 85–108.

Robinson, Francis. 1996. 'Islam and the Impact of Print in South Asia', in Nigel Crook (ed.), *The Transmission of Knowledge in South Asia: Essays on Education, Religion, History and Politics*. New Delhi: Oxford University Press, pp. 62–97.

Robinson, Francis. 1993. 'Technology and Religious Change: Islam and the Impact of Print', *Modern Asian Studies*, 27(1), pp. 229–51.

Robinson, Francis. 1974. *Separatism among Indian Muslims: The Politics of the United Provinces' Muslims 1860–1923*. Cambridge: Cambridge University Press.

Roy, Subrato. 2010. *Shanti, Sukh: Santushti*. Lucknow: Sahara India, 2010.

Rudolph, Lloyd and Susanne. 1978. 'To the Brink and Back: Representation and the State in India', *Asian Survey* 18(4), pp. 379–400.

Safadi, Y. H. 1978. *Islamic Calligraphy*. London: Thames and Hudson.

Sahasrabuddhe, P. G. and Manik Chandra Vajpayee. 1991. *The People Versus Emergency: A Saga of Struggle*. New Delhi: Suruchi Prakashan.

Sayeed, Mohammad. 2020. 'All That Happened Inside the Happening: Fear, Law and Politics after the Police Encounter at Batla House, New Delhi'. *Contributions to Indian Sociology* 54(1), pp. 51–75.

Schmitt, Carl. 2008. *Constitutional Theory*. Durham: Duke University Press.

Schmitt, Carl. 2005. *Political Theology*. Chicago: University of Chicago Press.

Scott, James C. 1998. *Seeing Like a State: How Certain Schemes to Improve the Human Condition Have Failed*. London: Yale University Press.

Scott, James C. 1990. *Domination and the Arts of Resistance: Hidden Transcripts*. New Haven, CT: Yale University Press.

Sen, Amartya. 1999. 'Democracy as a Universal Value', *Journal of Democracy* 10(3), pp. 3–17.

Seshan, T. N. (with Sanjoy Hazarika.) 1995. *The Degeneration of India*. New Delhi: Viking.

Sevea, Iqbal Singh. 2012. *The Political Philosophy of Muhammad Iqbal: Islam and Nationalism in Late Colonial India*. New York: Cambridge University Press.

Shaikh, Farzana. 1991. *Community and Consensus in Islam: Muslim Representation in Colonial India 1860–1947*. Bombay: Orient Longman.

Shani, Ornit. 2021. 'Women and the Vote: Registration, Representation and Participation in the Run-Up to India's First Elections, 1951–52', *South Asia: Journal of South Asian Studies* 44(2), pp. 228–246.

Shani, Ornit. 2018. *How India Became Democratic: Citizenship and the Making of the Universal Franchise*. Cambridge: Cambridge University Press.

Shannon, Claude E. 1998. 'The Mathematical Theory of Communication', in Claude E. Shannon and Warren Weaver. *The Mathematical Theory of Communication*. Urbana: University of Illinois Press, pp. 29–125.

Sharma, Aradhana and Akhil Gupta. 2006. 'Introduction: Rethinking Theories of the State in an Age of Globalization', in Aradhana Sharma and Akhil Gupta (eds), *The Anthropology of the State: A Reader*. Oxford: Blackwell Publishing, pp. 1–41.

Shaw, Graham. 1998. 'Calcutta: Birthplace of the Indian Lithographed Book', *Journal of the Printing Historical Society*, 27, pp. 89–111.

Singh, Ujjwal Kumar. 2012. 'Between Moral Force and Supplementary Legality: A Model Code of Conduct and the Election Commission of India', *Election Law Journal*, 11(2), pp. 149–69.

Singh, Ujjwal Kumar. 2004. *Institutions and democratic governance: A study of the Election Commission and Electoral Governance in India*. New Delhi: Nehru Memorial Museum and Library.

Skaria, Ajay. 2016. 'The Warrior's Sovereign Gift', in *Unconditional Equality: Gandhi's Religion of Resistance*. Minneapolis: University of Minnesota Press, pp. 91–118.

Smooha, Sammy. 1997. 'Ethnic Democracy: Israel as an Archetype', *Israel Studies*, 2(2), pp. 198–241.

Stark, Ulrike. 2007. *An Empire of Books: The Naval Kishore Press and the Diffusion of the Printed Word in Colonial India*. New Delhi: Permanent Black.

Stark, Ulrike. 2003. 'Politics, Public Issues and the Promotion of Urdu Literature: *Avadh Akhbar*, the First Urdu Daily in Northern India', in *The Annual of Urdu Studies* 18(1), (2003), pp. 66–94.

Tandon, B. N. 2003. *PMO Diary - 1: Prelude to the Emergency*. New Delhi: Konark Publishers.

Tarlo, Emma. 2003. *Unsettling Memories: Narratives of the Emergency in Delhi*. New Delhi: Permanent Black.

Thompson, Dennis F. 2004. 'Election Time: Normative Implications of Temporal Properties of the Electoral Process in the United States', *The American Political Science Review* 98(1), pp. 51–64.

Thompson, Dorothy. 1984. *The Chartists: Popular Politics in the Industrial Revolution*. Hounslow: Temple Smith.

Vishvanathan, Shiv. 1998. 'Revisiting the Shah Commission', in Harsh Sethi and Shiv Vishvanathan (eds), *Foul Play: Chronicles of Corruption*. New Delhi: Banyan Books, pp. 45-87.

Weber, Max. 2013. *Economy and Society, Volumes 1 and 2*, ed. Guenther Roth and Claus Wittich. Berkeley: University of California Press.

Weiner, Myron. 1983. *India at the Polls, 1980: A study of the Parliamentary Elections*. New Delhi: Munshiram Manoharlal Publishers Pvt. Ltd.

Weiner, Myron. 1978. *India at the Polls: The Parliamentary Elections of 1977*. Washington: American Enterprise Institute for Public Policy Research.

Woolard, Kathryn A. 1998. 'Introduction to Language Ideology as a Field of Inquiry', in Bambi B. Schieffelin, Kathryn A. Woolard and Paul V. Kroskrity (eds), *Language Ideologies: Practice and Theory*. New York: Oxford University Press, pp. 3–47.

Young, Iris Marion. 2000. *Inclusion and Democracy*. Oxford: Oxford University Press.

Zelliot, Eleanor. 1972. 'Gandhi and Ambedkar – A Study in Leadership', in Michael J. Mahar (ed.), *The Untouchables in Contemporary India*. Arizona: University of Arizona Press, pp. 69–95.

Index